When Food Is Comfort

"We desperately need solutions for the overeating epidemic that is contributing to the rise in obesity and the consequences that fill my cardiology practice. Julie Simon offers a seven-step mindfulness practice as an answer to emotional eating. I am going to share these steps with my patients immediately. *When Food Is Comfort* is exactly what we need to heal during these challenging times."

— JOEL KAHN, MD, FACC, author of *The Plant-Based Solution*

"If or when emotional eating is a challenge, Julie Simon's book *When Food Is Comfort* will enlighten and empower you with effective methods for healing deep emotional wounds through self-nurturing. With an authentic ring of empathetic authority, Julie Simon provides powerful, practical tools to help us liberate ourselves from the tyranny of our tongues. Indeed, those who control their appetites possess a great power, and *When Food Is Comfort* can help you and your loved ones attain and maintain this empowerment. Highly recommended!"

— MICHAEL KLAPER, MD, author of *Vegan Nutrition: Pure and Simple*

"*When Food Is Comfort* is a fantastic resource with a refreshingly new perspective. Written in a supportive and encouraging voice with moving personal and case stories, this practical, easy-to-follow book offers innovative strategies for anyone seeking freedom from unhealthy eating habits. I highly recommend it!"

— HYLA CASS, MD, coauthor of *8 Weeks to Vibrant Health*

"*When Food Is Comfort* is an excellent guide to gaining self-awareness, understanding, attunement, love, and, ultimately, loving self-control. It is also extraordinarily comprehensive and well written....If you thoroughly read, incorporate, and follow Julie's comprehensive, uplifting, and meticulous guidance, it will benefit you as much as years of therapy....You will change your relationship to food, using it for health and well-being rather than to try to fill unmet emotional needs. And best of all, you will enjoy a healthier, slimmer *you*."

— PRISCILLA SLAGLE, MD, author of *The Way Up from Down*

"How often do you eat when you're not really hungry, eat too much, or choose to eat comfort foods you know aren't good for you? If you do these things more than you'd like, this book is definitely for you. It will help you recognize the signs of emotional eating so that you can instantly tell the difference between emotional hunger and actual physiological hunger. And it will help you nurture yourself so that every part of you — including your body, your emotions, your thoughts, and your relationships — is truly and wonderfully well fed."

— JOHN ROBBINS, *New York Times*–bestselling author of *Diet for a New America* and president of Food Revolution Network

"As a wellness activist, I've observed firsthand how challenging overcoming emotional eating can be. Despite our best intentions, many of us find ourselves regularly snacking mindlessly and overeating at meals. Clearly, emotional eating is a symptom of deeper issues. Well written and comprehensive, *When Food Is Comfort* helps us understand the role early nurturance plays in both the etiology and the continuation of eating challenges. Julie Simon's simple yet powerful plan, developed in her highly successful twelve-week program, gets at the root causes of the problem. She gives readers all the tools they need to address the disconnection fueling their eating. If you or anyone you care about struggles with emotional eating, this book is a must-read."

— KATHY FRESTON, *New York Times*–bestselling author of *The Lean*

"As one whose recovery from binge eating dates back over thirty years, I am reluctant to recommend any work on the subject, as nearly all seem to lack a genuine understanding of the disorder and of the emotional eater as whole human being. *When Food Is Comfort* is the rare exception. Gently and astutely, Julie Simon guides the reader from confusion and entrapment to clarity and freedom. With solid science and a caring heart, Julie breaks through in this book to a place where few have ventured: a place of healing, restoration, and liberation." — VICTORIA MORAN, author of *The Love-Powered Diet*

"So many people struggle with emotional eating. *When Food Is Comfort* is a fascinating and eminently practical guide to making sense of what is going on and fixing it at the most fundamental level."

— NEAL D. BARNARD, MD, author of *Breaking the Food Seduction*

WHEN
FOOD
IS
COMFORT

Also by Julie M. Simon

The Emotional Eater's Repair Manual:
A Practical Mind-Body-Spirit Guide
for Putting an End to Overeating and Dieting

WHEN
FOOD
IS
COMFORT

Nurture Yourself Mindfully,
Rewire Your Brain, and
End Emotional Eating

JULIE M. SIMON, MA, MBA, LMFT

Foreword by Omar Manejwala, MD

New World Library
Novato, California

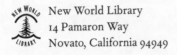 New World Library
14 Pamaron Way
Novato, California 94949

The sidebars on pages 82, 95, 139, 143, 185, 223, 231, and 239 and the tables on pages 91 and 159 are adapted by the author from her book *The Emotional Eater's Repair Manual*.

Text design by Tona Pearce Myers

Library of Congress Cataloging-in-Publication Data
Names: Simon, Julie M., [date] author.
Title: When food is comfort : nurture yourself mindfully, rewire your brain, and end
    emotional eating / Julie M. Simon.
Description: Novato, California : New World Library, [2018] | Includes bibliographical
    references and index. |
Identifiers: LCCN 2017055083 (print) | LCCN 2017055751 (ebook) | ISBN 9781608685516
    (Ebook) | ISBN 9781608685509 (alk. paper)
Subjects: LCSH: Compulsive eating—Psychological aspects. | Compulsive eating—
    Alternative treatment.
Classification: LCC RC552.C65 (ebook) | LCC RC552.C65 S472 2018 (print) |
    DDC 616.85/26—dc23
LC record available at https://lccn.loc.gov/2017055083

First printing, March 2018
ISBN 978-1-60868-550-9
Ebook ISBN 978-1-60868-551-6

Printed in Canada on 100% postconsumer-waste recycled paper

 New World Library is proud to be a Gold Certified Environmentally Responsible Publisher. Publisher certification awarded by Green Press Initiative. www.greenpressinitiative.org

10   9   8   7   6

For those who look outside themselves
for comfort and nurturance:
may this book inspire you to heal and discover
that your true source lies within.

CONTENTS

FOREWORD

Food, water, shelter. Most people are familiar with this list of basic human needs. And, of course, a basic need, like the need for food, is something that absolutely must be met. Yet every day millions of people struggle with how to eat food in a manner that doesn't destroy their health, sanity, or sense of self-worth. For something that seems like it *should* be so simple, making a decision about what to eat and following through with it has proved for so many to be so difficult as to be essentially impossible. As a psychiatrist who has spent my entire career treating addictions of varying sorts, I've seen nearly every possible variation of this struggle. As a former medical director of one of the oldest and largest treatment centers in the world, Hazelden, I've helped countless people and their families recover from the devastation that compulsive behaviors can cause. And as the author of the bestselling book *Craving: Why We Can't Seem to Get Enough* (Hazelden Publishing, 2013), I've explored both the science behind why cravings occur and the strategies for how to manage and prevent them effectively. I've appeared on all the major television networks discussing the devastating impact of cravings — most of these, including CNN, the CBS *Early Show*, and ABC's *20/20*, have described me as one of the nation's leading experts on addiction. Yet I've always understood that although we know so much about drug and alcohol addiction, compulsive overeating remains a poorly understood phenomenon.

As part of my research for *Craving*, I spent the majority of 2012 speaking with scientists and experts of all kinds on why compulsions are so difficult and how specifically to address them. I found and explained new insights that have helped countless people achieve freedom from cravings. One observation I made is that shame drives many self-defeating behaviors and that there is only one effective method of eliminating it: only love can neutralize shame. This means that food, water, and shelter are not the only basic human needs — love, too, is essential to survival. I also observed that needs that cannot be met in a constructive manner will be met in a destructive manner — they are needs and must be fulfilled one way or another.

During that time I came across Julie Simon's first book, *The Emotional Eater's Repair Manual: A Practical Mind-Body-Spirit Guide for Putting an End to Overeating and Dieting*, and was impressed — I recall reading it in one sitting. In that book, Julie essentially writes a clear, frank, and effective prescription for emotional eaters. She begins by explaining the problem and making the important observation that the latest-and-greatest diet can't possibly be the solution. By framing the problem as emotional hunger, she then explores how various forms of self-care can resolve the insanity that goes along with chronic overeating. I shared that book with many of my colleagues, who agreed that it was worth sharing with patients and friends. Since then, I've known many people who've used her methods to heal from the wounds that drive self-destructive eating.

In *When Food Is Comfort*, Julie builds on her earlier book with a deeper exploration of the critically important relationship between nurturing, comfort, and eating. Beginning with a simple checklist to assess emotional eating, she explores how inner nurturing is essential, and why and how its absence leads to a search for external sources of nurturing and comfort. She presents this information in a compelling manner with specific, and often personal, examples of how overeating results from an inability to self-nurture. Julie herself has suffered from these problems and unabashedly takes the reader through how she achieved freedom.

She focuses on the practical: part 1 explores the connections between child-hood experience and the need to seek validation and comfort externally, and part 2 presents seven specific skills and exercises that can restore inner nurturing and eliminate the dependence on food for emotional comfort.

I found each of the skills easy to understand, the examples straight-forward, and the exercises gentle and clear. I suspect that the majority of people who struggle with overeating will identify with her examples and benefit from the methods she prescribes.

My own research confirms that these conditions are essentially rela-tionship disorders — playing out in both how we relate to ourselves and how we connect with others. Julie ends with part 3 and an exploration of how to attract nurturing relationships and how to support and grow them. Just as isolation, loneliness, and dysfunctional relationships can be powerfully destructive forces, their opposite — nurturing, loving, sup-portive connections can lead to deeply fulfilling and satisfying experi-ences in recovery.

When Food Is Comfort is gentle, compassionate, and clear. At a time when one-third of Americans are overweight, another one-third are obese, and even many with "normal" weight struggle with the challenges of overeating, and in a culture in which diet books and fad diets emerge at an alarming rate, this book couldn't have come at a better time. It's my hope that the reader who struggles with the chaos of emotional eating can hear Julie's simple message of hope — that "your history is not your destiny" and that change and recovery are possible.

— Omar Manejwala, MD, author of
Craving: Why We Can't Seem to Get Enough, www.manejwala.com

INTRODUCTION

Have you ever wondered why some people can keep many of their favorite comfort foods in the house, eat one small portion at a time, and save the rest for later? Perhaps they even forget that they bought those special imported cookies or chocolates, and, God forbid, they go stale. Those same folks can go to a buffet or social gathering with an abundance of delectable foods and fill up one level plate, go back for a small amount of dessert, and that's it. They're done. They don't go back for seconds and thirds. *And they don't keep thinking about food.*

If having too many favorite "trigger" foods around overwhelms you and leads to mindless or excessive snacking, overeating, or bingeing, then you've picked up the right book. You probably prefer to keep your cupboards and refrigerator bare of too many favorite comfort foods, because they call to you when they're in the house. If these foods are in the house for the kids, your spouse, or company, you're keenly aware of them, right?

Most likely, you have to prepare yourself to avoid overindulging in restaurants or at social gatherings or holiday meals where there will be many of your favorite foods. Lack of planning on your part can lead to feeling food focused, overeating, and then suffering that familiar remorse, guilt, and shame. And let's be honest — sometimes you come home after overindulging at social events and eat more!

Maybe you've convinced yourself that your excesses aren't really all that bad. You love good food — perhaps you even label yourself a foodie. Is that such a crime? Everyone you know eats and drinks to excess at times, so what's the big deal? It could be worse — you're not shooting heroin or gambling yourself into bankruptcy.

But, truth be told, you've picked up this book because you're tired of feeling out of control with food and tired of the control it seems to have over you. You've had enough food hangovers for one lifetime. Somewhere in the recesses of your mind, you know that your life feels out of balance and that your excesses have something to do with it. You suspect, or you know, that your health is not optimal. You may not be satisfied with your weight. Perhaps you feel guilty about and ashamed of your eating behavior — at times you may hate yourself for it — and you're tired of having a poor body image. Take heart: you're not alone.

I know firsthand how frustrating it can be to feel so food focused all the time. I spent a good portion of my life stuck in a cycle of overeating comfort foods, gaining weight, and dieting. I found it especially difficult to stay away from my favorite foods, like bread, scones, muffins, crackers, pretzels, chips, cookies, and candy, as well as caffeinated beverages like diet soda, coffee, and tea.

If I kept my favorite foods in the house, inevitably I ended up feeling obsessed with them, overeating or bingeing, and then throwing them out. For many years, every time I brought them back into the house for a trial run, in any quantity larger than a single serving, I'd do okay for a day or two and then, unable to think about anything else, I'd start feeling compulsive and — well, you know the drill.

I was definitely an emotional eater. I had difficulty regulating my emotions, and I could get stuck for long periods in painful emotional states like anxiety, anger, sadness, hurt, shame, loneliness, frustration, depression, and hopelessness. Food altered my brain chemistry, helping to numb the pain of unpleasant emotions, self-doubt, and other negative thoughts. It also helped relieve stress. And because food is pleasurable and exciting, it was a good distraction. It temporarily filled up the inner emptiness and restlessness I regularly felt, a sort of spiritual hunger.

Throughout my overeating days, I always believed that eating and maintaining a healthy body weight — not overweight and not underweight — should be easy, comfortable, and intuitive. I knew we weren't designed to count calories, track carbohydrate or fat grams, or weigh and measure food — or our bodies, for that matter. After all, our earliest ancestors did not count calories or weigh and measure food, and they maintained their weight in an optimal range. And so can you!

Decades of research have confirmed that our bodies, those phenomenal machines, do all those behind-the-scenes calculations for us. They signal us with hunger pangs and cravings, calculate the caloric and nutrient density of the food we eat, and attempt to shut off our appetite by signaling us with fullness cues. Restrictive dieting is not necessary, and it is not the answer to resolving weight challenges. In fact, it has disconnected many of us from our intuitive body wisdom. Clearly, there are more pieces to the overeating puzzle.

I'm guessing that like me, you've tried to improve your relationship with food many times. You've been on every diet and eating plan known to humankind. But you've found it difficult to stick with restrictive eating plans. Even though you initially lose weight and feel a renewed sense of control, hope, and motivation, at some point a craving or a discomfort sends you right back to that tried-and-true form of comfort, soothing, pleasure, relief, excitement, and distraction — food.

You know others who have conquered these demons, but, for whatever reason, you haven't yet been successful. Perhaps you've concluded that these folks have more willpower or are more disciplined than you, or that they have less stress. Or that they have a nurturing partner, close friends, and a loving family, and you don't. Or that they have more balanced brain chemistry or better genetics. Or that you have an "addictive personality."

Although these factors may well represent pieces of the overeating puzzle, there is a more important piece that is often overlooked. The self-control other people seem to exhibit around favorite comfort foods may actually be the result of the quality of the caregiving they received as infants and small children; of the way their brain circuitry, brain chemistry, and stress-response mechanisms developed in a nurturing environment; and of the self-care skills they acquired early in life. *Mastering the skill of self-regulation depends to a large extent on experiencing consistently kind, supportive, and nurturing early interactions with our caregivers.*

The Complexities of Overeating

We all enjoy eating and, on occasion, eat when we're not hungry or over-eat just because the food is incredibly tasty or because it enhances our per-sonal or social experiences. Enjoying food beyond simple sustenance is a normal part of life. It becomes problematic, however, when we overeat to the extent of causing a significant weight gain or posing a health risk.

Overeating may seem like a simple act, but it's actually a complex behavior. All overeating behaviors (mindless or excessive snacking, over-eating at meals, and bingeing) are the result of complex interactions among emotional, cognitive, biological, neurological, social, and spiri-tual factors. Temperament and constitution, genetically inherited brain and body imbalances, insufficient nurturing, traumatic childhood experi-ences, chronic stress, chronic dieting, and the easy availability of high-calorie, nutrient-deficient foods all play a role. Resolving the problem of overeating requires a comprehensive, multidimensional approach.

When we regularly eat in the absence of physical hunger cues, rou-tinely choose unhealthy comfort foods, or keep eating when we're full, something is out of balance somewhere. These tendencies suggest that we are missing important self-care skills that are generally learned in child-hood. We may be lacking the ability to connect to and be mindful of our internal world — to consistently regulate uncomfortable emotional and bodily states, calm and soothe ourselves, and address our unmet needs. We may find it difficult to reframe self-defeating thoughts and self-belief distortions and to practice self-acceptance and self-love. Perhaps we never learned how to effectively grieve losses and disappointments, remind ourselves of our strengths and resources, and hold hope for the future. Without these skills, regulating our behaviors and setting effective limits for ourselves can feel like a daunting task.

Rewiring Your Brain and Your Response to Stress through Mindfulness

Throughout my own recovery from emotional eating, I was slowly piecing together the self-care skills I had been missing since childhood. As I practiced them, I noticed that something was happening to my brain that I wasn't able to articulate until years later, when I began to understand the neuroscience behind the changes I had experienced.

Scientific discoveries of the last twenty years have demonstrated that the mindful, self-reflective skills I was practicing were activating and connecting the self-regulatory circuits of my brain and, in so doing, were actually changing the physical structure of my brain. As new brain circuits develop and strengthen, they facilitate more adaptive responses and behaviors, creating resilience and well-being. All of this translates into better handling of stress and less obsessive thinking and wayward eating.

Through therapy and the intentional exposure to other kind souls, I began to learn the language of self-nurturance: unconditionally loving, affirming, validating, supportive, compassionate, empathic, calming, and soothing words and phrases that could actually turn my mood from anxious to calm, from despair to a sense of possibility and hope. As I wrote these phrases in my journal, I was amazed to find that, over time, something was shifting inside. Slowly I was developing the voice of my very own Inner Nurturer and, with it, self-acceptance and self-love.

I found myself turning less often to external sources of comfort. As I strengthened this inner voice, I no longer felt obsessed with or compulsive about food. My weight and mood stabilized. I felt less overwhelmed. I procrastinated less. My inner chaos and outer clutter diminished. I felt more emotionally balanced than I had ever been in my life. And, as a side benefit, my relationships improved: as I was able to meet more of my needs on my own, I was more emotionally available to others. Connection and intimacy began to replace the emptiness and loneliness I had lived with for so long.

Learning to Nurture Yourself

In my previous book, *The Emotional Eater's Repair Manual*, I covered these self-care skills in depth. I also covered key body-balancing principles (such as adding whole, unprocessed, plant-based foods to your eating plan and addressing body and brain imbalances) and soul-care practices (like practicing mind-quieting exercises and learning to let go). I introduced the very important skill of self-connection, which simply means regularly checking in with your emotions, bodily sensations, needs, and thoughts and accessing an internal nurturing voice capable of reassuring and comforting you and helping you meet your needs.

After the book's release, I received emails from readers all around the world describing how these skills, principles, and practices had helped them. They told me that they had never realized that they could learn how to nurture themselves. Over and over again, participants in my seminars, workshops, emotional eating groups, and Twelve-Week Emotional Eating Recovery Program echoed these sentiments and told me they felt encouraged by the notion that learning to nurture themselves could be the way out of a lifetime of food and weight obsession.

In this book, I expand on the concept of mindful self-nurturance and share with you the seven skills that constitute the practice I call *inner nurturing*. While it isn't necessary to read *The Emotional Eater's Repair Manual* prior to reading this book, if you are struggling with emotional eating, becoming familiar with the skills, principles, and practices of my first book is an invaluable first step.

My goal in this book is to show you how to nurture yourself by building and strengthening your Inner Nurturer voice and related skill set. You'll learn to soothe and comfort yourself, calm your stress-response apparatus, and grow and strengthen the regulatory circuits of your brain. You'll learn to meet your needs without turning to food or other unhealthy substances or habits. As a bonus, you'll enhance your resilience and sense of well-being.

Given that our early childhood environment has a powerful influence on brain development, and that you can't go back in time for a redo, it can be easy to feel hopeless about your chances of altering your brain's functioning, improving your self-care and your response to stressors, and resolving eating challenges. But there is good reason for hope.

Neuroplasticity refers to the brain's ability to reconfigure itself — to establish and dissolve connections between its different parts in response to experience. Our brain is an incredibly resilient and plastic (moldable) organ, and we continue to develop and expand our brain circuits throughout our lives. Research suggests that well into old age, our experiences can actually change the physical structure of the brain. In other words, it's never too late to learn to nurture yourself with the loving-kindness and self-compassion that you deserve, rewire your brain for optimal long-term emotional health, handle stressors more easily, and give your wayward eating the boot.

Ending Your Emotional Eating without Going on Another Diet

If you routinely snack mindlessly or excessively, overeat at meals, or binge, this book offers you a way out from a lifetime of suffering. If you're ready for an alternative to dieting, this book will help you address the true causes of your overeating or imbalanced eating.

Whether you were fortunate enough to have been raised by loving, kind, well-intentioned caregivers or had the misfortune of being reared by unkind, abusive, or neglectful elders, this book gives you the tools you need to connect to and pay attention to your mind, body, and spirit signals and respond to them with love and care.

If you're the parent, therapist, teacher, caregiver, spouse, sibling, or friend of someone struggling with emotional eating, this book will help you better understand, nurture, and support those you love and care for.

This book will also be helpful for anyone, not just emotional eaters, who may have missed out on consistent and sufficient emotional nurturance in childhood. You may not overeat, but you may overuse alcohol, drugs, sex, pornography, or drama, or surf the internet to excess. You may spend money compulsively or gamble irresponsibly. Perhaps you're a workaholic or an overexerciser or use busyness as your drug of choice. Maybe you have trouble controlling your anger and routinely lash out at others. Perhaps you're chronically late or struggle with procrastination. If you have difficulty controlling your behaviors and disciplining yourself or activating yourself, this book can help you.

How to Use This Book

Since each chapter of this book builds on the previous one, it's best to read the chapters in order. The Emotional Eating Checklist, which follows this introduction, will help you get clear on your particular emotional eating challenges.

Part I discusses how we develop self-regulation, or the ability to manage our emotions, moods, thoughts, impulses, and behaviors. In order for our brains to develop and connect the proper circuitry for self-regulation, we require *attuned* or "tuned-in" experiences with our early caregivers. These experiences help create secure attachments, activate certain pathways in the brain, strengthen existing connections, and enable new connections to be made.

Throughout the book, I share actual cases (with the individuals' names changed to protect privacy) that demonstrate how insufficient emotional and physical attention, chronically stressful interactions with our caregivers, separations, or traumatic experiences early in life can cause significant alterations in the structure and chemistry of the developing brain. These can result in difficulties in regulating emotions, moods, and behaviors; chronic disconnection; and self-abandonment. They can also result in poor emotional and physical awareness, lack of emotional endurance and resilience, and difficulty activating ourselves throughout our lives.

In part 1 you'll learn how you can enhance the structure and chemistry of your brain for improved self-regulation. You'll also learn about your body's stress-response apparatus. When, as infants and young children, we encounter responsive and nurturing adults, we develop healthy stress-response mechanisms. When we are exposed to chronic stress and negative emotional arousal, we are forced to manage this high-intensity activation through tension in many parts of our body. When we have developed these patterns in childhood, it is highly likely that we will continue to use these same patterns throughout life. Continual high emotional arousal can lead to physical changes that contribute to poor nervous-system regulation and multiple health challenges.

If you happen to be an overeater or imbalanced eater who had kind and loving parents and a great childhood, I show you how even the most well-intentioned caregivers may inadvertently fail to meet their children's early developmental needs.

In part 2, you'll learn that even if you missed out on emotional attunement early in life, or if you experienced insufficient or inconsistent nurturance as a child, you can still strengthen your neurological circuits and change the physical structure of your adult brain for improved self-regulation. By understanding how your brain works, you can learn to pay mindful attention, or *internally attune*, to your emotions, bodily sensations, needs, and thoughts. I show you how you can relate to yourself and others in ways that create and support healthy brain connections and facilitate learning and growth. Psychological and neurological maturation can continue throughout our lives.

Part 2 presents the seven skills that make up what I call *inner nurturing*, along with information, tools, and special tips that will help you begin using these skills to practice self-connection and self-nurturance. It's best to practice the skills in the order in which they are introduced, as they are designed to regulate emotional and physical arousal (and to begin rewiring your brain and altering your stress response) before attempting to problem-solve and meet your authentic nonfood needs.

Through practicing these skills, you'll learn to access an internal nurturing voice: a mature, wise, validating, affirming, unconditionally kind, loving, soothing, comforting, encouraging, protecting, hopeful, and helpful adult voice. This is the part of you that can help you stay with and process your unpleasant feeling states, reframe self-defeating thoughts, remind you of your strengths and resources, and help you meet your needs. Without this voice, a very young part of you — your *feeling self* — is running the show too much of the time.

As you establish and reinforce the alliance between this mature, wise part of you — your Inner Nurturer — and your *feeling self*, you strengthen the connection between the parts of your brain necessary for self-regulation. You can also apply these seven skills to other areas of your life where you're having difficulties with self-regulation, such as exercising, spending, or procrastinating.

In part 3, we complete our work on nurturance by learning some strategies for attracting nurturing others into our lives. Many emotional eaters have had little exposure to nurturing people. Lacking consistent and sufficient *external* nurturance when they were young, they have difficulty establishing nurturing connections with other people and often settle for undernourishing relationships. If you're dissatisfied with the quality of the nurturance you're receiving, you can find solutions here.

We'll also look at the four habits you'll want to cultivate in order to better nurture others. The people closest to us, as well as those we interact with in our communities, benefit when we strengthen our nurturing skills. Giving is truly receiving: learning to nurture others helps you nurture yourself.

Inner Nurturing:
Not a Quick Fix, but a Forever Fix

Building new skills takes practice and patience. You will not master them overnight. Allow yourself the time you need to proceed through the three parts of this book. A slow and steady approach is needed to conquer your emotional eating and meet your goals.

As you work on these skills and habits, watch any tendency toward perfectionism, which may imbalance you further. It's more important to practice what you're learning consistently — not perfectly. In the beginning, the skills may feel challenging. Learning to turn inward and use a kind, supportive inner voice may feel awkward. But as you build the integrative circuits of your brain, it will get easier, and you'll feel better equipped than ever to address your needs and set limits on unwanted behaviors. That's the power of inner nurturing. Now, let's get started!

Emotional Eating Checklist

If you regularly eat when you're not hungry, eat beyond fullness, or choose to eat unhealthy comfort foods, there is a good chance that your eating has an emotional component. A craving, or an exaggerated desire to eat in the absence of true physiological hunger cues, represents an emotional appetite. Emotional hunger often *feels* the same as physical hunger.

Please place a check mark next to any of the following that apply:

❑ I use food as a tranquilizer to dull emotions that are difficult to cope with, such as anxiety, anger, sadness, frustration, hopelessness, loneliness, shame, guilt, and even happiness, excitement, and joy.
❑ I use food to calm me when I'm experiencing an unpleasant bodily sensation, such as agitation, nervousness, or muscle tension.
❑ I turn to food for soothing and comfort.
❑ I use food for pleasure, escape, fulfillment, and excitement.
❑ I eat when I'm stressed out.
❑ I eat when I feel numb.
❑ I use food to silence negative, critical, self-defeating thoughts and quiet my mind.
❑ I eat when I'm overwhelmed and feeling paralyzed.
❑ I eat to distract myself from low-motivation states like boredom, lethargy, or apathy.
❑ I eat as a way to procrastinate.
❑ I eat because my life lacks purpose, meaning, passion, and inspiration.
❑ I try to fill up an inner emptiness with food.
❑ I eat because I feel so much regret regarding my life.
❑ I eat because I feel deprived in life.

- ❑ I eat to reward myself.
- ❑ I eat to punish myself.
- ❑ I eat to rebel against someone or something.
- ❑ I eat because feeling full makes me feel safe.
- ❑ I eat to ward off sexual attention.
- ❑ My preoccupation with food and weight keeps me from moving forward in life.
- ❑ I can't imagine life feeling satisfying without my favorite comfort foods.
- ❑ Food is my best friend.

If you have checked off one or more items, your eating may have an emotional component to it. And if that's the case, you'll benefit from the mindfulness practice presented in this book.

PART ONE

Parental Nurturing
Beyond Food and Shelter

CHAPTER ONE

The Importance of
Early Caregiving

Brain development in the uterus and during childhood is the single most important biological factor in determining whether or not a person will be predisposed to substance dependence and to addictive behaviors of any sort, whether drug-related or not.

— Gabor Maté, *In the Realm of Hungry Ghosts*

Most of us have been taught that genetics determines everything about us, from our eye and hair color to our personality traits, temperament, athletic abilities, height, weight distribution, susceptibility to certain diseases, and even eating habits and preferences. And as any dieter will tell you, certain inherited patterns, like body weight distribution and a gnawing sweet tooth, can seem nearly impossible to alter. But recent brain science shows that our brain development is hugely influenced by our environment, perhaps even more than by genetic factors. This fact has profound implications for our ability, as both children and adults, to self-regulate: to manage our emotions and moods, regulate our nervous system, control or redirect disruptive impulses and behaviors, and think before we act.

Large-scale research studies have examined how early life experiences, in addition to hereditary predispositions, shape brain pathways and affect brain development. Studies in rats have shown that those who received more licking and other types of nurturing contact from their mothers during infancy had more efficient brain circuitry for reducing anxiety as adults. All mammalian mothers nurture their infants. Right after giving birth, a newborn rat, puppy, or kitten nuzzles into the mother, and the mother begins licking it. She continues to lick her baby throughout the rearing period. Humans touch, kiss, cuddle, caress, hug, and hold their babies. Parental nurturing is critical to the normal development of the infant's brain.

A child's self-regulation skills are nurtured by her caregiver's ongoing, patient, tuned-in attention to the child's internal world and her developing interest in the external world. Literally thousands of moment-to-moment interactions between a caregiver and a young child take place during childhood, and these interactions are involved in building the child's emotional, cognitive, and social skills. Everything we experience in the womb, infancy, and early childhood — the kind of care we receive, the food we're given, the people we're surrounded by, the music we hear, the stories we're told, the lessons we learn, the stressors we're exposed to — has a significant effect on our brain development. If all goes well, we develop emotional and relational skills that allow us to live meaningful, well-balanced lives and enjoy healthy relationships with ourselves and others.

It Takes a Village to Raise Healthy, Well-Adjusted Children

In the past sixty to seventy years, parents in Western societies have faced new challenges in nurturing their children. The small nuclear family has become the norm, divorce and single parenting are common, and many parents are forced to cope with a lack of support — physical, emotional, and financial. Extended family members often live many miles, if not countries, apart. Families, couples, and singles living in close proximity barely know one another. A neighborhood is no longer automatically a community. When we lack the comfort and support of extended family, close friends, and neighborhood communities, it becomes more difficult to raise and nurture our children.

Parents who are raising many children and coping with stress or physical or mental illness may find it especially difficult to consistently meet their children's emotional needs. Depressed, anxious, or ill parents inevitably find parenting more challenging, and infants and children of such parents may become uncooperative and aggressive. Poor maternal nutrition and prenatal alcohol and drug exposure produce infants whose brain functioning is impaired.

Infants and children exposed to neglect and abuse live in a constant state of high arousal that alters the normal functioning of their stress hormones. They are easily aroused and ready to fight or flee. These children often fail to develop the ability to regulate their emotions and behaviors and end up on a life path that involves attention difficulties, poor performance in school, aggressive social behavior, criminal activities, and substance abuse, including disordered eating patterns.

Even emotionally and physically healthy, well-intentioned parents can miss the mark if they themselves missed out on the right kind of emotional nurturance in infancy and childhood and failed to learn skills for caring for themselves and others. Milder forms of parental misattunement in early childhood, such as a regularly distracted or overwhelmed parent, can also affect a child's brain development and result in behavioral challenges like eating disturbances.

Early in life, we may seek comfort, calming, and pleasure from external sources, like thumb sucking (I still have the bump on my thumb), favorite objects (I had a special doll that went everywhere with me), and favorite foods. Food is like medicine: it alters our brain chemistry and, like a thumb or favorite doll, it's readily available, soothing, and predictable. But when we miss out on the right kind of emotional nurturance early in life, and routinely turn to external sources, we fail to develop optimal brain circuitry. And when our brains don't develop properly, there is a high probability that our emotional life, thought processes, and behavioral patterns will be derailed. Rather than acquiring self-care skills that will last a lifetime, we end up with skill deficits that can have lifelong consequences.

Lacking appropriate self-soothing and comforting skills, we may have difficulty regulating our emotions, bodily sensations, impulses, thoughts, and behaviors. We are more prone to have difficulty focusing and concentrating and a limited tolerance for frustration. Perhaps we lack patience with ourselves and others. We may be hypersensitive, highly reactive, and lacking in emotional endurance and resilience. We may relate to others in immature ways. We may have trouble motivating ourselves. Basically, we grow up with an emotionally starved, very young inner child running our lives.

Stopping the Blame Game

This book is *not* about blaming parents and caregivers: parenting is one of the hardest jobs in the world. Rather, it's about understanding what you may have missed out on as an infant and small child and the effects this lack may have had on your brain development and ultimately on your eating behavior.

This is a sensitive subject, as parents, especially mothers, often feel blamed for not raising well-adjusted children. Parenting abilities, often passed down through generations, are limited by our own psychological issues, life circumstances, and challenges. In many cases, poor self-regulation is not necessarily the result of bad experiences in your childhood but rather of a lack of the sufficient nurturing, attuned experiences needed for optimal brain development. And if you had the misfortune of experiencing abuse, neglect, or loss at the hands of difficult and unkind caregivers, most likely they too were the victims of challenging early experiences. The blame game serves no purpose.

Growing and Strengthening Brain Circuits

When you understand how your brain works, you can learn to pay mindful attention, or become *internally attuned*, to your emotions, bodily sensations, needs, and thoughts. You can also learn to relate to yourself and others in ways that create and support healthy brain connections and facilitate learning and growth.

In this section of the book, you'll discover

- why infants and small children need more than proper nutrition, safety, and secure shelter;
- why emotional nurturance is so critical when we are young;
- the importance of a secure attachment to one or more caregivers;
- how shame and criticism can lead to insecure attachments and chronic, lifelong states of shame;
- how early attuned experiences with our caregivers activate certain pathways in the brain, strengthen existing neural connections, and enable the forming of new connections;
- which parts of the brain are involved in self-regulation;
- why it's never too late to strengthen connections and rewire the brain;
- which part of your brain is in charge when you have a strong urge to eat;
- why you often act before you think;
- how early relationships influence the development of the body's system for regulating stress;
- how chronic high emotional arousal can tear down the body and result in a myriad of health challenges; and
- how even well-intentioned caregivers can fail to meet their children's developmental needs.

Among the detailed cases that follow of clients struggling with overeating challenges, some may seem more relevant to your situation than others. It is, however, important to read them all carefully. Each case illustrates key concepts and principles that will facilitate your understanding of your own relationship with food as a source of comfort.

Even though your personal history is unique, you'll find elements in these cases that you can relate to. Some of them may bring up unpleasant emotions and memories from your childhood. This is normal and to be expected. Be gentle and patient with yourself as you work through the book. Take it slowly; there is no rush. Hopefully, the path will be exciting and illuminating as you begin to see the pieces of your own emotional eating puzzle.

CHAPTER TWO

What's Love Got to Do with It?

> Children whose parents are reliable sources of comfort and strength
> have a lifetime advantage — a kind of buffer against the worst that
> fate can hand them.
>
> — Bessel van der Kolk, *The Body Keeps the Score*

I could tell when I entered the waiting room of my office that Liz was having a bad day. Her eyes were puffy, and her mascara was smudged. Usually she sat comfortably in the large, cushioned chair, distracting herself with her phone or a magazine. Today she was sitting on the couch, her body tense and rigid and her hands clasped tightly on the edge, like a bobcat ready to pounce. When her eyes met mine, her body softened, and she began to cry.

As we walked down the hall to my office, I could feel her desperation. On her drive home from work, she had an argument with her mother, and on her way to see me, she did something that she hadn't done in six months. She stopped at her favorite donut shop and bought a coffee, four donuts, and two cream puffs. Only one cream puff was left in the bag. She had begun to lose weight in the past couple of months, and she was furious with herself for slipping back into old patterns.

Her mother, whom she described as a "controlling and domineering woman," had offered to throw a fortieth birthday bash for her, and in trying to firm up the plans, Liz asserted herself and suggested a restaurant she liked. Her mother quickly dismissed her choice as too expensive. And she shamed Liz, accusing her of choosing "an overpriced hole-in-the-wall with fattening food that you don't need to be eating." Her mother continued the tirade by highlighting Liz's high blood pressure and failed attempts at weight loss, reminding her that she wouldn't have many birthdays left if she didn't change her ways.

Even though Liz described feeling some anger toward her mother, the bulk of the feelings that came up as we discussed the conversation were about herself and about how she couldn't ever measure up. Liz often doesn't feel heard and understood by her mother, who regularly overreacts and dismisses, criticizes, or ridicules Liz's feelings. As Liz put it, "My mother always wins every argument."

These repeated misses in communication with her mother, which began as far back as Liz can remember, always leave her feeling bad about herself. Her mother's support is unpredictable: at times she is very supportive, but at other times she can be highly critical. Liz personalizes these attacks, which leave her feeling ashamed, inadequate, unworthy, and lonely. She feels bad about her abilities to make "grown-up" decisions, ashamed of her body (she inherited a body type very different from her mother's naturally slim figure), and sad about her relationship with her mother.

Liz's mother has shown little patience for discussing and processing their troubled interactions. They rarely transition from these negative interactions back to positive ones during the same conversation. After an interaction like this one, Liz and her mother typically go through a week or more of what Liz describes as "cold war" before reconciling, and Liz is the one who "crawls back" and tries to please her mother. It's just too difficult for her to tolerate her mother's displeasure and risk abandonment. Liz regularly abandons her own needs for understanding and validation in order to seek approval and secure the attachment with her mother. And Liz shames herself even further because she feels that as a social worker, she should know how to create a healthier relationship with her mother.

Liz's mother has had difficulty offering Liz a type of care and attention essential to the development of the brain's self-regulation circuits: *attunement.* This is the subtle process of adjusting to and resonating with another person's internal states: that is, being "in tune" with someone else's internal world. It's an instinctive process for a parent, but it may be lacking when a parent is stressed, depressed, distracted, or impatient.

Love is not the issue: Liz has never had any doubt that her mother loves her and would do anything she could for her. And Liz likewise loves and respects her mother, whom she describes as "a bright, articulate, and funny woman." They often have very pleasant times together. The problems generally arise when Liz is anxious or upset and turns to her mother for comfort and soothing, or when her mother strongly disagrees with the way Liz is handling something, like the upcoming birthday party.

Poor Attunement, Insecure Attachments

Attunement is an important component of another process that begins in infancy and childhood and continues throughout our lives: *attachment.* A vulnerable infant has an innate need to be close to a nourishing and protective other. Our drive for attachment is essential for our survival. Compared to most other mammals, we depend on our caregivers for an extended period. Yet, according to the child psychiatrist Daniel Siegel, a founding co-director of the Mindful Awareness Research Center at the University of California, Los Angeles, only about one-half to two-thirds of the general population have had what researchers call a "secure attachment."

When we have a secure attachment to a caregiver, we feel safe: we can count on them to protect us from harm and to calm, comfort, and soothe us when we are distressed. We feel that another person senses and observes our inner world and that our needs will be met. We develop positive expectations of interactions with other people and trust that these too will be fulfilling and rewarding.

In contrast, when we have experienced repeated, highly stressful interactions with our caregivers, our ability to form safe, secure relationships with them becomes compromised. This is true even with kind and well-meaning caregivers if they don't have enough time for us or have difficulty relating to us and meeting our needs. Liz's father, for example, is a kind and gentle man, but Liz has trouble relating to him because he is forty-five years older, often distracted, and a bit out of touch with her world.

Early attachment patterns create mental maps for our relationships throughout life and guide our expectations of others. Because of her insecure attachment to her parents and a history of being criticized and shamed by her mother, Liz has persistently high levels of anxiety and shame. She doesn't feel safe and secure in her body or in the world. The shaming she has suffered has created what John Bradshaw, the author of *Homecoming*, calls "toxic shame: the feeling of being flawed and diminished and never measuring up." Her shame makes it difficult for her to embrace both her strengths and weaknesses and to develop a healthy level of self-esteem and self-acceptance.

Liz is hyperreactive to intense emotions like shame and their associated bodily cues, such as heart palpitations, muscle tension, and what she describes as "a frozen feeling." Her internal world is fragile: she is easily derailed by external stressors like her mother's aggression and her boss's unpredictable moods. Neural pathways connecting the emotional region of Liz's brain to the thinking and regulating region have failed to form properly, while other circuits, geared toward handling stressful interactions, have been strengthened. She tends to be hypervigilant: her brain has become hard-wired to perceive threat quickly.

Feelings of shame are common in children whose parents are emotionally unavailable or repeatedly fail to attune to them. Children who feel invisible or misunderstood often experience this lack of attunement physiologically in the form of a shrinking or slumping sensation, or a feeling of heaviness in the chest, back, and shoulders. They often appear sad, with a downcast posture.

When brain cells, called *neurons*, repeatedly fire simultaneously in response to an experience, those neurons become connected to each other. As the Canadian neuropsychologist and researcher Donald Hebb puts it, "Cells that fire together wire together." They form a network and become hard-wired in the brain: in essence, they become part of our conditioned, habitual responses to the world. The strength of these connections is influenced by many factors, including the frequency of their use.

According to Daniel Siegel:

> These isolated states of being — shame intensified by humiliation — burn themselves into our synaptic connections.... In the future, we'll be vulnerable to reactivating the state of shame or humiliation in contexts that resemble the original situation. The state of shame becomes associated with a cortically constructed belief that the self is defective. From the point of view of survival, "I am bad" is a safer perspective than "My parents are unreliable and may abandon me at any time." It's better for the child to feel defective than to realize that his attachment figures are dangerous, undependable, or untrustworthy. The mental mechanism of shame at least preserves for him the illusion of safety and security that is at the core of his sanity.

Liz's early stressful experiences with her mother have been encoded as maladaptive emotional and cognitive patterns in her brain. After experiencing her mother's shaming look repeatedly when putting food on her plate, grabbing a snack, or trying on clothes, Liz regularly feels anxiety and shame even when no one else is around. She is quick to interpret an innocent glance from a stranger or store clerk as shaming. She has a tendency to overreact, because at times of stress, she can't access the neural circuits that would help her calm down and regulate her emotions. At times like these, indulging in her favorite, tranquilizing comfort foods, like donuts and cream puffs, is the fastest way to quiet the agitation in her body and the storm in her brain.

Regulating Emotions and Behaviors
through Attunement

A caregiver's role is to meet a child's basic physical needs (food, clothing, shelter) and to provide consistent emotional nurturance. Emotions — reactions in the brain that cause a change in our internal states — signal us, and our caregivers, to act. As infants and small children, we cannot regulate our emotions and behaviors alone: we rely on our primary caregivers to soothe and comfort us. Attuned interactions — experiences that let us know that someone else perceives and understands what we are feeling — allow preverbal infants, not yet capable of understanding emotions or using language, to feel close, connected, safe, and loved.

Most caregivers do a pretty good job of tuning in to an infant's distress and offering an appropriate and soothing emotional response. For example, when a toddler hits her head on the edge of the table and starts to scream and cry, her mother identifies and acknowledges her emotions and pain: "Oh, sweetie, I see that you are sad because you bumped your head. That really hurts! Let Mommy kiss your boo-boo." The child's mother helps to regulate or lessen the intensity of the child's emotions with her attuned words. By identifying the bumped head, the sadness, and the pain, the parent is teaching the child to name her emotions, her bodily sensations, and the things that cause pain.

At the same time, the mother conveys caring and empathy through her actions, kissing and cuddling the child in her arms. These behaviors help her baby feel safe and secure. An association is established between intense feeling states and the possibility of a return to safety and comfort. This is the necessary foundation for building the skills of self-soothing, self-nurturing, and self-regulation. Once her child is calm, the mother might use this situation to engage her child in problem solving for the future: "Corners of tables are sharp; it's best if we don't play near them."

This tuning-in session may only last a few minutes, but situations like this will occur thousands of times in the child's early years, not only with Mom but also with other caregivers. We need our caregivers to help us identify and name our emotions, to allow us to feel and express all of our emotions, and to help us tolerate and navigate challenging emotional and bodily states by soothing us and teaching us how to soothe ourselves. This requires an atmosphere of patience, warmth, empathy, understanding, acceptance, fairness, respect, and above all, nondistracted emotional availability.

These attunement experiences not only develop and strengthen the caregiver-child attachment but also play a role in the child's brain development. Research suggests that good attunement promotes the growth of the self-regulation region of the brain.

Over time, as the child's brain develops, her reliance on her mother to "coregulate" her emotions lessens, and she begins to self-regulate, or manage her emotions independently. This ability is crucial. Children with good emotional self-regulation do better in school. They have an easier time making friends because they can manage their emotions and relate to others without aggression or impulsiveness and without alienating them. And they are less likely to engage in substance use or abuse.

Young children who do not experience this kind of attunement will most likely experience difficulties with self-regulation. In the words of the addiction specialist Gabor Maté, the author of *In the Realm of Hungry Ghosts*: "Children who suffer disruptions in their attachment relationships will not have the same biochemical milieu in their brains as will their well-attached and well-nurtured peers. As a result, their experiences and interpretations of their environment, and their responses to it, will be less flexible, less adaptive, and less conducive to health and maturity."

A Good Kid in a Not-So-Good Environment

Stop for a moment and reflect on the type of caregiving you received as an infant and small child. Were your parents or caregivers kind and empathic? Were they good listeners? Did they tune in to your emotions and bodily states? Were they patient, soothing, and comforting when you were upset or discouraged? Did you feel that you wouldn't be judged or ridiculed, no matter what you did or said? Did you feel safe and secure?

Did your caregivers show you how to deal with worrisome thoughts? Did they make time for you when you needed them to? Were you treated with fairness and respect? Did you feel loved and valued? Did you feel that they appreciated and honored your uniqueness?

If your caregivers were stressed, anxious, distracted, or depressed when you were young, they may have had difficulty tuning in to your emotional states on a consistent basis. They may not have had their own basic emotional needs adequately met when they were young. Their parenting style may have been controlling, domineering, intimidating, hypercritical, angry, or shaming. They may have been overprotective, indifferent, or out of touch.

Even well-meaning, loving caregivers can be distracted by their own struggles. They may be working too many hours or have excessive responsibilities. They may have physical or mental health challenges. A parent can deeply love her child and feel a loving attachment but be unable to adequately tune in to her child's emotional states. Children in these types of relationships will know that they are loved but feel that their parents don't "get" them or don't have time for them.

When our caregivers cannot assist us in regulating our emotional and physical arousal and understanding our experiences, we are left in distress. Overwhelmed by unpleasant emotions, uncomfortable bodily sensations, and self-defeating thoughts, our ability to self-regulate, or keep our emotional environment on an even keel, is compromised.

The Importance of Internal Attunement

If, like Liz, you missed out on consistently nourishing attunement experiences and secure parental attachment in your childhood, take heart. Your adult brain can be influenced and altered by your current life experiences. Mindfulness practice — a form of *internal attunement* — can help you fill developmental skill gaps resulting from early attachment misses and nurture and strengthen the circuitry of your brain for improved self-regulation. We'll explore that practice in part 2.

In later chapters we'll revisit my sessions with Liz, focusing on her difficulty with staying with her feelings, validating them, and regulating them by soothing and calming herself. We'll also look at her challenges in relating to her mother. Without clear personal boundaries, Liz lives with a constant source of stress that taxes her physically and emotionally and fuels her overeating.

In the next chapter, we look at how this distress overwhelms our brain's self-regulation circuitry and chemical communication systems. Chronic distress also taxes our stress-control mechanisms and can lead to a residue of energy becoming trapped in our nervous system, where it wreaks havoc on our body, mind, and spirit. When we cannot regulate emotional and physical arousal in any other way, the lure of brain-numbing foods like donuts and cream puffs becomes irresistible.

CHAPTER THREE

It's All in Your Head

One of the most striking peculiarities of the human brain is the great
development of the frontal lobes — they are much less developed in
other primates and hardly evident at all in other mammals. They are
the part of the brain that grows and develops most after birth.

— Oliver Sacks, *An Anthropologist on Mars*

It's your mind that gets you into trouble when it comes to overeating.
On your way home from another exhausting day at work, you can't
stop thinking about pizza, so you stop and buy one. You did well at managing your eating all day, and you had the best of intentions when making
that last stop at the supermarket to pick up some fruit and vegetables. But
somehow that cheesecake sampler ended up in your cart. You know these
foods aren't the healthiest choices and that buying more than a serving
size of any of them isn't wise. You rationalize that you'll just have one
piece of pizza and one slice of cheesecake and save the rest for later. And
that Zumba class you were going to take — well, you're just too tired
tonight, but you'll go tomorrow for sure.

When tomorrow comes and your friend invites you to dinner, you
accept the invitation without hesitation and once again skip the dance

class. After all, you still have many more days this week to fit in exercise. On the drive to the restaurant, you promise yourself that you'll order soup and salad — you almost don't remember ordering the cheesy noodle dish and that second glass of wine. What happened between making that promise to yourself and now? Truly, you want to do better, but something always gets in the way.

It's your brain. And it's not your fault! When we have not received consistent and sufficient emotional nurturance during our early years, we are at greater risk of seeking it from external sources, like food and alcohol, later in life. Many of us have been raised to interpret undisciplined behavior patterns, like overeating and underexercising, as a sign of character weakness or laziness and a general lack of control. This kind of judgmental labeling is not only inaccurate — many overeaters I work with are extremely disciplined in many areas of their lives — but also unhelpful. Disordered eating patterns represent resourceful survival strategies for regulating emotional or physical arousal (or lack of arousal), coping with adverse experiences, and increasing pleasure. Understanding this takes the shame out of recovery and shows us the way forward.

When you have a strong urge to detach from unpleasant emotions or bodily sensations, turn off painful thoughts, distract yourself, numb out, and comfort, soothe, and pleasure yourself with food, the part of you that turns to food is very, very young. You can't manage or modify your behavior with logical arguments, because that very young part of you doesn't respond to reason. You are under the influence of an emotionally dominant part of your brain about the shape and size of an almond, called the *amygdala* (pronounced uh-MIG-duh-luh).

This part of the brain is like your central alarm system, and it plays a key role in the way you respond emotionally and behaviorally to perceived threats (in this case, a stressful day at work). This young part of you wants what she wants, when she wants it. She doesn't care about health or weight consequences. She doesn't care about fitting into the outfit you bought last month. She lives in this moment, and right now she is unsatisfied and demanding. Her motto is "I don't care; I want it *now*."

The mid to lower part of your brain (the limbic region), which houses the amygdala, runs from the brain stem, at the top of your neck, to about the level of the bridge of your nose. Although it's already well developed at birth, it's sometimes referred to as *primitive*, because it's responsible for regulating basic functions like breathing, heart rate, digestion, and wake and sleep cycles. It's ready at a moment's notice to activate the body's fight, flight, or freeze response. This part of the brain allows you to act before you think. It's responsible for strong emotions, impulses, and instincts, like the intense fear you feel and your quick reaction when your toddler runs out into a busy street, or the panic that sets in when you see a coyote cross your front lawn and you frantically search for your cat. This part of the brain is the source of our reactivity, and while it's lifesaving at times, it can also get us into trouble.

The upstairs part of your brain comes online later in development. This outer layer, called the *cortex*, runs from your forehead to the back of your head, covering the lower brain, and it doesn't reach full maturity until we're in our mid-twenties. The cortex, and more specifically an area called the *prefrontal cortex*, is part of our self-regulation system, and it depends on properly working connections and input from lower parts of the brain. This area of the brain is responsible for cognitive, emotional, and relational skills: it helps you regulate your emotions, observe your thoughts, take in insight, adjust your behaviors, learn from your mistakes, stay flexible and adaptive, make wise decisions and plans, and feel empathy and compassion for yourself and others.

This part of the brain allows you to think before you act and to evaluate emotionally driven impulses — like the urge to eat more than a couple of slices of pizza or buy an entire cheesecake sampler. With normal development and sufficient early nurturance, integrative circuits grow and strengthen between our upstairs and downstairs brain regions. We gradually develop the ability to apply mature, top-down control strategies that help us regulate our behaviors. When the downstairs part of the brain sends out signals to grab the pizza and the cheesecake, the upstairs part might remind us about an upcoming social event and the outfit we want to fit into. It might help us access a nurturing, limit-setting adult voice that reminds us we *can* have pizza and cheesecake if we like, but it's best to buy single servings. This area of the brain can become compromised, however, by insufficient, stressful, or adverse early experiences with caregivers. It may feel inaccessible when we are experiencing intense emotions and stress, especially if we are fatigued or sleep deprived.

Self-regulation, or the ability to manage our emotions, moods, thoughts, impulses, and behaviors, is a developmental achievement. Life experiences activate certain pathways in and between different regions of the brain, strengthening existing connections and creating new ones. Developing and connecting, or *integrating*, the proper brain circuitry for self-regulation requires certain conditions. In his book *The Developing Mind*, Daniel Siegel states that "optimal relationships are likely to stimulate the growth of integrative fibers in the brain, whereas neglectful and abusive relationships specifically inhibit the healthy growth of neural integration in the young child. Experience early in life may be especially crucial in organizing the way the basic regulatory structures of the brain develop."

In order to curb our emotional reactivity and wayward impulses and make wise decisions about food, we need the upstairs brain to step in and perform its duties as the captain of the ship. When our self-regulation circuitry is working well and all parts of the brain have open communication, we find ourselves less dependent on external supports, such as food or chemicals, to calm us down, lift us up, or get us going.

The Triune Brain

This simple model of the brain describes the three areas of the brain that are designed to process information separately and to function as a whole. (*Triune* means "three in one.")

The *brain stem* regulates basic processes like heart rate and respiration, as well as states of arousal. This area receives input from the body and communicates with the areas above it.

The *limbic region* is the emotional brain, responsible for our basic drives and emotions, and it is home to the emotional-processing *amygdala* and the *hippocampus*, which is responsible for converting our feelings and experiences into words and memory.

The *cortex* is the thinking brain, responsible for higher-level cognitive functions and relational skills and helping to coordinate the connections among all brain regions.

Left Brain, Right Brain

The brain is organized into lateral as well as vertical regions. Like the upstairs and downstairs regions of the brain, the left and right sides of the brain need open channels of communication. The right side develops earlier than the left and communicates more directly with the lower brain areas and the body. This side of the brain receives emotional information: it is home to our emotions, intuition, gut feelings, imagery, nonverbal communication, and autobiographical memory. As very young children, we're right-brain dominant: we live completely in the moment and have little concern for concepts like right and wrong or following the rules. Our left brain, responsible for logic, language, and linear thinking, develops a bit later.

Generally, the two sides of the brain work together fairly smoothly, even in people who seem to favor one side over the other. However, traumatic memories appear to activate the right hemisphere and deactivate the left. One of the results of this imbalance is that when something reminds us of a traumatic event, we can feel as though the event were happening in the present, not the past. Unable to access our rational left brain, we may feel flooded and overwhelmed by our feelings. At times like these, there's a high probability that our emotional response will be bigger than the crime and that we'll resort to a maladaptive coping behavior in an attempt to stop the emotional overload and restore tranquility. We may grab our favorite comfort foods and overeat. We might ignore the alarm messages from our emotional brain, even though our bodies are registering the threat, and deny the existence of our feelings. But the right side of the brain keeps working, as stress hormones signal the muscles to prepare for fight, flight, or freeze. Eventually, the physical effects on the body will demand attention.

Similarly, when we function predominantly from our left brain, we cannot harness the full potential of both sides working together. Cut off from our emotions and intuition and the richness and creativity they offer, our lives can feel dull and unsatisfying. We may find that delectable foods offer the excitement and bliss our left-brained lives seem to be missing.

Brain Chemistry and Overeating

Consistent and sufficient parental nurturing in infancy and childhood plays a major role not only in the normal development of the structure of the brain regions and circuits, but in the brain's chemical communication systems as well. Brain chemicals, called *neurotransmitters*, allow messages to pass from one cell to the next and are essential for communication between brain cells. Brain chemicals regulate our mood and mental energy, alertness, focus, and calmness. The quality of our lives is highly determined by our brain chemistry.

There is a specific area of the upstairs brain, called the *orbitofrontal cortex*, that is heavily involved in our ability to regulate our emotions, impulses, and behaviors. This area has a dense network of connections to the lower brain structures, where our most primitive emotions, like rage and fear, are generated, and the brain stem, where our physiological body states are managed. This area of the brain is at the center of our reward and motivation system, and it contains a large supply of the reward chemicals — endorphins and dopamine — associated with soothing, calm, joy, and pleasure.

Endorphins: Molecules of Emotion

Endorphins alleviate physical and emotional pain and facilitate emotional bonding. If you've ever had a serious injury and didn't feel pain immediately, you can thank your endorphins for that — and for the deeply relaxed and calm feeling that comes after lovemaking, because a flood of endorphins is released during orgasm. (Leave it to nature to make sure the propagation of the species is an enjoyable process!) Endorphins are also the brain chemicals responsible for "runner's high," the euphoric state some runners describe after an extended period of aerobic exercise. Some overeaters are also overexercisers, and this tendency may be due in part to a subconscious effort to boost low endorphin levels.

Researchers have identified more than twenty different types of endorphins. In addition to alleviating emotional and physical pain, these chemicals are involved in the regulation of blood pressure, heart rate, breathing, and body temperature. We have endorphin receptors (think of these as the loading docks of your cells) in different types of cells throughout our bodies, playing different roles. For example, in the nervous system, endorphins act as painkillers and tranquilizers, whereas in our mouths, they diminish secretions and lead to the familiar "cotton-mouth" sensation.

Endorphins also govern our attachment instinct. A mother's attention and loving presence trigger an endorphin release in an infant's brain. Nature didn't forget the brains of mothers, either: mothers experience huge endorphin surges when they nurture their babies. Conversely, if a mother or other caregiver fails to respond adequately to an infant's needs on a consistent basis, endorphins are not released in the baby's brain. She is left to self-soothe with alternative coping mechanisms like thumb sucking, rocking, or shutting down and tuning out.

When our levels of this natural pain reliever (named for its resemblance to morphine) are low, we may find that we are highly sensitive to both emotional and physical pain. We seem to feel pain more than others do. Perhaps we cry at the drop of a hat. Stress can deplete our scanty levels of endorphins even further.

Alcohol and drugs (especially opiates), as well as drug-like components in foods such as refined flours and sugars, can attach to our brain-cell receptor sites and take the place of our natural brain chemicals. As our brain perceives these receptor sites as full, it produces *less* of our natural chemicals. This partly explains the vicious cycle many overeaters know so well: cravings, indulgence, relief, and more cravings.

Dopamine: Energy and Focus

Our main energizing brain chemical is called *dopamine*. It's like our natural caffeine. It promotes a sense of satisfaction, drives assertiveness, and pumps up our libido. Dopamine keeps us feeling energized, upbeat, and alert. By helping us focus and concentrate, it plays a role in the learning of new behaviors. Pleasurable experiences such as dinner with a dear friend, a good tennis match, or the anticipation of a vacation tend to elevate dopamine levels.

Joyful, nurturing interactions with primary caregivers stimulate the development of dopamine receptors in the infant's brain. Early separations, insufficient emotional and physical attention, or regular stressed interactions with caregivers can cause significant alterations in the dopamine system, including reduced dopamine production as well as a diminished number of dopamine receptors.

If you're low in this important brain chemical, you may experience low or flat moods, including depression. You may have difficulty getting out of bed in the morning or tend to sleep long hours. You may find it challenging to concentrate and focus on tasks. Your motivation, drive, and enthusiasm for life may be low, and you may have difficulty activating yourself. You may experience boredom or apathy more often than you'd like. You may feel easily overwhelmed and inclined to procrastinate. Your brain and your life may feel cluttered.

Studies have demonstrated that 12 to 40 percent of adults in the United States are born with a gene that reduces the number of dopamine receptors. A diminished number of dopamine receptors in the brain appears to play a role in the diagnosis of attention deficit disorder. People with fewer dopamine receptors are at greater risk of engaging in substance abuse, compulsive gambling, internet and sex addiction, and compulsive overeating. Some overeaters have been born with an altered gene that also results in lower production of dopamine.

When your dopamine levels are low, you may be attracted to stimulating substances like coffee, tea, soda, chocolate, tobacco, and street drugs like amphetamines and cocaine. You may also have cravings for sweets, starches, alcohol, marijuana, and foods and drinks sweetened with aspartame. Foods high in fat, like fried foods, chocolate, cheese, and meat also increase dopamine levels, so if these are your go-to comfort foods, low levels of this chemical may be playing a role. And, as with endorphins, when our brains perceive our dopamine receptor sites as full, whether from drug-like foods or beverages or from actual brain chemicals, our natural production declines. We're back to that vicious cycle.

Serotonin: A Sense of Well-Being

Another key brain chemical is *serotonin*. When you have enough of this important chemical, your mood tends to be stable (assuming your other brain chemicals are in balance). Animal studies have demonstrated that parental nurturing determines the production of serotonin. Even minor imbalances in the availability of this chemical can manifest in behaviors such as fearfulness and hyperactivity.

Serotonin deficiency is by far the most common cause of mood problems in the United States. Low serotonin levels can make you feel anxious, panicky, irritable, agitated, cranky, constantly worried, or depressed. You may act impulsively, obsessively, and perfectionistically. Your thoughts are likely to be negative, fearful, and critical. You may experience phobias, fibromyalgia, migraines, PMS, and tension in your jaw. You may suffer digestive difficulties, since a large percentage of the serotonin in your body is in your gut (which has been called the second brain). You might find it difficult to get a good night's sleep, as serotonin is converted to melatonin, the so-called sleep hormone. Your mood may worsen with season and daylight changes, a condition called *seasonal affective disorder*.

Low serotonin levels play a role in food obsession, compulsive binge eating, and exercise addiction. If you find that you're drawn to high-carbohydrate snacks in the late afternoon and evening, it may be because your serotonin production is dropping. Daylight, physical exercise, and foods containing the amino acid L-tryptophan increase serotonin levels in the brain and the body. You may crave dairy products high in this substance, like ice cream, hot chocolate, pudding, or a warm glass of milk. Marijuana and alcohol can enhance serotonin levels, and this explains why you might find yourself wanting to unwind, as the sun goes down, by smoking pot or drinking wine, beer, or your favorite cocktail.

Unfortunately, overuse of marijuana and alcohol can lead to addiction and end up inhibiting serotonin production.

GABA: Soothing Emotional Eruptions

GABA, or gamma-aminobutyric acid, is probably the least-known brain chemical. It is our natural Valium, and it helps us feel relaxed. It's called an inhibitory neurotransmitter because it turns off certain kinds of brain reactions, such as the production of excitatory chemicals like adrenaline. GABA helps to calm our emotional storms without recruiting our brain-stem areas into the all-too-familiar fight, flight, or freeze reactions. If the integrative fibers that connect our upstairs and downstairs brains are working properly, this brain chemical is released when we experience stress.

When GABA levels are low, we may experience mood disturbances and cravings for alcohol, drugs, and comfort food — particularly substances that calm us down, such as alcohol, marijuana, sedatives, sweets, and fatty foods.

Glutamine: Sweet Cravings and Good Digestion

There is one final key player worth mentioning that affects mood and food cravings. Amino acids are the building blocks of all proteins. Glutamine, the most abundant amino acid in the muscle and plasma of humans, is a stimulating, excitatory organic substance that acts like a brain chemical. Traditionally considered a nonessential amino acid, it now appears to be an essential nutrient in the body's response to stress, injury, or illness. It is critical for optimal brain function, boosting mood, increasing alertness, and enhancing memory. It also increases libido and facilitates digestion.

Our brains can use glutamine as an emergency substitute fuel, in place of glucose, when we haven't eaten or when our blood sugar levels are low. If we have enough of this important amino acid, we are less likely to hit the candy machine when our blood-sugar levels drop. When we are under stress, the right amount of glutamine can stop our sugar cravings and save our adrenal glands from overworking. The brains of sugar addicts and alcoholics tend to be low in this important organic substance.

Circuits, Synapses, Chemicals, and Environment

Whether because of insufficient early nurturance, inherited deficiencies, or lifestyle factors, many overeaters have brain chemistry imbalances that make them more susceptible to the energizing, soothing, and calming effects of particular foods and more prone to overeating them.

For some overeaters, a few simple lifestyle changes can help correct these imbalances. I discuss these in further detail in *The Emotional Eater's Repair Manual*. Eating more unprocessed, whole plant foods (especially raw vegetables and foods high in amino acids and essential fatty acids) and reducing your intake of processed foods, alcohol, and stimulants like caffeine are a good start. Exercise is critical to good health, and aerobic exercise, in particular, releases mood-enhancing chemicals and promotes the growth of brain cells.

Good sleep is important, as is good sleep hygiene — habits conducive to getting the right amount and quality of sleep. These include exercising early in the day, refraining from stimulating activity and avoiding bright lights in the evening, and preparing for bed by calming down and dimming the lights. If you are having trouble getting yourself to make any of these lifestyle adjustments, your brain chemistry may be holding you back.

If you feel that the symptoms you're experiencing and the substances you're craving suggest a deficiency or imbalance in any of these chemicals, an adjustment to your brain chemicals may be warranted. There is a good chance you could benefit from a trial of natural supplements prescribed by an informed health-care provider. These include amino acids, essential fatty acids, enzymes, herbs, vitamins, and minerals. Medications also have a place in restoring brain chemistry. Once a prescribed medication has accomplished the initial restoration, the gentler natural supplements can often sustain it.

A medical examination must always be the first step in ruling out physical causes of brain chemical imbalances and any associated symptoms. Do not stop using any prescription drugs or begin taking any supplements without consulting your physician.

Chemical imbalances are caused not simply by an absence or decreased amount of any particular brain chemical but rather by the complex interplay of brain function and chemistry with environmental factors. All overeating behaviors are the result of a complex set of mechanisms that may include inherited deficiencies as well as faulty neurological programming from insufficient early nurturing and traumatic experiences. These, as well as our internal psychological state and our adult interpersonal connections, must be taken into consideration to facilitate recovery.

A multipronged approach is most effective for healing overeating patterns. If your symptoms and cravings are not too bothersome or severe, you may want to practice the mindfulness skills outlined in part 2 before addressing any brain chemistry imbalances. These skills, in addition to the lifestyle adjustments mentioned above, may be sufficient to strengthen the integrative circuits of your brain.

Learning *internal attunement* through mindfulness practice will help you connect to your inner world of feelings, unmet needs, thoughts, beliefs, and memories. By building and strengthening an inner nurturing voice and associated skill set, you'll enhance the self-regulation circuitry in your brain, connecting top to bottom and left to right. At the same time, you'll sharpen your self-soothing skills and learn how to calm your stress response. When all the parts of your brain are communicating and working properly, you'll begin to notice that your favorite comfort foods have less of a hold on you.

CHAPTER FOUR

The Body Remembers

Our bodies contain our histories — every chapter, line, and verse of every event and relationship in our lives. As our lives unfold, our biological health becomes a living, breathing, biographical statement that conveys our strengths, weaknesses, hopes, and fears.

— Caroline Myss, *Anatomy of the Spirit*

When I asked Jan her reason for seeking therapy, she expressed concern that her weight had been creeping up over the past few years and she couldn't seem to get a handle on it. A quiet and reserved fifty-four-year-old endocrinologist with a busy practice, Jan was mindlessly grabbing bags of chips, crackers, and cookies at work and drinking "a ton of coffee" to get through her long days. She was overeating at dinner, and on many nights she consumed two to three glasses of wine. She was also struggling with anxiety and low-grade depression, fatigue, migraines, bouts of fibromyalgia, gastric reflux, and an irritable bowel.

As a physician, Jan knew that part of the weight gain and physical symptoms might be related to diminishing hormones, general stress, food allergies, and blood sugar spikes caused by poor food and beverage choices, lack of exercise, and insufficient sleep. But she wondered if her overeating and physical complaints also had something to do with the challenges she was experiencing at home with her youngest daughter and the arguments she and her husband were having over the situation.

Vanessa, age fourteen, was getting poor grades in school, and any attempt Jan made to intervene and help was met with "rage-filled meltdowns." Jan's husband, Sam, had a better relationship with Vanessa, but he also was having trouble helping her with her studies or motivating her to do her homework.

Sam, a fifty-five-year-old software engineer who had been out of work a couple of times in the last few years, had more-regular hours than Jan. According to Jan, Sam was supportive of her, but he was concerned that she was working long hours and not taking very good care of herself. He complained about her lack of patience with Vanessa's emotional struggles. Their older daughter, Tracy, age sixteen, presented no parenting challenges: she was a straight-A student and heavily involved in extracurricular activities. But Jan was concerned that Tracy was also gaining weight.

When I asked Jan if her marriage was satisfying, she said she was so busy working and raising the kids that she didn't have time to think about her marriage. Even though she and Sam hadn't been intimate for over a year and their sex life was "never thrilling," she described Sam as a good husband and father; but she resented his inability to bring home a consistent income.

Jan added that she felt uncomfortable both in her body and with body contact. "I don't feel good about how my body looks, and I don't feel very sexual or sensual. Even though I'd like to have a hug here and there, I don't feel up for anything more than that. I feel bad because I know Sam wants to be intimate. I felt more connected to my body when I was younger and more active. But I haven't had that connection to myself in decades."

As Jan shared her concerns with me, she showed little emotion, even as she described her daughter's outbursts, the challenges of running a busy medical practice, and her resentment of her husband. She recounted her story as if she were reading a news report — her mouth was moving, but her body was stiff and motionless. There was a deeper disconnect that concerned me, and I was feeling the pain she couldn't allow herself to feel. Clearly, she was stressed out and eating emotionally, but she didn't seem to be *feeling* any emotions.

Running Away from Emotions

Most of us find it difficult to tolerate emotions for very long. Sure, we're okay with pleasant, even arousing, emotions, like joy, contentment, happiness, and excitement. But we're uncomfortable with deflating emotions such as sadness, hurt, loneliness, and hopelessness, or low-arousal psychological states such as boredom and apathy. Some of us are uncomfortable with anger — ours or anyone else's. We have limited tolerance for what have been called the master emotions, shame and guilt. When we experience these painful emotions, or witness someone else experiencing them, we want to run away as fast as we can. We've been taught to quickly access our rational, upstairs brain and distance ourselves from unpleasant feeling states.

We don't have much patience for uncomfortable bodily sensations either, as evidenced by all the drugstore shelves filled with pain-relieving pills and ointments. To seek pleasure and avoid pain is instinctual, part of our most primitive neural wiring. Part of the problem is that most of us have never learned the purpose and value of emotions and sensations. We haven't been taught to pay attention to and embrace the wisdom of our bodies.

What were you taught in childhood about emotions and bodily sensations? Did anyone actually take the time to help you identify and name these important signals from within? When you expressed your emotions, were you heard and were your feelings validated? Did anyone try to talk you out of them? Did it feel safe to express *all* your emotions, or were you criticized or shamed for having particular emotions, such as anger, disappointment, or grief? Were sensations such as butterflies in your stomach, or headaches, addressed or minimized? Did your caregivers allow time for processing feeling states, or did they rush to solve your problems? I always knew my emotions were about to be dismissed and I was about to receive a lecture when my mother began a sentence with "Look, Julie..." How did your caregivers handle their own emotions and bodily sensations?

If it isn't safe to express our emotions within the family, we resort to acting them out. Thumb sucking, bed-wetting, temper tantrums, moodiness, defiant behaviors, hurting ourselves, and substance use or abuse are behaviors we turn to instinctively to cope with emotional pain. We also unconsciously adopt defense mechanisms to push unpleasant experiences and memories out of awareness. Perhaps when painful memories surface, you distract yourself from the pain you feel by minimizing it through rationalization or intellectualization: "My parents did the best they could. Everyone has had challenges. It's the past, and I'm over it." Maybe you have a long-standing pattern of disconnecting from yourself and going numb: this is known as *dissociation*. You may notice that you have trouble remembering painful childhood events: this is known as *repression*.

Emotions and bodily sensations are like street signs, precious signals from within that point us in the direction of our needs. They do not go away when we disconnect from them. They do damage behind the scenes, until they finally get our attention, one way or another.

Hidden Hurts

I asked Jan what she remembered from her early childhood experiences, as I was sure that her emotional disconnect had begun a long time ago. She didn't remember much before age five, when her mother was hospitalized for a nervous breakdown, seemingly related to postpartum depression. Her father, a hot-tempered, distant man, told her that her grandmother would be coming to stay with them and that Jan needed to be a "good girl" and take care of her younger siblings. Her father, a litigator, worked long hours and retreated to his study every evening after dinner. While Jan never saw him drunk, he did have a few drinks every night. She was afraid of him: he rarely hit the kids, but he had a tendency to be verbally abusive, especially with their mother. One of the reasons she married Sam was because he was "the exact opposite of my father — he was even-keeled, kind, and patient, and he loved children."

Jan recounted an incident when she accidentally burned the collar of her father's shirt when learning to iron. "I feared for my life — the veins in his neck bulged out, and he grabbed me by the arm so hard I thought it would break off. He cursed at me and sent me to my room without supper. My mother did nothing, as she was quite passive and was also afraid of his anger." As Jan recounted the story, I inquired as to whether her daughter's "rage fests" felt similar to her father's bouts of anger. She said that she had never made this connection because of their age difference, but agreed that they were similar and that her response was the same to both — to run for cover. Clearly this wasn't helping Jan or her daughter.

The year her mother was hospitalized was a difficult and lonely year for Jan. She remembered being afraid that her mother would die. But it was no use sharing her concerns with her father or grandmother. "My father couldn't be bothered with us kids, and my grandmother was a cold and stern woman. If I complained about anything, she would remind me how hard she had had it in her childhood, as one of nine children."

Her mother's recuperation lasted over a year. Jan remembered wanting to be closer to her mother but finding it difficult because her mother suffered from anxiety and depression, and was overwhelmed with raising three kids and coping with a volatile husband. She often went to bed early, leaving Jan to tend to the little ones. As Jan described this period of her life, her head and shoulders drooped, and her body slumped in the chair. I was sure that I could see some sadness in her eyes, but when I inquired, she said she felt nothing. She knew it was a sad experience and that she *should* feel sad, but she felt numb.

Escaping from the Pain

When I asked Jan if she remembered feeling sad or lonely in her childhood, she replied that she learned early in life to block out unpleasant emotions and retreat into food and things she was good at. From elementary school on, she excelled at schoolwork, and, like her father, she was a voracious reader. She was also athletic and took part in team sports like soccer and volleyball. Studies, reading, sports, and caregiving duties at home kept her away from "all those terrible memories and feelings." I had a hunch that her older daughter might be following in her footsteps.

"Because I was a good student, I was allowed to stay in my room for hours on end, and I could block out all the family drama." Jan told me she rarely invited friends over because she never knew what to expect with her father's moods. "During elementary school, my brother and sister started fighting regularly, and I would retreat to my room with my books and a stash of my favorite treats. I know this sounds crazy, but sneaking and hiding bags of cookies, pretzels, chips, and candy was really exciting. I always looked forward to coming home to my books and my stash. I think that's why the ever-changing array of junk food at the office is so appealing to me."

Jan was aware that the environment she grew up in might be playing a role in her current inability to cope with and manage relationships. She recounted a recent experience of being humiliated by a colleague in a professional meeting. Unable to process the flood of emotions, she described the experience as "feeling like I was falling apart." When she left the meeting, she grabbed a box of four ice-cream bars from the freezer at work and ate them all on the drive home. A couple of glasses of wine at home finished off any residue of emotion.

Jan also revealed that she found it difficult to stay in the exam room when she had to share disturbing lab reports with her patients. While no physician enjoys delivering bad news, Jan found her patients' emotional pain and occasional outbursts unbearable. She usually called in her nurse, a sweet older woman, to do the comforting and soothing. I didn't need to be Sherlock Holmes — or a seasoned psychotherapist, for that matter — to see the parallel with her difficulties in handling her adolescent daughter's outbursts.

Leaning to the Left

In traumatic, undernourished, emotionally empty childhoods, one side of the brain may be understimulated, while the other becomes more dominant. The right side of the upstairs brain is more directly connected to the downstairs brain: information flows up from the body to the brain stem, the limbic areas, and the right cortex. The right side, which develops earlier, offers us a more direct connection to our whole body and the electrical, chemical, and hormonal discharges that we call emotions. The left side of the upstairs brain is more removed from these sources of input.

Jan was raised in an academic family that emphasized education and work. She had learned to "lean to the left" — to stay logical, literal, and linear and to avoid right-hemisphere-generated emotion and body awareness. The right side of her brain's neural circuits had, perhaps, been underutilized for decades. Jan strenuously avoided any situation — discussions with her daughter, intimacy with her husband, or interactions with upset patients and staff — that might trigger uncomfortable emotions and bodily sensations.

Jan's adaptations to a traumatic childhood, including her determination to have a better life than her parents', were resourceful and had helped her move through life and achieve professional success. But her unconscious "leaning to the left" was keeping her from connecting with herself and others. Imprisoned in a rigid and unemotional world, she was surviving but no longer thriving.

Listening to the Body

Infants and small children depend on their caregivers to help them regulate emotional and physical arousal. Our earliest social relationships are formative in the development of the stress-response apparatus, our body's system for regulating arousal. The body's stress apparatus involves the lower brain centers where emotions are perceived and processed, the immune system, the endocrine (hormonal) glands, and the nerves and nervous system. All these systems are joined together into a mind-body continuum through several pathways.

Children in the care of responsive, nurturing adults develop healthy stress-response mechanisms. Infant observation studies suggest that we are born with a high degree of "relational knowing." We are keenly attuned to our caregivers' subtle emotional shifts, such as the muscle changes in a mother's face that convey softness or tension, fear or joy. We react to the tone and speed of their voices. We notice that their eyes are wide open or nearly shut. All these subtle or not-so-subtle shifts are linked together for us by a single regulatory system called the *autonomic nervous system* (ANS).

The ANS has two branches. The *sympathetic nervous system* (SNS) acts as our body's accelerator and is responsible for arousal, and the *parasympathetic nervous system* (PNS) serves as the brake. The SNS includes our fight-or-flight response — it is responsible for the shot of adrenaline that speeds up our heart rate and prepares us for action when we almost rear-end the car in front of us. The PNS calms down arousal by slowing the heart rate, returning our breathing to normal, and relaxing our muscles when the danger has passed.

When we are exposed to chronic stress and negative emotional arousal in infancy and early childhood, we experience this high-intensity activation as contraction of our internal organs, muscles, and joints and tension in other parts of our body, like our eyes, our ears, and the base of the skull. When we have developed these patterns in childhood, it is highly likely that they will persist throughout life. High emotional arousal, or, as in Jan's case, repression of emotion and arousal, can lead to physical changes that contribute to nervous system dysregulation and conditions such as fibromyalgia and irritable bowel syndrome.

The Sixth Sense

Fortunately, the majority of physiological processes necessary to ensure our survival, from electrolyte balance to regulation of our heartbeat, happen outside our awareness. Our incredible machines are constantly making behind-the-scenes calculations and adjustments to keep us healthy and in balance. If external adjustments are required, our body and brain send us signals, generally in the form of sensations. When our body needs fuel and proper nutrition, it signals us with hunger pangs and cravings for particular foods. Thirst is a signal that fluid levels are low. When we need sleep, we become drowsy. Our sensations vary in intensity. If we feel a mild ache in a knee, we may continue the tennis game; if we feel a sharper pain, we call it quits.

If all parts of your brain are communicating properly, it is easy to read your body's signals and respond appropriately. Not only do you quickly perceive and make sense of your body's various sensations, but you can also pick up more subtle cues using your intuition, or what some call the sixth sense.

Suppose you're walking in an empty parking lot or on a dark street and have a sense that someone is behind you and perhaps following you. Or you step into an elevator and get a gut feeling that it isn't safe to ride with the unsavory character already in there. Your heart beats faster as your nervous system sends out an alarm. You feel tension in your body as your brain stem, limbic area, and cortex work in concert with your body to assess the threat. You instinctively grab your keys, walk faster, scan the area for help, or pretend you forgot something and back out of the elevator. When the threat has passed, without your thinking about it, your body releases the tension, and you feel calmer.

If you have experienced chronically high levels of emotional arousal in your early years, the various regions of the brain may not be communicating properly, and the region responsible for fire alarms and vigilance may be running the show more often then you'd prefer. Not only do you risk misreading situations and perceiving danger in too many situations, but you also most likely fail to pick up subtle yet important cues about the world around you.

The Effects of Stressful Early Childhood Experiences

Early parental deprivation (even in mild forms) can lead to a decrease in the production of the brain chemicals necessary for experiencing a sense of well-being and joy. These chemical deficiencies can manifest themselves in behaviors such as fearfulness, hyperactivity, and withdrawal and can set a child up for an increased sensitivity to stressors for life.

Deprivation and stressful early childhood experiences can also lead to a chronic excess of stress hormones such as adrenaline and cortisol. Stress hormones are a critical part of our response to biological or physiological threats, but high levels of these hormones in the womb, in infancy, and in early childhood can damage the brain. Cortisol, in particular, can damage certain brain systems, like the midbrain dopamine system, and shrink others, like the hippocampus, a structure important for the processing of emotions and the verbal and narrative memories that help us make sense of our world.

When our world is chaotic and unpredictable, our stress apparatus gets wired for easy triggering, and we are more likely to be reactive, overactive, anxious, agitated, panicky, and depressed. Too much stress early in life can reduce a child's ability to handle stress throughout life, which in turn can increase the risk of the child's turning to external sources, such as food, for short-term relief, soothing, and comfort.

The Destructiveness of Chronic Stress

In the past quarter century, Western researchers have confirmed what ancient wisdom traditions have always asserted: *our bodies do not exist in isolation from our minds.* We can't separate biology from psychology: everything is interconnected. Psychological stressors contribute to biological breakdown and vice versa. Stress affects virtually every tissue in the body.

Both external and internal stressors were contributing to Jan's physical complaints of fatigue, migraines, fibromyalgia, gastric reflux, and an irritable bowel. Long, exhausting days at work, lack of sleep and exercise, and the consumption of alcohol and unhealthy convenience foods were putting strain on her body and causing her adrenal glands to secrete high levels of stress hormones. She was often anxious or depressed, and because her nervous system had been highly sensitized by early stressful experiences, she suffered from a heightened perception of pain.

Some of us handle stress better than others. Our ability to handle stress without turning to substances is determined not only by our innate constitution but also by the social support we experience early in life. Hans Selye, a respected physician and researcher and the author of *The Stress of Life*, points out that people can become addicted to their own stress hormones. Some people who are habituated to high levels of external and internal stress from early childhood need a certain level of stress to feel alive. For these folks, a life that is calm and stress-free leaves them feeling boredom and emptiness. I was concerned that this might be the case with Jan.

Chronic unpleasant feelings and thoughts, even when pushed out of awareness, are an insidious form of stress, taxing our physiology and resulting in a myriad of physical ailments and "dis-ease" states. When we disconnect from the wisdom of our bodies and tune out our bodily symptoms, we fail to benefit from the messages they convey and the richness and joy life has to offer.

The Body Never Forgets

Jan's needs for attunement in childhood were not met: she didn't feel seen, heard, safe, or loved. Instead, her earliest experiences were often harsh, shaming, depressing, and sometimes terrifying. Her attempts to be close to her caregivers were thwarted. She was exposed to chronic stress, and her home life did not allow for the healthy physiological responses of fighting or fleeing. She had to stay, and she coped with it as best she could by blocking out the hostility and neglect and acting as if they didn't matter. Retreating to her private and safe world of books and food was an instinctive, resourceful, and adaptive way to survive.

But her body has not forgotten what she endured as a child. It has become wired to keep a constant watch for threats she regularly pushes out of her consciousness, prepared to ward off attack, emotional outbursts, rejection, and shame at any moment. Areas of her brain like the prefrontal cortex are in a state of constant hypervigilance. This is why she runs for cover when her daughter has meltdowns and why she leaves the room when her patients are upset. And because she has few skills for processing her own emotions and bodily sensations, her main tranquilizers are food, alcohol, and anxiety medications.

As a grown woman, Jan is living a stifled and deadened emotional existence. It feels normal to her: it's all she has ever known. While those around her — her daughters, husband, siblings, staff, and patients — are experiencing the routine emotional ups and downs of life, she is stranded in an emotional desert, and her body is keeping the score.

It's Never Too Late to Start Feeling

Near the end of our session, Jan told me that she had seen other therapists in the past for her weight challenges and bouts of depression, boredom, and emptiness. Previous therapists, she said, had tried to get her to feel and asked her to track and write about her feelings. She had dropped out of therapy a few times because she couldn't seem to experience her feelings, and she felt like a failure. When she tried group therapy, she witnessed other members "feeling all over the place" but still felt blocked.

I reassured Jan that I wouldn't try to get her to feel; rather, we would work on enhancing her right-brain awareness of bodily sensations, such as hunger and fullness signals and muscle tension and relaxation. If Jan could become more aware of her bodily sensations and able to stay with and tolerate them, they would offer her important messages about the state of her internal world. We would allow her body to tell us her story and lead us to the pain she had long ago learned to push away and stuff down.

I commended Jan for finding resourceful ways to handle an emotionally painful and difficult childhood. When I praised her for her strength and resiliency, she began to feel something behind her eyes that she said "could be sadness." She had experienced so little praise in her life that this little tidbit had begun to open the floodgates. It was clear that I could help

Jan access her inner world not only by offering her the attunement she so desperately needed and deserved, but also by highlighting her strengths.

The Way to Vitality

I explained to Jan that slowly and gently learning to pay mindful attention to her bodily sensations would help her reside more in her body. Over time, we would carefully draw out the sensory information that had been stored in her body and frozen by trauma. She could learn to connect these sensations to any associated emotions, as well as to current or past physical and psychological events. As we nurtured and strengthened an underdeveloped set of circuits in Jan's brain, she would be better able to tolerate and regulate her emotions and soothe and calm her nervous system. This would give her more ease and comfort in handling other people's emotions.

Feeling more connected to herself in this way could also help her feel more comfortable in her body. Jan's earlier connection to her body through sports was a resource that she could draw on. Exercise that she enjoyed would be a way for her to reconnect to her body and perhaps to tolerate and enjoy the comforts of touch, including more intimacy with her husband.

Learning Mindfulness

If, like Jan, you were exposed to severe attunement failures or early traumatic experiences, an overall sense of threat has been stored in your nervous system and in every cell of your body. But it's never too late to release this locked-up energy, increase your zest for life, and reduce your attraction to food for comfort.

In part 2, we'll see how Jan learned to use mindfulness to become more aware of her bodily sensations, stay present to them, and allow them to inform her as they shifted and dissipated. As her tolerance for unpleasant feeling states increased, she began to release and free the energy that had been frozen inside her. As her vitality increased, she felt better equipped to transcend her painful history and transform her life.

CHAPTER FIVE

Yes, but I Had Great Parents

To some degree everyone is a prisoner of the past.

— Judith Lewis Herman, *Trauma and Recovery*

One thing most emotional eaters have in common is that their childhoods didn't feel particularly nurturing. Even if their parents or caregivers were loving, supportive, and kind, often there just wasn't *enough* quality attention, listening, good attunement, understanding, empathy, soothing, comfort, and *consistent* nurturance for optimal development of the brain's self-regulation circuitry.

You may be thinking, "Hold on, this doesn't fit my situation — my parents were very loving and caring, and I didn't experience any traumatic events in my childhood. My problem is that I just love food and eating." I understand. And I believe you. I also believe that if you're having trouble managing your eating habits and maintaining your weight in an optimum range, there's a good chance that your brain's self-regulation circuits could use some strengthening, and your self-soothing and self-comforting skills could use some sharpening. There's *some* reason you're having difficulty consistently regulating your behaviors and meeting your needs without turning to your favorite foods.

Even well-meaning caregivers can unintentionally neglect their children's emotional needs at critical points in terms of brain development. Sometimes caregivers are unskilled at handling their children's routine emotional challenges, including disappointments and losses, and they offer food as a source of comfort. Perhaps your parents baked cookies for you or took you out for ice cream when you were upset. "I'm sorry those kids were so mean. Come on, let's go get a chocolate shake." Maybe they unintentionally dismissed or denied your feelings in an attempt to calm you: "The shot at the doctor's office will only hurt for a second. Then we'll have pizza for lunch." Or "Don't worry. I'm sure you'll do fine on the spelling bee; you always do. When you get home, I'll bake your favorite cupcakes."

Perhaps they were skilled enough to inquire how you were feeling, but once you shared your feelings, they quickly attempted to distract you or to solve the problem. "I know you're sad today about saying goodbye to Fluffy. Let's go to the movies and take your mind off of it." Or "I can understand your being upset that you weren't picked for the team. Maybe there's another sport you could try." No doubt they loved and cared about you, but you were left with uncomfortable and confusing emotions, and without the skills for exploring and processing your inner world of feelings and worrisome thoughts, calming yourself down, and learning from these experiences.

If your caregivers missed out on the right kind of emotional nurturance in their own infancy and childhood, they may have failed to learn critical self-and-other care skills somewhere along the way. Or challenging situations may have taxed their coping abilities: even the most loving caregivers can be overwhelmed by a death in the family, a needy or difficult relative coming to stay, caring for a family member suffering from a mental or physical illness, or a devastating relationship breakup.

Emotional challenges and skill deficits resulting from unmet developmental needs often become more apparent *after* we address any physical imbalances that may contribute to overeating. Most overeaters have some body and brain imbalances, such as hormonal irregularities, food allergies, and brain-chemical deficiencies, that contribute to cravings and overeating. These imbalances may be caused by both genetic and lifestyle factors. The easy availability of nutrient-deficient, addictive processed foods, foods of animal origin, and caffeinated and alcoholic beverages also plays a role, for sure, in wayward cravings and imbalanced eating. Most of us are stressed out, sitting for too many hours and sleeping for too few. And our increased exposure to endocrine disruptors, including the toxic chemicals in plastics, perfumes, and pesticides that are ubiquitous in our environment, is wreaking havoc on our bodies and brains.

Teasing Out the Pieces of the Overeating Puzzle

Lenny, a thirty-four-year-old art director for a large advertising firm, approached me at the end of a seminar I was giving on emotional eating. Looking tense and exasperated, he said:

> I sure hope you can help me. I'm really frustrated. I've been binge-ing ever since the holidays, and I've gained a lot of weight. I'm stuck in a pattern of avoiding the things I need to get done and doing everything other than what I need to do. I'm depressed, sleeping long hours, and most mornings I don't want to get out of bed. I have a ton of clutter at home and at work, and I cannot get myself to start back exercising. I'm sure I eat emotionally, especially when I'm lonely. I'm single, I work long hours, and I don't have much of a social life. Or much of a sex drive, for that matter. Truthfully, I'm disgusted with myself and my life, and I'm embarrassed sharing this. I just don't know what to do. I can never stick to any eating plan, so I don't want to go on another diet.

When I suggested to Lenny that, in addition to emotional eating, he might be struggling with body and brain imbalances that were contributing to his overeating, he felt relieved.

> LENNY: So maybe it's not all emotional? That's a relief. You
> know, I love to eat, and I have little willpower to resist my
> favorite foods. And I'm kind of lazy and don't like exercising

that much. But it's never been this bad before. I'm not sure what's changed, but I feel totally out of control. What kind of imbalances do you think I might have?

JULIE: Well, your body may be hormonally challenged — adrenal, thyroid, insulin, and sex hormone imbalances can cause sweet and carbohydrate cravings, low energy and fatigue, blood-sugar fluctuations, overeating, and weight gain. You may be struggling with food allergies and possibly food addiction. Your brain chemicals may also be out of balance, and in addition to overeating, this may be contributing to sleeping long hours, procrastinating, and feeling depressed.

LENNY: Wow, this feels so hopeful. It does feel like I'm addicted to certain foods, and that's why I can't stop eating them. One of my sisters has celiac disease, and she steers clear of wheat products. I wonder if I might be suffering from this as well, although I don't have the same symptoms. And thyroid problems, weight issues, and depression run in my family, so it's probably all related, right? [*Speaking with his shoulders erect and chin up, sounding more hopeful.*]

JULIE: Yes, there may be a genetic component, and in addition to body and brain imbalances, your early childhood experiences might play a role in your binge eating, depression, clutter, procrastination, and difficulty consistently exercising.

Lenny stopped me at this point and asked, "How could that be? I had a great childhood. My parents were very loving and committed, and they were always there for me and my siblings."

Addressing Body and Brain Chemistry Imbalances

Lenny's twelve-hour-plus days at the advertising firm were stressful. Most mornings he stopped for coffee and a muffin on his way to work. If he didn't have a client meeting, he would skip lunch, getting by all day on more coffee, diet soda, and energy bars. At least a couple of nights a week, he dined with clients, and these dinners usually involved heavy meals and bottles of wine. On the other evenings, when he was ravenous and drained from work, his nighttime meals turned into large, unwind-from-the-day binges. He exercised infrequently because of time constraints, low energy, and a lack of motivation.

Lenny is representative of the many clients who come to see me for help with their eating challenges. Most believe their overeating is emotionally driven. They label themselves as lazy, weak-willed and undisciplined, primarily when it comes to eating and exercise, and they feel ashamed and guilty. Like Lenny, many have an intuitive sense that their overeating may be partly due to cravings triggered by body and brain chemistry imbalances.

It's often helpful to start addressing overeating challenges by looking at these imbalances, because it can be difficult to work on emotional issues when you're feeling fatigued and depressed and struggling with food cravings. Most diet books and weight-loss programs fail to address the body and brain chemistry imbalances that fuel overeating. Even the most balanced eating plans can inadvertently trigger body and brain imbalances in sensitive individuals.

Overeating may seem like a simple act, but it's actually a complex behavior. All overeating behaviors are the result of complex interactions among emotional, cognitive, biological, neurological, social, and spiritual factors. Temperament and constitution, genetically inherited brain and body imbalances, insufficient or traumatic early childhood experiences, chronic stress (including loneliness), chronic dieting, and the easy availability of food all play a role. When we regularly eat in the absence of physical hunger cues, choose unhealthy comfort foods, or eat when we are already full, something is out of balance somewhere. Most overeaters have some body and brain imbalances that need to be resolved, and most are missing or have poorly developed self-regulation skills — especially the ability to connect to, or attune to and be mindful of, their internal world, and to regulate their feelings, moods, impulses, and behaviors.

It is beyond the scope of this book to address the symptoms and resolution of body and brain chemistry imbalances that underlie overeating behaviors. If, like Lenny, you believe your imbalanced eating behaviors may be, in part, due to body and brain chemistry imbalances, the first step is to pay attention to your symptoms. Some symptoms may represent underlying conditions that require the assistance of a qualified health care provider. You might also want to consider looking at part 2 of *The Emotional Eater's Repair Manual*, where I discuss the symptoms of and possible treatments for body and brain chemistry imbalances that may contribute to overeating.

There are steps that you can take right away, such as reducing your intake of processed foods and adding more fiber-rich, unprocessed, plant-based foods to your eating plan. Make sure any animal products you are eating are organic and hormone- and pesticide-free. Reducing your use of stimulants like caffeine and nicotine will help rebalance your chemistry, as will reducing or eliminating your use of alcohol. Getting your vitamin D levels checked is important, as is making sure you're getting enough essential fatty acids, especially the omega-3s.

Increasing movement during the day, such as through walking and gentle stretching, is helpful. And allowing time for adequate sleep and rest gives your body the downtime it needs to heal and repair itself.

"It's Almost Like There Are Two Versions of Me"

I suspected that Lenny might be struggling with a mood disorder — an inherited brain chemistry imbalance — because depression ran in his family and he had experienced low moods for as long as he could remember. I also suspected brain imbalances of contributing to his difficulties with focus, procrastination, and clutter. His low sex drive and history of dieting suggested hormonal imbalances might be at play as well.

Although Lenny came from a loving family, he was the fourth of five children with parents who had a lot on their plates. His early needs for attunement, comfort, and soothing might have unintentionally gone unmet at critical points in his childhood, leading to developmental skill deficits. And those unmet emotional needs could also be playing a role in his workaholic tendencies and the chronic emptiness and loneliness he experienced.

Lenny's blood tests did, in fact, show a number of hormonal imbalances. His adrenal and thyroid glands were taxed, and his testosterone levels were very low, contributing to his low moods and lack of sex drive. His integrative health-care practitioner prescribed bioidentical hormones and a supplement regimen that included vitamins, minerals, glandular support, and essential fatty acids.

He and I worked on his depression and focus issues by adding specific amino acids and herbs to his supplement regimen. We also addressed his food allergies and food addiction by slowly adding whole, unprocessed plant foods he enjoyed, like sweet potatoes and sugar snap peas, to his eating plan. This made it easier for him to reduce his consumption of potential allergens, like wheat and dairy products. And he significantly reduced his intake of caffeine and alcohol.

A few months into our work together, Lenny was feeling much better. He was waking up rested and getting out of bed easily. He wasn't feeling depressed, and his focus was better. He was finding it easier to clear his clutter. His libido was perking up, and he was feeling more energetic. He joined a gym near work and hired a personal trainer.

Once Lenny's body and brain chemistry were in better balance, it was easier for us to determine to what extent his overeating was due to emotional imbalances. Even though he was losing weight and had stopped bingeing, he was still snacking mindlessly and overeating at meals.

LENNY: I'm eating something healthy for breakfast and lunch, so I'm fine there. I get into trouble if I'm under stress and there are unhealthy snack foods at work — I'll grab them without thinking. But the most challenging times are when I'm out with clients for lunch or dinner, or when I get home after work and I'm all alone. It's almost like there are two versions of me. One is paying attention and is excited about all the healthy habits I'm practicing and the prospect of losing more weight. The other doesn't seem to care. That part of me rebels and uses food either for pleasure or to numb out. Or even to punish myself. I told you, I think there is this lazy part of me that sabotages my progress. [*He looks somewhat dejected, as his shoulders drop and his body sinks into the chair.*]

JULIE: I don't think it's about laziness, Lenny — you're very motivated, driven, and disciplined in many areas of your life. You have quite a few internal resources that you are able to access and rely on: you're hardworking, dedicated, determined, and ambitious. You're very friendly and personable. You're excited about learning and growing, and when you set your mind to something, nothing stops you. I'm wondering if there might be a very young part of you that feels invisible and is clamoring for attention and acting out with food.

LENNY: Somehow, that feels right on, but I don't really know what that's all about. [*He sits up with his eyes wide open.*]

Unintentional Neglect and Self-Abandonment

Lenny grew up in a small, idyllic New England town, the son of a successful orthopedic surgeon and a stay-at-home mom he described as "sweet, loving, artistic, and creative." He couldn't remember any problematic experiences in his early years: no one had abused him or his siblings, and there was no violence in the family. His parents weren't alcoholics; no one raged or even raised their voice in his house. His parents were always engaged and involved in their children's lives. I explained to Lenny that emotional imbalances are not always the result of something horrific or terrible happening in the past, but rather, in the words of the British psychoanalyst D. W. Winnicott, they may be caused by "nothing happening when something might profitably have happened."

JULIE: When did your challenges with eating begin?

LENNY: Even as a young kid, I remember sneaking food, especially cookies and candy, and hiding the wrappers in my closet. I have two sisters and two brothers, and our household was busy, but it wasn't like there was a shortage of food. I was always looking for snacks after school, overeating at dinner, and coming back for more food later. I was chubby, and my mom started taking me to diet doctors around age ten or eleven. It was really embarrassing, but I'm sure they were just trying to help.

JULIE: Tell me what it was like being the next-to-last of five kids.

LENNY: Well, you may be right about unintentional neglect. When I was in first or second grade, my mom's father died suddenly, and everyone was reeling from the loss. My grandmother was battling depression, and she came to stay with us. My younger brother Tom was a fussy kid, and he threw a lot of tantrums — my needs may have fallen through the cracks. I'm sure my parents were overwhelmed. My mom didn't work, but my father was rarely home before all of us kids were in bed.

When I asked Lenny how he coped during this time, once again he demonstrated his resourcefulness.

LENNY: I usually went to my best friend Dan's house after school. If I wasn't there, I'd be in my room, eating and playing video games. Dan's mom kept their pantry full of every goodie you could think of. I always felt so food focused at his house and wanted to go back for more snacks, but I was embarrassed to have anyone see me eat so much. Of course, Dan was skinny and couldn't care less about food.

JULIE: During your intake session, you said that you were moody and struggling with depression near the end of middle school. Do you have any idea what the moods were about?

LENNY: Yes, that's when Dan and I had a falling-out over a new friend, and I got pushed out of the picture. We broke up, and I stopped hanging out with him — it was a lonely time. We had been friends since kindergarten. And that meant I lost a second family as well. I think I felt really lost and alone. [*Lenny sighs and sinks into the chair once again.*]

JULIE: And who did you turn to for comfort and soothing then?

LENNY: No one, really. Two of my siblings were heading off to college, and one of them, Sally, who I generally confided in the most, was crazy busy. Lori, two years older than me, didn't have a best friend, so I didn't think she would understand. Tom was really acting out, so I tried to steer clear of him. He was later diagnosed with depression and attention deficit disorder.

JULIE: What about your mother, father, or grandmother? Do you have any memories of them comforting you?

LENNY: Not really. My dad's a great guy, but like me, he's a workaholic. My mother is very sweet and always available, but she doesn't really get me like Sally does. When I tried to share my problems with her, she would offer advice, in a kind way, but it wasn't very helpful. My grandmother was also very loving, but she usually wanted to distract me by baking something for me or getting me to play cards with her.

JULIE: It sounds like you felt your parents and grandmother were somewhat out of touch with your world and your needs.

LENNY: Yes, exactly. But doesn't every kid feel that way? I've always said, after middle school, I kind of raised myself. After the breakup with Dan, I had trouble making new friends in high school — I guess I wasn't very trusting. So I put my focus into my schoolwork. My parents emphasized education and the importance of a college degree. I realized early on that the way to get my parents' attention was to get good grades, so I worked hard to be a straight-A student. While they weren't happy about my weight, they were very pleased with my grades. I think this is why I'm so driven with my career. It's where I derive my self-esteem. But truly, I think my parents did a pretty good job with all of us. None of us are into drugs or alcohol; some of us are married with kids. Isn't my situation fairly typical?

When we know that our parents were kind and loving and did their best to offer us a wonderful childhood, it may be difficult to see where they might have made mistakes or lacked skills. We all have a tendency to deny what we don't want to believe to be true. We don't want to blame them, and if they are no longer alive, we may feel guilty for thinking poorly of them. We also may experience shame when we lift the veil of denial and look at what might have gone wrong in our rearing.

Stop for a moment and reflect: Were there events in your childhood that you experienced as threatening or traumatizing? Did you feel comfortable sharing these experiences with your caregivers? Did they *routinely* help you process your feelings regarding upsetting events? Did you hide certain experiences from them? If so, why? Did you feel they wouldn't be able to handle them or help you with them? Did you feel you needed to protect them? Did you fear they might judge, criticize, or shame you?

Were your caregivers raising many children and coping with undue stress or physical or mental illness? Were they regularly depressed, anxious, worried, self-absorbed, or preoccupied? Even milder forms of parental misattunement in early childhood, such as a regularly distracted or overwhelmed parent, can affect a child's brain development and result in behavioral challenges like eating disturbances.

Our goal here isn't to look for someone to blame; rather we're trying to determine whether your childhood environment provided sufficient emotional nurturance for your brain circuitry, brain chemistry, and stress-response mechanisms to develop optimally. Because Lenny's parents were overwhelmed with caregiving duties and out of touch with his world, there just wasn't enough quality attention, listening, good attunement, understanding, empathy, soothing, comfort, and *consistent* nurturance.

When our caregivers fail to consistently meet our needs for emotional nurturance, even unintentionally, we are forced to abandon our needs and conform to whatever our situation requires. All children naturally adjust their emotional expressions, behaviors, and needs to conform to parental demands, expectations, and preferences.

Unintentional Neglect of Developmental Needs

CAREGIVERS ARE OVERWHELMED: they are coping with many children, illness or death in the family, relatives coming to stay, or excessive work or community obligations.

CAREGIVERS ARE REGULARLY DISTRACTED: they have difficulty handling and juggling the demands of work, household, and childcare.

CAREGIVERS ARE UNSKILLED AT NURTURING: they have difficulty offering attention, attunement, good listening, validation, empathy, support, comfort, soothing, encouragement, and hope.

CAREGIVERS ARE UNSKILLED AT HANDLING DISAPPOINTMENT AND LOSS, including traumatic events.

CAREGIVERS ARE CRITICAL OR FIND FAULT: they highlight shortcomings and faults rather than strengths and resources.

CAREGIVERS ARE SHAMING: they highlight challenges such as weight, mood disturbances, shyness, learning disabilities, acne, bed-wetting, and thumb sucking.

CAREGIVERS SET RIGID RULES AND UNREALISTIC EXPECTATIONS: they may allow children little autonomy regarding free time, cleanliness, chores, etiquette, dating, studying, homework, bedtime, and so on.

CAREGIVERS LACK RESOURCES: they may be short of financial, emotional, spiritual, and material assistance and support.

CAREGIVERS ARE DECEASED: when a parent or caregiver dies, children may not receive the necessary support in processing the loss.

Unintentional neglect of our developmental needs at critical points in time can be due to many factors. Caregivers may be overwhelmed by the needs of many children, a death in the family, the needs of a grieving, depressed relative, or a child with mood or behavioral challenges. Caregivers may be unskilled at handling major losses or disappointments — their own or those of the people closest to them, like the breakup Lenny experienced. Taking young children to diet doctors and highlighting or criticizing body size can lead to painful shame states that derail developmental skill building, making it difficult for children to develop a healthy level of self-esteem and self-acceptance. Although some of these factors, such as highlighting and criticizing body size, may appear intentional and deliberately cruel, they may stem from a caregiver's desire to encourage good self-care or high achievement, or the belief that this is the best way to motivate a child to change.

Survival Strategies

Lenny's family was thrown into a challenging situation when his grandfather died suddenly and his depressed, grieving grandmother came to stay with them. Lenny's mother had to cope with the loss of her father and her mother's resultant depression, all while maintaining a household and raising five children, including a fussy baby boy. This perfect storm could overwhelm even the best of caregivers. Lenny's older siblings were often required to watch over and babysit the younger ones. But no matter how kind and loving they may be, older siblings are themselves children, and they cannot possibly take the place of mature, well-attuned, empathic, emotionally available elders.

When we find ourselves in challenging situations, we instinctively adopt survival strategies that help us adjust and adapt to our circumstances and the expectations and demands of our caregivers. Lenny recalled being told that he was a good baby and toddler, easy to take care of and good-natured. He learned early in life to disconnect from his internal world of feelings, thoughts, and needs to conform to the expectations and demands of others. Fortunately, he was able to access many internal resources that helped him cope with a hectic childhood environment in which it was often challenging to get his emotional needs met. His pleasant nature, flexibility, innate curiosity, interest in learning, and drive to work hard for good grades allowed him to please his parents and receive praise. By accommodating others with his people-pleasing behaviors, he maintained a best friendship with Dan and acquired a second family. When those around him were unable to provide comfort, he figured out how to soothe himself with distractions like food and games.

Drawbacks of Survival Strategies

Lenny is friendly, ambitious, and passionate about his work, but his personal life is not satisfying, and his life feels out of balance. Trust issues resulting from the unintentional lack of parental attunement in his early years, and the betrayal and abandonment by his best friend, have left their mark. While he has many casual acquaintances and work relationships, he has had difficulty establishing close relationships with both men and women.

Lenny regularly distracts himself from the emptiness and loneliness he experiences by overeating and watching television. He's still a people pleaser, accommodating everyone else's needs ahead of his own. And he has continued the pattern he began in childhood of disconnecting from his inner world and driving himself hard in his career, thus abandoning a very young part of himself. Even though he has resolved many of the body and brain chemistry imbalances that were contributing to his overeating, food still plays a larger role in his life than he would prefer.

Lenny and I discussed how the resolution of his emotional eating would have to take into account his internal psychological world — the emotions, needs, thoughts, beliefs, and memories that fuel his addictive impulses and behaviors — as well as his external world. Resources and strategies that helped him survive benign neglect, betrayal, and abandonment in his childhood would now have to be supplemented by new resources, both internal and external. As he learned and practiced the self-care skills he was lacking, he would create and strengthen brain circuits that would enable him to develop adaptive capacities and strategies for satisfying his needs.

Learning Mindful Self-Nurturance

If your caregivers were kind, loving, and well intentioned, you've got a head start on resolving your overeating challenges. But, as Lenny's experience shows, unintentional neglect of developmental needs can and does happen, and this may be contributing to your difficulties regulating your behaviors.

The mindfulness practice described in part 2 will help you fill developmental gaps and repair the brain derailment caused by early attachment deficiencies. We'll follow Lenny's progress, examining his difficulty in staying with his feelings, learning to soothe and calm himself, and reframing the self-defeating thoughts and core beliefs that have made it hard for him to trust others and form close bonds.

Part 3 offers empowering strategies for transforming sabotaging interpersonal patterns like people pleasing, and for bringing kind and loving others into your life. While you can't go back and change your early childhood environment, you can make your present and future experience more joyful and satisfying by mindfully nurturing yourself and changing your internal environment.

And don't worry — if you can't relate to Lenny's situation because your early years were truly happy, nourishing, and untroubled, you'll still benefit from the mindfulness practice. You've most likely picked up this book because something feels out of balance — you're having difficulty consistently regulating your behaviors and meeting your needs without turning to food or other substances. You're dissatisfied with your weight or your health, or both. The seven skills I present in part 2 will help you strengthen the self-regulation circuitry of your brain so that you can act in a way that helps you achieve your goals.

PART TWO

Inner Nurturing
Becoming Your Own Best Friend

CHAPTER SIX

Developing a Supportive
Inner Voice

Mindfulness is awareness, cultivated by paying attention in a sustained and particular way: on purpose, in the present moment, and non-judgmentally.

— Jon Kabat-Zinn, *Mindfulness for Beginners*

Imagine that you just had an argument or an unsettling discussion with someone. Now you are by yourself, and as you begin to process what just happened, you feel an overwhelming urge to go get your favorite comfort food. Rather than giving in to this desire, you pause for a moment and attempt to set a limit with yourself. What does the voice in your head sound like? Does it sound like a neutral adult voice, helping you adjust your behavior by stating the facts: "Those donuts are fried and really high in calories"? Does it attempt to set a limit, saying something like "No, let's *not* get donuts — we've had enough sugar today"? Does it remind you of past experience: "Better not head to that drive-through; you're going to order something fattening and feel bad about it later"?

Is this voice critical and shaming, saying things like "You're never going to lose the weight, because you're just too lazy and undisciplined"? Or is it gentle, nurturing, and understanding: "Yeah, that chocolate chip muffin looks really good, but it's loaded with empty calories, and eating wheat makes our head feel stuffy, so let's find a healthier treat"?

If you're like many emotional eaters I work with, that voice in your head tends to be a mix of all three voices. But it's likely that the voice you hear most often is the neutral or critical voice, and the nurturing voice is underdeveloped.

As we grow and develop, we internalize the voices of our caregivers, extended family members, siblings, and mentors. After we spend years listening to these voices, they become automatic and habitual. We're often unaware of them. They represent our *thinking self*, the part of our personality that emanates from the upstairs part of our brain. This part, which includes experience, knowledge, intellect, wisdom, rationality, morality, and logic, drives and initiates action and makes decisions. Our *thinking self* can sound like a neutral adult voice, a helpful or destructive Inner Critic, or a caring and kind Inner Nurturer. Our Inner Nurturer must act, at times, as our Inner Limit Setter, capable of setting effective, nurturing limits. If our Inner Nurturer acts too often as an Inner Indulger ("Yeah, that was a stressful meeting — we deserve a pastry"), we get into trouble with overeating and other unhealthy habits.

Our *feeling self*, the emotional, childlike part of our personality, represents our intuitive, sensing, vulnerable, feelings-centered, spontaneous, pleasure-seeking, wonder-filled, imaginative, authentic core being. We all have a playful, instinctual inner self, even though we may not be in touch with it. This part of our personality emanates from information received from our body and downstairs brain, and it does not change as we grow older.

If the adult voices of our childhood were primarily nurturing — warm, kind, validating, loving, soothing, calming, encouraging, hopeful, and helpful — we develop, early in life, a supportive inner voice that can restore us to emotional balance when needed. This voice also helps us regulate our behaviors. As we mature, this becomes the voice of our Inner Nurturer, our main source of validation, approval, reassurance, calming, soothing — and limit setting.

If we don't receive sufficient nurturance in childhood, we fail to internalize this kind, calming voice, and we continue to try to get our need for nurturance met from the outside. As adolescents and young adults, we may still seek comfort from our original caregivers, especially if they were able to comfort us some of the time. This approach, however, generally leads to frustration and disappointment as caregivers reopen old wounds by failing again to provide consistent, reliable comfort and support.

As adults, we may seek nurturance from those closest to us — our partners, spouses, close friends, mentors, and peers, and even our children. This often places too much burden on others. Close friends and family members aren't always available at a moment's notice when we're in distress. Our children are just starting their own lives and don't need us leaning on them. Other adults in our lives are busy, preoccupied, and struggling with their own issues. Sometimes those who care about us relocate or become ill and can't offer us support in the way they once did. Depending excessively on others for nurturing and support is draining for them, and one-sided; they probably feel that they could use some nurturing from us at times.

Some of us compensate for our unmet need for comfort and lack of self-nurturing skills by becoming super-independent, unconsciously disowning these needs. Denying our needs does not, however, get rid of them. To minimize the discomfort they cause, we may attempt to overcontrol our lives. We become rigid and inflexible, lacking the adaptability that good mental health requires. One way or the other, we end up expecting too much from others or from ourselves. Our lives become imbalanced, and we fail to develop this supportive voice within.

Self-Connection: Paying Attention to Your Inner World

It's important to understand *why* you regularly turn to food for comfort: it's likely because your inner world is full of uncomfortable emotions and bodily sensations, unmet needs, and self-defeating thoughts. You may be keenly aware of your feelings and needs but have a tendency to become overwhelmed by them and paralyzed by negative thinking. Or you may be only vaguely aware of these signals from within, cut off from the wisdom of your body and mind. In either case, food can seem like a quick fix.

In *The Emotional Eater's Repair Manual*, I introduced a very important self-care skill called self-connection — checking in regularly with your emotions, bodily sensations, needs, and thoughts. Learning to name, experience, and track our internal states is a skill that we begin to acquire in childhood and continue to develop throughout our lives. If you're disconnecting from your inner world because no one ever helped you learn this skill, it's not too late. Emotions, bodily sensations, and thoughts are like street signs pointing us in the direction of our needs, and you can learn to recognize and read these signs.

Becoming aware of your feelings, needs, and thoughts is a critical first step, but it isn't enough, on its own, to create lasting behavioral change. You'll need to learn how to stay with and process your feelings, reframe self-defeating thoughts, and meet your needs. For this you'll need the help of an internal nurturing voice — a mature, wise, loving, validating, unconditionally kind, affirming, encouraging, soothing, comforting, protecting, hopeful, and always helpful voice.

Because many of us did not receive consistent, sufficient nurturance from caregivers as infants and small children, and perhaps still, as adults, have little contact with nurturing others, we have never fully internalized this voice. Without it, our very young *feeling self* is often running the show.

Through therapy and contact with kind, nurturing people, it's possible to "borrow" and practice a soothing voice in order to manage unpleasant feeling states and reframe self-defeating thoughts. This alone can create new neural circuitry and change your brain functioning for the better. But one or two therapeutic sessions per week won't cut it — you need lots and lots of practice to develop this nurturing voice. You need a protocol to follow, a skill set, and a bag of tools.

Inner Nurturing:
A Transformative Mindfulness Practice

The *Random House College Dictionary* definition of nurturing is "to promote the development of [someone or something] by providing nourishment, support, encouragement, etc., during the stages of growth." In this part of the book, I show you how to build your inner support system and nurture yourself. If you've read *The Emotional Eater's Repair Manual* and have been practicing your inner conversations and catch-and-reframe exercises, you'll have a head start. If not, no worries. Inner nurturing incorporates both of these processes.

Inner nurturing comprises seven skills that help you regulate emotional arousal and calm your body. You'll learn to validate your feelings, form an alliance with the wisest and most loving part of yourself, and get clear on your authentic needs. You'll learn to reframe self-defeating thoughts, remind yourself of your strengths and resources, hold out hope for the future, and meet your needs without turning to food.

As you learn to focus your attention in particular ways, you create new neural-firing patterns that strengthen connections in the brain and your capacity for self-regulation. As you develop your Inner Nurturer voice and the associated skill set, you'll be better equipped to cope with eating challenges, and you'll improve your relationship with yourself and others. And by learning to nurture yourself — by putting your own oxygen mask on first — you'll be better able to nurture those closest to you.

Many of us, not just emotional eaters, are missing skills that are ideally developed in childhood, and this leads to emotional, cognitive, and behavioral imbalances. Perhaps someone close to you doesn't overeat but overindulges in alcohol, drugs, sex, drama, pornography, internet surfing, video games, or anger. Other common, related problems include compulsive spending and gambling, workaholism and chronic busyness, tardiness, procrastination, clutter, chronic anxiety, panic attacks, depression, apathy, lack of motivation, and difficulty forming and maintaining friendships. Many of these problems stem from difficulties with self-nurturance and self-regulation.

Inner nurturing consists of the following seven skills:

1. Pop the hood: name and track emotions and bodily sensations.
2. Practice self-validation.
3. Reinforce the alliance and offer love, support, and comfort.
4. Get clear on needs.
5. Catch and reframe self-defeating thoughts.
6. Highlight resources and provide hope.
7. Address needs and set nurturing limits.

Practicing Inner Nurturing

Try using this seven-skill mindfulness practice if

+ YOU WANT TO USE DISTRACTIONS such as food, alcohol, drugs, shopping, working, sex, gambling, drama, television, internet surfing, video games, busyness, or excessive sleeping;
+ YOU'RE EXPERIENCING UNPLEASANT EMOTIONS like sadness, anxiety, depression, anger, loneliness, fear, guilt, shame, helplessness, or hopelessness;
+ YOU'RE EXPERIENCING UNCOMFORTABLE BODILY SENSATIONS like muscle tension, aches and pains, a racing heart, or butterflies in your stomach;
+ YOU FEEL NUMB, which may be experienced as emptiness, boredom, apathy, lack of motivation, or feeling blah, lost, or disconnected;
+ YOUR THOUGHTS ARE OBSESSIVE OR NEGATIVE when you're thinking too much about things like food, meals, body image, or weight; regularly recycling self-defeating, critical, judgmental thoughts; or worrying constantly about anything;
+ YOU ENCOUNTER STRESSFUL SITUATIONS such as difficult people, relationship struggles, social encounters, losses, disappointments, financial hardship, or illness.

In this section of the book, you'll discover

- how to notice, experience, name, stay present to, and track your emotions and bodily sensations;
- how to deal with highly reactive emotional states;
- how to develop and strengthen your inner nurturing voice;
- how to practice unconditional acceptance and understanding of everything you feel;
- how to use self-soothing to regulate your nervous system;
- how to address powerless thinking and self-concept distortions;
- how to quiet an overdeveloped critical inner voice;
- how to acknowledge and draw on your strengths and resources;
- how to access the energizing power of hope;
- how to identify and meet your needs; and
- how to regulate your behaviors by setting effective limits for yourself.

Connecting to yourself in this way takes time, practice, and patience. The good news is that these are all skills you can acquire at any age.

The mindfulness practice presented here is truly transformational. These skills can free you from long-standing patterns that have kept you from living your life to the fullest. Consistently practicing the seven skills is a sign that you're making the transition from a derailed, hungry grown-up child to a satisfied, fulfilled, and confident adult, ready to meet life's inevitable challenges with ease, flexibility, creativity, and vitality.

CHAPTER SEVEN

Skill 1. Pop the Hood

Name and Track Emotions and Bodily Sensations

> By developing the ability to focus our attention on our internal world, we are picking up a "scalpel" we can use to resculpt our neural pathways, stimulating the growth of areas of the brain that are crucial to mental health.
>
> — Daniel Siegel, *Mindsight*

The primary cause of your emotional eating is disconnection from yourself. You're cut off from the most basic signals from your brain and body: your emotions and the way they present in your body as sensations. Of course, you still experience unpleasant emotions such as anxiety, frustration, anger, and sadness, as well as uncomfortable sensations like physical agitation, nervousness, tightness in your neck, and headache. But I'm guessing that when you experience these feeling states, you allow yourself to register them only briefly, and then you get on with whatever you're doing. Maybe you even deny having any feelings: some of us are quite skilled at cutting off from emotions we don't want to feel. Staying with intense emotions and uncomfortable bodily sensations is not easy.

You may find that sometimes, when you distract yourself, your feelings seem to disappear. At other times, you get stuck in them for hours or days on end, recycling the issues that cause the feelings and the pain. You get trapped in emotional reactivity and risk acting out your pain on yourself or others. You're more likely to experience physical ailments at these times, as your body contracts and braces in an effort to manage emotional pain.

The problem is that you don't know how to deal with these unpleasant states, either when you're experiencing them or after the fact. This lack of skill is keeping you stuck and turning to food. Your overeating or imbalanced eating is an attempt to comfort and soothe yourself and distract yourself from these feeling states. It's also an attempt to give yourself pleasure and fill up on something outside yourself.

Our inner world of emotions, bodily sensations, needs, and thoughts drives our behavior, yet most of us have never had any instruction or education in exploring this inner world. Many of us have been raised in a culture that prizes rationality and stoicism. We've come to believe that emotional expression is a sign of weakness and that emotions are best kept under wraps. We're encouraged to get over our problems, disappointments, and losses as quickly as possible.

Navigating our often-turbulent inner landscape doesn't come naturally to us. Just as we need music lessons to hone our musical talents and coaching to improve our athletic abilities, we actually need to have certain experiences in childhood or later that help us develop this important skill.

In childhood, we learn about experiencing and expressing our emotions by observing the behavior of our caregivers and significant others. Through trial and error, we discover whether it's safe to express emotion or whether we need to suppress it (for instance, when a caregiver says, "If you don't stop crying, I'll really give you something to cry about!"). We also register whether anyone pays attention to our physical sensations ("You're pressing on your head — is it hurting, honey?") and body movements ("You're curling up in a ball — are you cold?") or whether it's best for us to disconnect from these as well.

If you lack the capacity to name and track your emotions and the way they present in your body as sensations, you will be unable to learn from them or manage them in the future. Emotions and bodily sensations, as well as body movements (like a furrowed brow) convey important information about your internal and external environment. In order to understand the behavior of emotional eating, you have to tune in to and explore your inner world. Getting clear on what you feel is the first step in determining what you truly need and resolving your emotional eating.

In this chapter, I'll show you how to identify and stay with your emotions, rather than disconnect from them or act them out. You'll learn how to scan your body and become familiar with how emotions present in your body as sensations. I'll share with you a few mindfulness techniques for further exploring your sensations and ways to create a safe space to go to when feelings become too difficult to handle. You may be pleasantly surprised to find how easy it is to practice self-connection.

Pop the Hood: Learning Self-Connection

We begin our practice of inner nurturing by popping the hood and checking in with our inner world. Just like a master mechanic, you're going to monitor your internal world, listening for signals of distress and making the required adjustments to meet your needs and stay in emotional balance.

The best time to pop the hood is when you're experiencing distress and want to grab something to eat. These are the times when you're most aware of unpleasant emotions and corresponding sensations. You can also pop the hood when you want to snack even though you're not hungry, when you grab food mindlessly, or when you're already full and want to continue eating. You can also practice this skill when your thoughts are self-defeating or obsessive, when you feel numb, or when you aren't necessarily aware of emotions but want to turn to food for pleasure, distraction, and excitement.

Pop the Hood

STEP 1. Ask yourself, "What emotions am I experiencing in this moment?"

STEP 2. Pay attention to your bodily sensations. Just *notice* what you're feeling.

You can reverse the order of these steps if you like.

I use the term *emotions* to refer to the one-word labels we apply to describe our emotional experiences. I use the terms *sensations* and *bodily sensations* to refer to our sensory experiences of a situation, person, or event. When I use the term *feelings*, I'm referring to both.

Step 1. Ask Yourself, "What Emotions Am I Experiencing in This Moment?"

Whether or not we're aware of them, we all experience a full range of emotions and corresponding bodily sensations. It just takes time and practice to learn to identify and name them. Stop for a moment and reflect: Do you allow yourself to feel a full range of emotions? Are there particular emotions that you try to avoid at all costs, such as rage, shame, guilt, or grief, because they're too big or too dark to handle? Have you noticed that certain unpleasant bodily sensations go with particular emotions? For example, when you're anxious, do you notice a restless sensation in your chest? When you're irritated, do you feel muscle tension in your shoulders, neck, or head? Do you tend to grab comfort food the minute these feelings surface? How long are you able to tolerate them before seeking an external source of relief?

If it was safe for you to express your emotions during your childhood, you probably find it easy to identify and name them. But if no one helped you regularly process them, you may find it more challenging to stay with them. When you do allow yourself to feel your emotions, you may get overwhelmed by, obsessed with, or even paralyzed by the experience.

If it wasn't safe to express your emotions in your childhood, you may not even be sure what you're feeling most of the time. Emotions and bodily sensations may feel unfamiliar and uncomfortable. In my Twelve-Week Emotional Eating Recovery Program, workshops, and support groups, participants often tell me things like this:

> "I always try to distract myself from intense feelings. Who wants to feel that much pain?"
>
> "I'm afraid that if I allow myself to feel all my emotions, they'll overpower me, and I won't be able to cope."
>
> "I don't know what to *do* with my emotions or the sensations that go with them — they're so uncomfortable."
>
> "I can only experience my feelings briefly; then I disconnect from them somehow."
>
> "I can name many of my emotions, but I never associated them with physical sensations. This is all new to me."
>
> "I feel numb most of the time; I'm not sure I feel much of anything."

Perhaps in your childhood it was okay to express certain emotions but not others. In my family, it was okay to be sad or disappointed, but not to express anger, especially toward my mother. I learned to stuff it down to avoid confrontation and more pain. This, however, led to recurrent bouts of hopelessness, depression, and stomachaches.

You may also cut yourself off from particular emotions in an attempt to be different from your caregivers. Perhaps you made a decision long ago *not* to be like your sad and depressed mother. You may find yourself regularly suppressing your sadness, even if it means experiencing headaches and a chronic sense of disconnection from yourself and others.

IDENTIFYING YOUR EMOTIONS

You'll need to pull away from your busy world for a few minutes in order to access your emotions. With practice, you'll be able to do this anytime, anywhere. Find a quiet space where you can be alone — even your closet or a bathroom will do. In the beginning, it's best to sit upright and ground yourself — feel your feet on the floor and your rear end in the seat. As you gain more skill, you can try sitting in any comfortable position. Lying down isn't recommended, as it often leads to falling asleep, a sneaky way to avoid emotions. Take a few deep breaths as you quiet your mind. Ask your *thinking self*, the noisy, thought-generating part of your mind, to be silent for now.

When you ask yourself what emotions you're experiencing, you can use a neutral adult voice or your Inner Nurturer voice. If you choose to begin with your Inner Nurturer voice, access your most compassionate, kind, and curious adult voice, and ask the young part of you, your *feeling self*, "What emotions are *you* experiencing in this moment?" The terms for emotions are just single words, such as *scared*, *worried*, or *angry*. Begin identifying your emotions with "I feel…" statements. For example, "I feel scared," or "I feel excited." Use table 1, "Seven Core Emotions," to identify as many emotions as possible.

You may notice that you're experiencing multiple, conflicting emotions. When your best friend finds a great partner, you may be happy for her and also jealous. When you have to say goodbye to your beloved furry friend who has been ill for two years, you may feel extreme sadness and also relief. Just notice what you're experiencing, without judgment or criticism, as if you're watching an interesting parade pass by. See if you can allow yourself to feel all your emotions, without doing anything about them. Access your willingness and curiosity: rather than trying to get rid of unpleasant emotions, view them as important messengers from within, worthy of your attention and time.

Table 1				
Seven Core Emotions				
HAPPY*	AFRAID*	HURT*/+	GUILTY+	ANGRY*
Appreciative	Alarmed	Baffled	Bad	Agitated
Blissful	Anxious	Bewildered	Culpable	Annoyed
Calm	Apprehensive	Dazed	Regretful	Antagonistic
Centered	Avoidant	Dejected	Remorseful	Bitter
Comfortable	Concerned	Disappointed	Responsible	Contemptuous
Compassionate	Defensive	Discarded	Sheepish	Disdainful
Confident	Distressed	Insulted	Wrong	Disgusted
Connected	Disturbed	Invisible		Enraged
Content	Dread	Mystified	SAD+	Envious
Delighted	Edgy	Offended		Exasperated
Ecstatic	Frantic	Rejected	Blue	Fed Up
Encouraged	Frightened	Unimportant	Cranky	Frustrated
Energized	Helpless	Unwanted	Dark	Furious
Enthusiastic	Hesitant		Defeated	Guarded
Excited	Insecure	ASHAMED+	Depressed	Grumpy
Fulfilled	Mistrustful		Despairing	Hostile
Glad	Nervous	Chagrined	Despondent	Impatient
Grateful	Overwhelmed	Confused	Disappointed	Indifferent
Hopeful	Panicked	Culpable	Discouraged	Indignant
Inspired	Paralyzed	Disgraced	Disheartened	Irate
Joyful	Petrified	Dishonorable	Distressed	Irked
Loving	Powerless	Embarrassed	Down	Irritated
Moved	Rattled	Exposed	Empty	Jealous
Optimistic	Restless	Flustered	Gloomy	Mad
Peaceful	Scared	Foolish	Grieving	Outraged
Pleased	Shaky	Humiliated	Hopeless	Peeved
Radiant	Shocked	Improper	Irritable	Perturbed
Refreshed	Startled	Mortified	Miserable	Resentful
Safe	Suspicious	Ridiculous	Morose	Upset
Satisfied	Terrified	Self-Conscious	Sorrowful	Vengeful
Secure	Uneasy	Shocked	Unhappy	Vindictive
Strong	Vigilant	Unworthy	Unwanted	
Thankful	Wary	Visible	Withdrawn	
Tickled	Worried	Vulnerable		
Touched				

* These emotions tend to be energizing, even though they may not be pleasant.
\+ These emotions tend to be deflating.

You may find that you're limited in your emotional experience and tend to feel one or two main emotions. Perhaps you feel anxious and frustrated whenever you're really sad, disappointed, lonely, angry, guilty, or ashamed. Maybe you feel angry whenever your core, underlying emotions are sad, hurt, afraid, or hopeless. Some emotions, like anger, are more arousing and energizing, and you may prefer to experience these emotions than deflating emotions such as sadness, disappointment, or hopelessness. Using table 1, see if you can identify more emotions than you are usually aware of.

After you allow yourself time to experience your emotions, write them down. It's easy to get distracted by other thoughts if you try to do this all in your head. You may want to buy a journal specifically for this purpose, or you can just grab some paper and start writing. Don't edit or censor yourself. You can throw your writings away, or delete them afterward, if you're concerned that someone might read them.

Research demonstrates that the simple act of writing down our account of a distressing situation can lower our physiological reactivity and increase our sense of well-being. Lower reactivity means that our bodies are less flooded with stress hormones. It also means easier access to our upstairs, rational brain. This practice alone, over time, can significantly improve your health and reduce your wayward eating.

Mistaking Thoughts for Emotions

When I asked Liz (the social worker introduced in chapter 2) what she was feeling after the disturbing conversation with her mother about plans for her fortieth birthday party, she quickly stated that she felt anxious, ashamed, inadequate, and unworthy. I knew from our earlier work together that even though Liz found it fairly easy to identify and name her emotions, she resorted to her *thinking self* quickly, sharing with me the upsetting story and her thoughts about the story rather than her emotions. Staying with her emotions for any length of time and locating and experiencing associated bodily sensations were a bit more challenging.

Stuck in her dominant right brain, Liz often felt flooded by her emotions. She had a tendency to numb out quickly, saying, "My head is foggy," because intense feelings felt overwhelming and uncomfortable. Hence the purchase of the donuts and cream puffs immediately after the argument with her mother.

Liz was skilled at naming her emotions because she had been encouraged to express them in her childhood. But both her parents tended to be problem solvers — jumping to their *thinking selves* quickly, offering practical solutions and advice when Liz was upset. Neither of them had much skill at processing their emotions or their children's, and they lacked the patience required for the journey into Liz's inner world. They unintentionally failed to attune to her emotions and sensations and to teach her about the importance of these signals from within. Left alone with conflicting emotional states and uncomfortable bodily sensations, Liz learned early in life to model her parents' behavior and jump to her thoughts in a frenzied attempt to quiet the emotional storm within and experience some comfort. But at times like these, she had trouble accessing all the resources of her upstairs, logical, soothing, and regulating brain. When thinking didn't do the trick, she resorted to her favorite comfort foods.

When Liz expressed her emotions, she hardly experienced them, quickly retreating to her *thinking self*:

"I *feel* anxious. I *think* my mother is going to pound away at me until she gets her way."
"I *feel* ashamed. I *think* my mother will never take me seriously until I lose this weight."
"I *feel* inadequate. I *think* I'll never be good at making decisions."
"I *feel* unworthy. I *think* I'm not worthy of love and respect because I've made poor decisions in the past and because I'm overweight."

We all have a tendency to move away from unpleasant emotions by focusing on our thoughts. Problem solving feels more productive and energizing than staying with messy emotions. But thinking our way through a situation too quickly is often an attempt to avoid our emotions. Thinking about our challenges is helpful, but only after we've had time to gain insight by tracking and staying with our feelings.

See if you can differentiate between your thoughts and emotions. Tell your *thinking self* that you'll come back to the thoughts later. For now, just jot down any self-defeating thoughts you're aware of. (We'll focus on how to handle these in skill 5.)

Practice going back to your emotions by having your Inner Nurturer say to your *feeling self,* "Let's stay with these emotions." You can also ask your *feeling self,* "What *else* do you feel about this?" to access the full gamut of emotions and begin the process of identifying bodily sensations.

When I suggested that Liz stay with her emotions and asked her what else she was feeling about the situation, she was able to access additional layers of emotion, though she was still inclined to retreat quickly to her thoughts:

LIZ: I *feel* anxious. I *think* my mother is going to pound away at me until she gets her way.

JULIE (as Liz's Inner Nurturer): Let's stay with our emotions. How else do you *feel?*

LIZ: Hmm, I also *feel* angry and hurt. My mother does this to me all the time — she invalidates every decision I make. I know she's better at making decisions, but I can't be that bad.

In the beginning, it may feel exhausting to feel so many emotions. If you've been used to cutting off from these signals, you may also feel self-absorbed and hyperconscious. Keep in mind that in order to become your own best friend, you need to pay attention to these basic signals. Staying with them, for at least a few minutes — and longer, if possible — allows you to truly experience and learn from them. Be gentle with yourself: take your time. You're about to uncover important messages from within that will help you solve your personal emotional-eating puzzle.

SOOTHING BEHAVIORS

When we are distressed, our emotions are intense, and our thoughts can be anxious, obsessive, fearful, negative, and hopeless. We can't think clearly, and we're not functioning at our best. At these times, we might need to calm ourselves down with a soothing behavior, like breathing deeply or taking a warm bath or shower, before we're ready to pop the hood.

Soothing Behaviors

When you feel too upset or agitated to pop the hood, try calming yourself first with any of the following behaviors. Note that all of these are meant to be done alone.

- ✦ Breathe deeply.
- ✦ Hold or hug yourself.
- ✦ Stroke your face, shoulders, and arms.
- ✦ Change into comfortable clothing.
- ✦ Sit in a comfortable chair or couch.
- ✦ Hold a cuddly stuffed animal.
- ✦ Snuggle up with a beloved pet.
- ✦ Curl up in the fetal position with a pillow.
- ✦ Take a warm bath or shower.
- ✦ Listen to comforting music.
- ✦ Watch a music video.
- ✦ Listen to uplifting audio messages or affirmations.
- ✦ Read comforting passages.
- ✦ Play a musical instrument.
- ✦ Sing.
- ✦ Do yoga or stretching exercises.
- ✦ Take a walk or hike in natural surroundings.
- ✦ Garden.
- ✦ View or create artwork.
- ✦ Knit, bead, sew, or do needlepoint or woodwork.
- ✦ Do light housework or chores.
- ✦ Write about your feelings.
- ✦ Meditate.
- ✦ Pray or chant.

The purpose of soothing behaviors is to restore ourselves to calm, not to distract ourselves from our feelings. The goal is to calm down enough to be able to pop the hood. You do not want to use soothing behaviors to numb out. You already know how to do that with food, television, web surfing, sleeping, and shopping. When you tranquilize yourself, you do not learn or practice new skills.

CREATING A SAFE SPACE

If you find it overwhelming to experience and stay with your feelings, you may need to build up your inner resources first. One way to do this is to create a safe space to which you can always retreat to soothe and calm yourself. This can be an actual place, such as a comfortable chair or couch in your home stacked with pillows and blankets, the floor of a closet or small room, or, if you're an animal lover, in bed with your animals. It can also be an imagined or remembered space, such as a favorite vacation spot; a quiet, cozy beach cottage; or cabin in the forest. It can be a memory of being held by a caring other. I have a wonderfully comforting memory of spooning with my grandmother until I fell asleep. Take some time to create this safe space for yourself.

Spend a few minutes taking in all the sensations, sights, and sounds of your safe space. What bodily sensations are you noticing? What emotions are you experiencing? As you bask in this experience, you're creating a neural association between this image of your safe space and your awareness of pleasant emotions and bodily sensations. You're experiencing a state of receptivity and openness. And you're also building your inner resources — your ability to go to your safe space, regulate your nervous system, and calm and soothe yourself as needed. You are harnessing the regulatory and soothing functions of your prefrontal cortex to help you monitor and manage your internal states. As you increase your tolerance for handling uncomfortable emotions, sensations, memories, and issues by retreating to your safe space, your reactivity decreases, and with it, your need for comfort food.

IF THE FEELINGS ARE OVERWHELMING

If you've been disconnecting from your emotions for a very long time, you may feel raw and vulnerable when they surface. In addition to feeling overwhelmed, this vulnerability may trigger anxiety or panic. This is a sure sign that your self-soothing skills need sharpening. Your safe space is going to be a very important part of this work. Start with a soothing behavior, like changing into comfortable clothes and taking a few deep breaths. Go to or envision your safe space and ground yourself there: allow yourself to feel all the comfort and safety of this special place. Take your time. Then pop the hood, asking yourself what emotions you're experiencing in connection with the situation causing you distress.

If, after retreating to your safe space, you find it too overwhelming to allow emotions to surface and find that when you do, you feel an impending sense of loss of control, it may be an indication of unresolved trauma. When you allow yourself to feel these emotions, you may feel disconnected from yourself or the world, a state called *dissociation*. You may find that you feel this way when you're very anxious or depressed. If you have experienced trauma in the past, accessing emotions may bring up very painful material that you are not equipped to cope with on your own.

A professional psychotherapist can offer you the expertise and empathy required to help you move through your natural resistance to accessing old memories and experiencing unpleasant feelings. Please be gentle with yourself if this is the case: needing assistance is not a sign of weakness. If you do choose to try identifying and experiencing your emotions on your own, you might consider having a nurturing friend or family member available for added support. While addressing unresolved trauma is beyond the scope of this book, I do address trauma, and the healing self-care skill of grieving, in *The Emotional Eater's Repair Manual*.

Step 2. Pay Attention to Your Bodily Sensations:
Just Notice What You're Feeling

Bodily sensations are the physical feelings that are generated by many different activities within our bodies. The movement of muscles, the circulation of fluids, the release of hormones, the beat of our hearts, and the inward and outward flow of our breath all create a myriad of different sensations. Some sensations correspond to particular emotional reactions; others, such as pressure in your bladder when it's full or tension behind your eyes after reading for an extended period, are not necessarily associated with emotion.

Most of us have an easier time recognizing and naming our emotions than our bodily sensations. Our emotions tend to be more intense, demanding our attention. By contrast, we generally don't think about our sensations unless we're experiencing discomfort or pain. They are ever changing and shifting, sometimes subtle and often vague. We may struggle to find the appropriate words to describe them.

But if you stop and think about it, you're already an expert at noticing many bodily sensations. You associate that empty, rumbling feeling in your stomach with hunger. You've probably registered that uncomfortable fullness sensation, called bloat, more times than you care to admit. You're all too familiar with the tension called a headache and the unpleasant sensations associated with a sore throat. Ever notice your heart pounding and your mouth getting dry when it's your turn to speak up at an important meeting?

You may be wondering why it's so important to pay attention to your bodily sensations. Isn't labeling the emotions enough? The problem is that taking the time to figure them out is actually a mental activity involving our *thinking self*, and, as we saw with Liz, this act can remove us from our feelings. In fact, most of us don't stay with them long enough to receive their messages.

Focusing on the sensations accompanying any experience gives us more information than we can gather from our cognitive mind alone. For example, you may *think*, "I'm not bothered that Joe canceled our plans again." But the heaviness in your shoulders and the ache in your chest are telling you, "I'm tired of feeling unimportant. This *is* a big deal." By listening to what the body has to convey, we can experience a shift in the way we view an issue, and this, by itself, can lead to positive changes.

Paying attention to the moment-to-moment experience of how

emotions present themselves in our bodies — as sensations — and using language to describe them helps us *stay with* our feelings. As we do so, the sensations shift and dissipate, allowing us to better tolerate them and build resilience.

Resilience is the capacity of our nervous system to tolerate increasing levels of emotional arousal without resorting to maladaptive defense mechanisms, like denial or repression, or coping behaviors, such as overeating or lashing out. When we understand our bodily responses, we find it easier to accept them, work *with* them, and learn to regulate them. Awareness of our sensations also helps us live more fully in our bodies.

Everything we experience, from birth to the present moment, registers in the body on a cellular level, whether or not we consciously remember it. Paying attention to our sensations is especially important when we have been exposed to chronic threat or danger, as is the case with neglectful or abusive families, challenging relationships, or domestic violence. In these situations, our nervous system remains locked in a state of high arousal and vigilance, preparing for fight, flight, or freeze. When not discharged regularly, this arousal sets up an ongoing cycle of distress that affects all of our body's systems.

According to Laurence Heller, the author of *Healing Developmental Trauma*:

High levels of arousal, freeze, and dissociation held in the body foreclose a person's access to his or her life force and create a diminished range of resiliency. The tragedy of early trauma is that when babies resort to freeze and dissociation before the brain and nervous system have fully developed, their range of resiliency becomes drastically narrowed. In addition, their capacity for social engagement is strongly impaired, leaving them much more vulnerable and less able to cope with life challenges and later trauma.

Identifying bodily sensations enables us to locate the symptoms that represent this compressed energy. If we direct our attention to these sensations, stay with them, and allow them to dissipate, we can release energy that has long been held in check, perhaps for a lifetime. This energy can lead us to the internal and external resources that can then be used to transform our painful histories and our lives. (We'll cover this in skill 6.)

THE FELT SENSE

There is another kind of feeling through which we acquire information about ourselves and others that we can learn to pay attention to: the *felt sense*. The felt sense includes our intuition and gut feelings. It's such a natural part of our experience that we tend to take it for granted.

The felt sense is defined by Eugene Gendlin in his book *Focusing*:

> A felt sense is not a mental experience but a physical one. *Physical.* A bodily awareness of a situation or person or event. An internal aura that encompasses everything you feel and know about the given subject at a given time — encompasses it and communicates it to you all at once rather than detail by detail.

I remember a time when I was about to place my order at the counter of a small café. Two young men entered, and their body language and clothing suggested that they might be gang members. I immediately experienced a *felt sense* of danger and a lack of safety. One man moved to the counter as the other hung back near the door. As my heart began to race and my muscles tensed, my instincts took over. I slowly moved away from the counter, acting as if I wanted to grab a free newspaper near the door, and slipped out of the café. As I neared my car, I looked back and saw the young man near the door point a gun at one of the patrons and grab her purse. Fearing that they would come after me, I got in my car as fast as I could, sped away, and called the police. Had I not paid attention to my felt sense, I would most likely have been robbed, or worse.

Our felt sense can lead us to the instinctual resources we have for averting or coping with danger. We all have these innate, defensive action plans we can rely on. We just need to pay attention and tune in. Our felt sense informs us of positive experiences as well, like the overwhelming sense of relief, safety, and security I felt in my locked car once I was out of the parking lot and sure that no one was following me.

IDENTIFYING YOUR BODILY SENSATIONS

The following guided fantasy will give you a quick sense of what it means to experience bodily sensations along with your emotions.

> Imagine that you are on a hike and you come to the edge of a large cliff. Your friend asks you to step closer to the overhang to see the view. As you approach the edge, notice what you're experiencing in your body. What is the first sensation you experience? Are you aware of any emotions associated with this sensation?

Most likely, you're experiencing a rush of adrenaline — an intense, tingly sensation in your entire body. Perhaps you're experiencing shallow, rapid breathing and a racing heart. You may feel your muscles tighten and contract as they brace for possible danger. Maybe you feel a sense of exhilaration — an expansive, open sensation in your chest. You might feel an urge to jump, experienced as an urgent, pushy energy coursing through your body, especially your legs. Your sympathetic nervous system is on the job, preparing your body for quick action.

The typical emotions that most people report in connection with these sensations are anxiety, nervousness, fear, fright, and panic. Some report excitement, joy, and a sense of freedom — a connection to something larger than themselves.

> Now imagine that your friend calls you away from the edge, back to the safety of the trail. As you move away from the cliff, what do you notice happening in your body? Are you aware of any emotions associated with these new sensations?

Most likely, you feel yourself beginning to relax. The tingly sensation and tension in your upper body is dissipating, your breathing and heart rate are easing, and your muscles are relaxing. Any threat you experienced is over. You might be experiencing a sense of relief and calmness, perhaps even joy. You can thank your parasympathetic nervous system for sending out the message that the danger has passed and returning your body to a state of calm.

When you're practicing naming your bodily sensations, see if you can find several words that describe what you're experiencing in different areas of your body. The accompanying list can help you develop your vocabulary for these messengers from within. You may experience or "see" colors with your sensations — something may feel "red hot"; you may experience a "blueness" with your depression or headache. Resist the urge to interpret your sensations — just stay with them and allow yourself to fully experience them.

You may notice that they transform into something else — perhaps another sensation, an image, or an emotion. This may not happen immediately, so take as much time as is needed to allow a sensation to shift, change, and dissipate. If it doesn't change during a particular pop the hood session, that's okay. These changes are generally moving in the direction of releasing stored energy and increasing vitality. Just *notice* what you feel, without judging, analyzing, pushing, or forcing anything.

You may find that sensations are associated with emotions some of the time, but not all the time. For example, you may find that hunger pangs make you anxious when you have an extended morning meeting, but you don't associate hunger with anxiety when you're at home. Perhaps the sensation of fullness after dinner is associated with safety and comfort at home, but it's associated with shame and remorse after social events. Take note of these different experiences.

If you're not in the habit of noticing your bodily sensations, all you need is a little time and practice. See if you can maintain an attitude of openness and curiosity. Be patient and try not to get discouraged. As you slow down and quiet your mind, you'll begin to notice the many subtle sensations that you experience in a day — sensations you may never have paid much attention to.

Bodily Sensations

achy	dull	large	smooth
agitated	electric	light	soft
airy	empty	loose	solid
antsy	energized	mild	sore
big	faded	moist	spacious
bloated	faint	nauseated	steady
blocked	fiery	numb	sticky
blurry	fixed	on fire	stiff
breathless	flaccid	on pins and	strong
bright	floating	needles	stuck
bubbly	fluid	paralyzed	suffocating
burning	flushed	parched	sweaty
buzzing	fluttery	pressure	swollen
calm	full	prickly	tense
chilled	fuzzy	puffy	thick
churning	goose bumps	pulsating	throbbing
clammy	hard	quaking	tickly
clenched	heavy	quivering	tight
cold	hot	radiating	tingly
congested	icy	ringing	tiny
constricted	itchy	round	trembling
cool	jagged	shaking	twitching
damp	jerky	sharp	vibrating
dense	jittery	shivering	warm
depleted	jumbly	shuddering	weak
dizzy	knifelike	slimy	wet
dry	knotted	small	wobbly

If you've experienced poor attunement or trauma in your past, it may take time to trust that it's safe to allow yourself to feel what comes up. If you feel overwhelmed at any point, your body may be telling you it's too much. Trust the wisdom of your body and take it slowly. There is no reason to rush through this process.

Exercise: Noticing Bodily Sensations

Try practicing this exercise for the first time when you are not in a highly charged, emotionally aroused state. Find a place where you can be alone for ten to fifteen minutes. Sit upright in a comfortable chair, grounded with your feet planted flat on the floor, feeling your rear in the seat. Allow yourself time to get settled in and comfortable. Read through this entire exercise before you begin.

Bring your attention to your body. How does your body feel overall? Notice the sensations in your feet where they make contact with the floor. Sense your rear end making contact with the surface of the chair. Notice how your skin feels. Pay attention to your breathing. Notice any other physical sensations: do you feel anything in particular in your feet, calves, legs, hips, groin, tummy, hands, arms, chest, back, shoulders, neck, or head? Some sensations will be subtle; others will be more intense.

If you aren't noticing any sensations, it most likely means simply that there aren't any strong sensations calling for your attention at the moment. Just continue scanning your body until something grabs your attention. It could be as simple as a twitch or an itch. Take your time. With curiosity and patience, continue to scan your body.

Do any particular sensations call out to you? Select a sensation to focus on. Keep your attention on this sensation for a few minutes. Does this sensation stay the same? Does it change, become weaker or stronger, disappear, or become something else? Does it stay where it is or move? Just notice what happens. If you notice your attention wandering, gently bring it back to the experience of the sensation. Take it slowly, and don't attach any judgment or interpretation to what you are experiencing. If the sensation becomes uncomfortable, try shifting your attention somewhere else momentarily.

After a few minutes, explore whether this sensation has any emotion associated with it. Emotions are located in the body and are experienced as sensations. If there is an emotional quality to this sensation, take note of it. If there is no emotion associated with this sensation, or you're uncertain, just stay present to the sensation without attempting to analyze it further. If the emotion feels overwhelming, try shifting your attention somewhere else, imagine your safe space, or stop the exercise.

At the end of the exercise, notice how you're feeling in general. Are you feeling relaxed, calm, energized, curious, agitated, frustrated, or defeated? Are you feeling overly self-conscious? Whatever you're feeling is perfectly okay. All sensations and emotions are valid and acceptable. There is no right or wrong way to feel or to do this exercise.

Take a few minutes to reflect on your experience. Did you find it easy or difficult to locate your sensations? How was it to stay with them? Did it feel foreign and unfamiliar? Was it easy to identify emotions associated with your sensations?

If you found yourself resisting or avoiding the journey inward, you're not alone. Most of us find this process a bit slow and uneventful in the beginning. It's similar to our first attempts at meditation or paying attention to our breath. It's common to get bored and frustrated. You may find yourself more easily noticing the sounds outside than the sensations inside. Perhaps you began to daydream or distract yourself with your thoughts. You may want to try this exercise at a different time of day. You may find that certain moods are more conducive to your staying present to your internal world.

You'll also want to try this exercise again when you're in a highly reactive state, experiencing strong emotions. These are the times when you are most likely to act out with food or in other ways. Scan your body for sensations and stay with any intense sensations as long as possible, noting if they shift or disappear.

If you disconnect during the exercise, take note of how you do this. Do you shift to your *thinking self*, perhaps analyzing, evaluating, or interpreting? Do you begin to daydream? Are the emotions or sensations so intense that you go numb? Experiences like this highlight the importance of strengthening your self-connection skills.

What Are You Noticing in Your Body Right Now?

In my session with Liz, we went through a similar process to help her identify her bodily sensations. When I asked Liz what sensations she noticed, she was able to access additional layers of emotion and truly *feel* the way her emotions presented in her body:

JULIE (as Liz's Inner Nurturer): Let's try to stay with what you're feeling. What are you noticing in your body right now?

LIZ: I feel a tightness right here. [*Points to her chest, neck, and throat.*] It feels fluttery, racy, and tingly. I feel a tightness in the back of my shoulders and my arms.

JULIE: Allow your body the time it needs to process the sensations you're experiencing. Just notice what they feel like.

[*Liz takes a deep breath as a sad look comes over her face.*]

JULIE: What's happening in your chest, neck, and throat right now?

LIZ: It feels looser, and so do my shoulders and arms, but now I feel a heaviness behind my eyes and a lump in my throat. [*She starts to cry.*] I'm feeling really sad. My face feels droopy, and my lips are trembling.

JULIE: It's okay to feel all that you're feeling right now, Liz. It's all right to feel sad. I am here with you. I know this is painful, and I am here to help you. [*In the role of Liz's Inner Nurturer, I'm validating her feelings (we'll cover this in skill 2). I'm also reinforcing our alliance, reminding her that she is not alone, and offering her comfort and soothing (skill 3).*] How does it feel to allow yourself to feel sad and for your face to feel droopy and your lips to tremble?

LIZ: It feels better than the tight, racy feelings. It feels good to know that you are here with me and not judging me for my feelings. I actually feel like I'm starting to relax now. [*She smiles.*]

JULIE: Tell me more about the sense of relaxation you're experiencing. What are you noticing in your body right now?

LIZ: I was feeling looser — less tension — but now I feel some tension again, this time in my stomach. I'm feeling embarrassed. I feel a sinking feeling in my whole body — my body feels heavy. I feel like I want to collapse into this chair and become invisible. I'm frustrated — I was feeling better, and now I'm tight again.

JULIE: In this process, it's natural to go back and forth, experiencing contraction in your body when you're upset, then expansion as you release stored energy, and then contraction again as additional emotions surface. See if you can just notice what you're feeling without judgment. Take your time, Liz; I'm not going anywhere.

LIZ: [*Deep sigh.*] Okay, the tension is releasing in my chest again. Now the sadness is back, and I feel the heaviness around my eyes.

As Liz began to relax once again, we explored the emotions she was experiencing. Beneath her anxiety, anger, and hurt was a deep sadness. She longed to have a relationship with her mother that had more intimacy, comfort, and safety. She felt ashamed that she was still trying to get this from her mother at age forty and that she didn't "have it all together by now." She felt ashamed of her sadness — her mother often shamed her for crying. She also felt ashamed, as a social worker, to be exposing these aspects of herself to me, another mental health professional.

As she allowed herself to grieve for the relationship they never had, she noticed a sense of relief and calmness come over her again. Liz was, perhaps for the first time, truly experiencing her grief and her shame *in her body*, staying present to these states, and allowing them to inform her.

> LIZ: It feels so much clearer to me now. I act like a little girl around my mother. I'm still seeking her approval, but when I'm upset and insecure, she isn't the right person for me to turn to. She starts to give advice, and usually it has a judgmental, shaming quality. I try to get approval from my older sister as well. I'm also realizing that when either of them judges and shames me, I do the same to myself. Then I go into a shame spiral where I feel really chaotic on the inside. That's when I disconnect from myself and eat. I'm realizing that I don't have to do this anymore. I don't have to feel bad about who I am or how I want to live my life. I don't need to share everything I'm going through with them — I need better boundaries. It's funny — it's not like I haven't had these thoughts before, but somehow, after today's session, I feel like the message is going to stick. And I feel like this will get me back on track with my eating.

During the argument with her mother, Liz became dysregulated: her emotions were all over the place, and her nervous system was revved up as her downstairs brain sent out high-alert messages about danger and threat. Even though she had consumed the donuts and cream puffs before our session, she was still experiencing anxiety and agitation when we began our session. Only after we paid attention to her emotions and sensations was Liz able to access her soothing, logical upstairs brain for important insights about her relationship with her mother and sister.

Processing the emotions and bodily sensations associated with chronic attunement failures helps to release and resolve some of the traumatic memory stored in the body. The logic of the upstairs brain isn't the best resource for addressing painful issues such as unworthiness, low self-esteem, and shame. We can't talk ourselves out of these states. This is why Liz *felt* different in this session, even though she had *thought* about these issues many times before.

This Pop the Hood session was one of many opportunities for Liz to learn how to calm her stress response, release blocked energy, and strengthen the connection between her downstairs and upstairs brain for improved emotional regulation. As she continued her practice of inner nurturing, long-held core beliefs, such as "I'm basically inadequate" and "I'm unworthy of love" were beginning to feel less true and to have less of a hold on her self-esteem. Skill 5 offers ways of identifying and overcoming negative core beliefs.

Stuck in Freeze Mode? Start with Step 2

Remember Jan from chapter 4, the endocrinologist struggling with her daughter's adolescent meltdowns? Jan never had the opportunity, as a young girl, to learn to track her internal states in a safe and secure environment. Like many emotional eaters, she learned early in life to disconnect from painful emotions and unpleasant sensations. As she escaped into a world of books, sports, and comfort foods, she no longer felt much of anything.

As an adult, Jan continued the pattern of keeping herself too busy to feel. Busyness, food, and alcohol had become her drugs of choice. She wasn't, however, able to entirely escape unpleasant emotions: she regularly struggled with anxiety, low-grade depression, and a pervasive sense of emptiness. She experienced boredom on her days off and had trouble motivating herself to engage in creative hobbies like home decorating or playing the piano. Her body regularly sent her messages regarding the painful experiences, current and past, that she pushed out of consciousness. She experienced fatigue, migraines, fibromyalgia, gastric reflux, and an irritable bowel. Certainly, not every physical ailment is related to early trauma or has an emotional component to it, but it's difficult to separate mind, body, and spirit.

Like Liz, Jan tended to answer questions about her feelings by addressing her thoughts. Because she found it challenging to name and track her feelings and already felt like a failure at it, we added a few more mindfulness practices to her bag of tools.

Guided Tensing and Releasing of Muscle Groups

At the start of our therapy sessions, I asked Jan to close her eyes and systematically tense and release each individual muscle group, working slowly from her toes to her head. As she relaxed, she was better able to notice the subtle sensations in her body and any associated emotions.

Here's a transcript from a session I had with Jan after a particularly difficult weekend with her daughter:

JULIE: As you share with me the details of the weekend, what are you noticing in your body right now?

JAN: As usual, I'm not feeling anything. I feel numb. I had some anxiety earlier today, but I'm not feeling it right now.

JULIE: That's okay. Let's get grounded. With your feet on the floor, I want you to bring your attention to your feet. Can you feel them on the floor?

JAN: Yes, I can.

JULIE: Let's tense both feet, and then relax them. How is that feeling?

JAN: Good — it feels good to slow down and relax.

JULIE: Let's move to your shins and calves, tensing and then releasing. Are you noticing anything in particular in your body?

JAN: Just that I'm starting to release tension I didn't know I was even holding.

JULIE: That's it. Let's move on to your thighs, tensing both legs and gently releasing any tension.

After we did a full pass through Jan's body, her body, face, and demeanor were visibly relaxed, and we began to talk about what had happened.

JULIE: Tell me more about the weekend with your daughter.

JAN: I asked Vanessa about her homework and a test she needed to study for. She started screaming at me, something about not wanting me to hound her about her homework. It's ridiculous; I'm her mother, and I can't ask about her homework.

JULIE: I'm wondering what you're experiencing in your body as you're telling me this?

JAN: Well, I'm actually noticing that my upper body is somewhat tense, and my throat feels like it's constricting. My head is starting to hurt.

JULIE: Can you tell me more about those sensations?

JAN: I feel pressure in my chest and head — it's a dull pressure. My throat feels tight. I'm feeling like I'm not going to be able to handle all this discomfort. [*She looks panicky.*]

JULIE: All right. Let's have you go to your safe space. [*Jan's safe space was an image of the guest room in her aunt's home, where she spent some childhood summer vacations: a quiet, comfortable room filled with stuffed animals and pillows.*] I'd like you to imagine yourself in the guest room. Get comfortable and take in all the sensations, smells, and comforts of that room. Just notice what you're experiencing.

JAN: I feel safe. It's quiet in the room. The bed feels plush. The comforter smells great, like it's fresh out of the laundry. The lighting is soft. It's very peaceful. I love it here.

By having Jan go to her safe space, we were strengthening the neural association between her awareness of unpleasant bodily sensations and her mental imagery of a place of safety.

JULIE: What are you noticing in your body now?

JAN: The pressure in my chest is less. There's just a tiny amount of pressure in my head now. My throat is less constricted. I feel much better. Maybe I can handle the discussion about my daughter now. I'd really like to find a way to deal effectively with her screaming bouts. [*She appears tense again.*]

JULIE: I'm wondering what you're noticing as we revisit this subject?

JAN: My stomach feels like it's in knots, and I just realized I'm clenching my fists, and they feel tight and achy. Here I go again!

JULIE: It's important not to judge yourself, Jan. Which sensation is feeling the most uncomfortable?

JAN: My stomach — this is how it always feels when Vanessa and I fight. In fact, it feels this way when Sam and I argue about Vanessa. I think I eat to get rid of this feeling.

Placing Hands on the Sensation

JULIE: I'd like you to try placing your hands on the location of the sensations in your stomach. Gently and lovingly hold that area. What are you noticing?

JAN: I'm not noticing much change in the sensation, but it feels better when I put my hands there. It feels warm and soothing. Ah, actually, maybe it's a bit lighter now; more diffuse.

JULIE: You can also try placing one hand over your heart and the other over your abdomen. How does that feel?

JAN: That feels very calming and soothing. It really helps with my hand on my heart.

Research indicates that physical touch releases the feel-good hormone oxytocin into our brain and body. First associated with breast feeding, oxytocin is released into the bloodstream in response to soothing and connecting behaviors such as thumb sucking, hugs, back rubs, lovemaking, and even self-touch. Eating also stimulates the release of this calming chemical, as does drinking moderate amounts of alcohol, and this explains, in part, why these behaviors are soothing.

Oxytocin lowers blood pressure and levels of stress hormones and increases our tolerance for pain. It boosts our mood, encourages bonding and social connection, and can result in more positive and adaptive behavior. When we feel upset, a loving touch, even our own, can help us relax and feel safe.

Using self-touch in this way, Jan was able to stay connected to her sensations. As she increased her awareness of her sensations and widened her window of tolerance for them, she was initiating long-term synaptic changes in her brain and transforming the way she experienced her own body.

Breathing into the Sensation

Breathing is part of our life force: breath and emotion go hand in hand. We often hold our breath, or take quick, shallow breaths, when we are experiencing intense feelings. When the threat is over, we often exhale with a deep breath.

One way to stay with our sensations and really feel them is to locate them and breathe "into" them. We focus on a particular sensation, inhale and experience an expansive feeling, and then exhale any contracted energy. We revisit the sensation and notice how it is changing, if at all. We continue to breathe into the sensation until we feel it release or change. If it stays the same, that's okay: we just allow it to be. Three to five slow, gentle breaths should be adequate.

JULIE: I'd like you to try breathing into the sensation you're experiencing in your stomach. What happens to the sensation when you breathe into it?

JAN: [*Takes a deep breath.*] It feels like my breath is spreading the sensation out. Like it's elongating it, and it feels less knotted. It definitely feels lighter and looser.

Discovering What a Sensation Is Trying to Say

If you suspect that a particular bodily sensation might be associated with an emotional state, you can try directly asking the sensation about the message it's there to convey; for example, "Stomachache, what are you here to tell me?" Using your Inner Nurturer voice, you might ask, "What is this neck pain trying to tell us?"

What we're looking for is a quick response, a gut feeling about the emotion, not a prolonged analysis. There is no right or wrong answer; whatever comes up is important, even if you feel like you might be making it up. It's still a message from within, part of your innate wisdom. If you don't come up with anything, just be patient. With practice, you'll become a whiz at reading your body's messages.

> JULIE: What do you think the sensation in your stomach is trying to tell you?
>
> JAN: [*With hands still on her stomach and heart*] Hmm, maybe that I can't stomach all this fighting and tension with my daughter?
>
> JULIE: Okay. Just notice the sensation and allow any and all messages to come up. There is no rush to answer.
>
> JAN: Wow — I just had an image of myself doubled over in the bathroom with a bad stomachache when I was a kid. I totally forgot about all the stomachaches I had in my childhood. I had stomachaches almost every day with all the fighting in the house. Thinking about this is really making me tight again.
>
> JULIE: I'm wondering what you're experiencing in your body right now?
>
> JAN: Tension and tightness in my neck, throat, shoulders, and arms. I feel myself clenching my fists again. My stomach hurts more. Maybe some of this is panic. I'm afraid that my father won't stop screaming and that he'll hurt someone.

JULIE: It might be helpful to go to our safe space right now. [*Jan is talking about her father as if the incident is happening in the current moment — she is reliving the trauma.*]

JAN: I think I'll be okay. I'd like to try to stay with this process. I'm noticing that I'm feeling some pressure behind my eyes. [*Begins to cry, very lightly.*]

JULIE: It's okay to feel all that you're feeling right now, Jan. I am right here with you.

JAN: It was so terrible in that house. It was scary and depressing — I was always afraid. I never felt safe. [*Weeping more now.*]

JULIE: It's okay to feel sad and to grieve. It was really scary and depressing in that house. I understand. I'm so sorry you had to experience that. [*Jan takes the time she needs to grieve.*]

JULIE: What's happening in your neck, throat, shoulders, and arms right now?

JAN: The pressure is less. I'm just feeling really sad. And exhausted.

It's common, in the beginning, to feel exhausted or drained by this process, especially if you aren't used to feeling so many emotions and sensations. It's not a sign that anything is wrong. It's similar to the muscle soreness and exhaustion you feel when returning to exercising after an extended break. Your body and brain are getting a workout. Take a break from the work whenever you need to by shifting to a nourishing activity that doesn't involve food.

As Jan's experience shows, body scans, breath work, self-touch, and emotional inquiry can help us access the sensations, emotions, and stored memories from unresolved trauma. Moving from the experience of panic to comfort in her safe space helped Jan build confidence in her ability to regulate and tolerate intense and threatening feelings and thoughts. With this awareness, she was more willing to approach and stay with her internal experiences, rather than avoid them or withdraw from them too quickly.

As Jan continued to pay mindful attention exclusively to her bodily sensations, she realized that *sensations are just sensations* and that they did not necessarily mean that she was in any danger. This realization in and of itself was calming. She was learning to differentiate her sensations (tightness in her neck and throat) from her emotions (fear and panic) and trauma-related beliefs (that she was unsafe and trapped). In this way, she was interrupting a lifelong pattern of arousal, panic, and disconnection.

When Jan first came to me, she said she was numb most of the time and unaware of her feelings. Between our work and her practice at home of identifying and accessing her emotions and sensations, Jan was becoming aware of her internal world and learning how to manage emotional and physical arousal. I regularly modeled the voice of her Inner Nurturer so that she could get the hang of using this voice as she practiced popping the hood.

During one of our sessions, Jan shared an "aha" moment about her relationship with her daughter:

JAN: I'm realizing that my daughter's explosive anger is like my father's, and that I feel very young when she's screaming at me. I freeze: my body gets tense, my stomach gets knotted, and I feel hyped up and panicky. That's why I step away from her and head to the kitchen for comfort food or a glass of wine. But now that I can sense what's happening in my body when she's upset, I'm more able to calm myself down by reminding myself that these are just sensations, and I can handle them. I'm the adult, and I'm in charge. I'm not a child in my father's house anymore. In fact, when she lashes out, I'm now more aware of my emotions, and I feel some anger toward her. I guess I used to cut off from this as well. The bottom line is that now *I feel like the adult*. I'm even working on soothing and comforting her when she's having a meltdown. I discovered that if I talk in a soft voice and touch her shoulder and stroke her hair when she's upset, if she'll let me, she starts to calm down. This helps me connect to her and remember that she is my little girl. I now understand that her nervous system, like mine, is easily dysregulated — probably from my lack of proper attunement to her — and she needs me to help her calm down, not abandon her. I've also set some boundaries with her: if she is verbally abusive, there are consequences. Our relationship isn't yet where I'd like it to be, but it's much, much better. And so is my relationship with my husband. And so is my relationship with food!

Held Hostage by Unpleasant Memories

Most of us don't like to spend much time thinking about our disappointments, losses, or painful childhood experiences. We're reminded of them when something in our environment triggers unpleasant memories. We might see a young couple heading off to a school dance and remember how awful it felt not to have a date for the prom. We might notice a chubby child sitting by himself on the playground and immediately remember the shame and criticism we experienced as an overweight kid. We might observe a small child demanding her mother's attention in the supermarket and for a moment remember what it felt like to have a distracted mother.

Do we really need to dredge up all of those painful memories to stop our emotional eating? The answer is no. In fact, often it's counterproductive and retraumatizing to revisit them. But if there are painful experiences that you haven't processed properly, they may be fueling emotional reactivity, anxiety, depression, relationship difficulties, and emotional eating.

While you may attribute your overeating simply to a lack of willpower and difficulty coping with current problems or situations, your current pain is often just the tip of a big iceberg of old pain. As painful memories surface during your Pop the Hood practice, take note of how you experience these memories in your body, and go to your safe space if the sensations become too arousing and dysregulating.

To maintain good emotional health, you need to be capable of grieving your significant losses and disappointments. Revisiting, processing, and grieving your old pain can be a transformative process, one that can lead to renewal, hope, and the possibility for creative change.

When I asked Lenny, the art director we met in chapter 5, how he was doing with his goal of making new friends, he responded, "Terrible."

LENNY: I've noticed that when a new male friend tries to pursue a friendship with me, I start to put up walls. I do this with women I date as well. I don't let anyone get too close.

JULIE: Can you think of a recent example of when you started to put up a wall?

LENNY: Yes. My client's in-house art director, Jonathan, invited me to join him for various events. I really like him — he's funny, and I have a good time with him. But when he calls, I can feel myself pulling back.

JULIE: And what exactly do you feel?

LENNY: I really don't know — just an overwhelming desire to say no and pull away.

JULIE: Stop for a moment and imagine Jonathan calling you. What are you experiencing in your body right now?

LENNY: This is going to sound really weird, but it's a mix of panic and anger. The panic makes me feel jittery and like I want to run and hide. I feel light-headed and a bit dizzy, with a racy feeling in my chest. The anger feels like tension in my shoulders, neck, and arms. [*He grits his teeth and stamps his feet.*] I feel these same feelings when I date someone I like.

JULIE: That doesn't sound weird at all. It makes sense that you're experiencing those feelings. Let's stay with them. What do you think these sensations are trying to tell you?

LENNY: [*Yelling*] It's not safe to get close to anyone! I'll just get hurt again. I should run away now. [*He looks very panicked.*]

JULIE: As you're having those thoughts, Lenny, what are you experiencing in your body?

LENNY: I feel pressure — some tension and heat in my face. I think I'm actually going to cry. [*Tears well up, and he places his hands over his face.*]

JULIE: It's okay to feel sad, Lenny. I am right here with you.

LENNY: But I've been through this before in therapy — I know what it's about — the breakup with Dan. I don't think I'm ever going to get over it. [*He looks angry.*]

JULIE: As you're thinking that thought, Lenny, what are you experiencing in your body?

LENNY: Tense again, and I want to pound this pillow. It's not fair that this happened to me — I was always a good friend to him. I want to move past this! [*He pounds his fist into the chair.*]

JULIE: You're in the process of doing just that, Lenny.

Grief is a mixture of many emotions. Like Lenny, you may experience many different emotions, such as panic, anger, and sadness. You may feel like sobbing, wailing, ranting, screaming, hitting a pillow, and stomping your feet. *This is your old pain.* There is nothing to do with it except to be with it, feel it, and allow it to run its course.

Moving through the many emotions and stages of grieving requires willingness, patience, and courage. It also demands a leap of faith — believing that if you go through this dark tunnel, you will find relief and comfort on the other side. At some point, the grief will lessen, and you will begin to feel a sense of renewal and gain an expanded perspective.

Lenny thought he had finished grieving his childhood experiences of neglect and betrayal in therapy years earlier. But he realized that even though he had told his story many times, he had never really *felt* his old pain in this way. Lacking an Inner Nurturer, he had often resorted to numbing himself with food after therapy sessions. For the first time, he was learning to connect with his *feeling self* in a more intimate and soothing way, and it was paying off.

In a subsequent session, Lenny shared a new realization:

LENNY: I got a call from this girl I like over the weekend, and I started to feel my heart racing and my body getting tense. I didn't return the call immediately — I wanted to pop the hood first. The session I had with myself was amazing. I allowed myself to feel everything that was coming up. I even allowed myself to cry. I have never cried like this before, by myself. I've always avoided feeling those emotions. I also hit this big pillow and let myself feel my anger. I wrote all of this in my journal and had this realization: even though I felt powerless as a kid when Dan pushed me away, I'm not powerless now. I can set the pace and get to know someone, friend or lover, slowly. And *I* can decide if it feels safe to get closer. You've taught me that the best guide is how I feel in my body. I know I'll never have a crystal ball and be able to predict betrayal — or prevent it, for that matter — but giving myself permission to take it slow and pop the hood as I go gives me a lot of hope. And as I'm developing my Inner Nurturer voice, I'm feeling less alone and eating less when I'm alone.

Following Up

After you complete a Pop the Hood session, take some time to journal about your experience. What emotions and bodily sensations did you notice during the exercise? Did your feelings change or dissipate? Was it challenging to stay with particular feelings? Could you tolerate some more than others? Did you experience yourself in a new way? Did you learn anything new? Keep in mind that you can practice the two steps of the Pop the Hood process in either order. Many of my clients prefer to start with noticing sensations and then move on to naming associated emotions.

The most important thing is to continue practicing this skill until it is second nature. As you strengthen your skills of self-connection and internal attunement, you're increasing your capacity for self-observation, self-compassion, self-soothing, and self-regulation. You're increasing your tolerance for unpleasant feeling states, and building patience and resilience. And you're rewiring your brain, initiating long-term synaptic changes that will transform the way you handle challenging feeling states in the future.

What If I Still Feel Like Eating after I Pop the Hood?

It's best to pop the hood before you eat, especially if you're not hungry or you feel like overeating or bingeing. Pop the hood when you have a strong urge to head to your favorite takeout restaurant and order comfort food, buy more than a serving size of a treat at the market, stop at the bakery for your favorite pastries, bake in quantity at home, get a second serving of food when you're full, or go browse through the refrigerator or kitchen cabinet after you've eaten. Stay with your feelings as long as possible before you begin the next skill.

In the beginning, you may still want to comfort yourself with food after you pop the hood. Try to move on to the next two skills first. Give yourself permission to use food for comfort afterward, if you need to. Skill 2 involves learning to validate your feelings, and this will calm you even further. Skill 3 reinforces the alliance between your Inner Nurturer and *feeling self* for added support, love, and comfort. When you're aware of your feelings and also better able to tolerate them, process them, and calm and regulate your nervous system, it will be much easier to resist the lure of comfort foods.

You did not become an emotional eater overnight, and eating challenges will not go away overnight. As you get more practice with this skill and those that follow, you will feel less stuck and more motivated to work on underlying issues. Your life will feel more manageable. You'll have more vitality. And you'll be amazed at how quickly you're able to restore yourself to emotional balance and find ways to meet your needs without comfort food.

CHAPTER EIGHT

Skill 2. Practice Self-Validation

A moment of self-compassion can change your entire day. A string
of such moments can change the course of your life.

— Christopher K. Germer, *The Mindful Path to Self-Compassion*

Not a day goes by in my psychotherapy and life-coaching practice
where I don't hear a client say something like this:

"It's ridiculous that I'm upset about this."

"I know it's wrong to feel this way."

"It's idiotic that I can't stop a behavior that is clearly destroying
my health."

"It's stupid to feel anxious about this at my age."

"It's crazy that I think about my ex-husband this many years later."

"It's silly to be so bothered by this person."

"It's insane that I'm holding on to this and making myself ill over it."

"It's mind-blowing that I'm concerned about something so insig-
nificant."

"I feel like a baby for being stuck in these feelings and needing
comfort — it's infantile."

"It's shameful that I'm this heavy."

"I shouldn't feel this way — there is nothing I can do about the
   situation."

"It's not okay that I'm letting her get to me in this way."

"It's unbelievable that I still feel hurt about this."

How often do you say critical things like this to yourself? Be honest.

When you're experiencing recurring unpleasant feelings or familiar
unmet needs and self-defeating thoughts, are you generally kind and gentle with yourself? Do you unconditionally accept all of your emotions,
sensations, needs, and thoughts? Do you give yourself the empathy, compassion, warmth, and understanding you'd offer a close friend or family
member? Are you patient with yourself? Or do you have a tendency to
invalidate what you're feeling, needing, and thinking by criticizing and
ridiculing yourself?

I am saddened when I hear the stream of invalidating, critical, judgmental, negative, unloving comments that my clients verbalize about themselves.
Most of us have past or present situations, events, issues, and relationships
that we find difficult to accept. It's challenging to forgive ourselves for
mistakes and perceived failures. Emotional states such as disappointment,
frustration, shame, remorse, guilt, and regret are not easy to live with or
process. We're often hard on ourselves, not only for the states we find ourselves in, but also for not getting over them quickly enough.

Unfortunately, our self-invalidation doesn't stop there. Most of us
have aspects of our bodies and personalities that we would change if we
could. It's difficult for us to accept our excess body fat, double chin, wrin-
kles, cellulite, acne, or body parts we believe to be too big, too small, or
out of proportion. We long to have been born with different genes. We
might wish we were younger, smarter, funnier, or more entrepreneurial,
driven, or athletic, and we find it hard to accept what we believe are our
shortcomings.

We compare ourselves endlessly with others and envy those who
have the traits and bodies we would like to have. We find it challenging to accept and love ourselves unconditionally — flaws, bulges, scars,

inadequacies, and all. Like a 24/7 newsfeed, a stream of invalidating commentary plays in our heads:

"I'm unattractive and dumpy looking at this weight."
"I look like a cow in this outfit."
"My thighs are huge and disgusting."
"I've never had a good body, and I probably never will."
"My hair is thin and looks like crap."
"My skin is a total mess."
"I hate my big boobs, rear end, large ears, wide hips, etc."
"I'm just not smart enough to change careers."
"I dislike my passive, introverted nature; I wish I were an extrovert."
"I don't have an engaging personality."
"I'm not driven enough to be successful."
"I'm not the kind of woman men go for."
"I'm too old to find a partner."

In addition to voicing these explicit self-criticisms, we invalidate ourselves in sneaky ways. We may deny that we're upset about something, disregarding our true emotions and invalidating our *feeling self* with an assertion like "I'm not bothered by this at all." We might minimize our feelings and needs: "It's not really a big deal that I got passed over for the promotion." We might ignore or disregard our feelings, needs, or thoughts by distracting ourselves with pleasurable pastimes like watching television or eating.

But whether or not we're aware of the many ways we invalidate ourselves, our minds, bodies, and spirits register this lack of compassion. Our relationship with food will remain imbalanced as long as we continue to treat ourselves poorly.

What Self-Validation Means

We continue our practice of internal attunement by offering our *feeling self* the developmentally critical experience of validation. As you work on this skill, you'll get lots of practice using your Inner Nurturer voice — that kind, wise, warm, empathetic, compassionate, ever-loving part of you that can help restore your *feeling self* to emotional balance.

Self-validation involves three distinct steps. First, our Inner Nurturer communicates unconditional acceptance of our internal experiences. This means that when you're anxious about the presentation you're about to give, worried that you're going to blow it, and in need of reassurance, your Inner Nurturer makes space for you to be nervous. Rather than judging, ignoring, or denying your inner experience, or trying too quickly to cheerlead you out of it, she gently and compassionately acknowledges it and lets you know that it is real, valid, and okay to feel everything you're feeling, and that it's all right to have worrisome thoughts and need reassurance.

This means that when you're beginning to raise your voice because of something your partner just said, rather than blaming, shaming, or judging you, your Inner Nurturer reminds you that it's acceptable to feel anger and to experience agitation in your body when you feel misunderstood. Your Inner Nurturer reassures you that it's okay to have angry thoughts and need quality listening from your partner.

Unconditional acceptance means that when you get annoyed, tense, and grumpy because your elderly mother asks you the same question for the fifth time in ten minutes, your Inner Nurturer, rather than criticizing and making you feel guilty, kindly acknowledges these feelings as acceptable, okay to feel, and a natural part of eldercare. When you are thinking that you'll never be able to handle all of your mother's needs, your Inner Nurturer lets you know that it's all right to have that thought and to have your own needs.

In the second step of self-validation, your Inner Nurturer offers understanding to your *feeling self*. When you're nervous before the presentation, your Inner Nurturer not only reassures you that it's okay to feel this way, but also lets you know that it makes sense to feel this way, that it's normal to feel anxiety when making a presentation to a large group. When you're angry with your partner, your Inner Nurturer reminds you that not only is it acceptable to feel anger when you don't feel heard, but it's also understandable. When you're frustrated with your elderly mother, your Inner Nurturer offers you understanding by saying something like "Of course you're feeling frustrated — it's exhausting to repeat yourself so many times."

In the third step of self-validation, you notice what you're experiencing in your body when you practice kind and compassionate self-talk. You may notice that your anxiety subsides and the agitation in your body is reduced. Perhaps you notice that your shoulders are relaxing, the churning in your stomach has stopped, and the tension in your jaw is gone. By noticing the effect your loving self-talk has on your body, you are strengthening the association in your brain between your Inner Nurturer's soothing and comforting words and the easing of your unpleasant emotions and sensations. In the future, you'll be able to calm down quickly just through knowing that your Inner Nurturer is on the scene, the same way a baby is soothed when she sees her mother's face.

Why Self-Validation Matters

We've all experienced the comforting and soothing effects of external validation. When someone unconditionally accepts our internal experiences and offers us understanding, we immediately feel less reactive. Empathy and compassion always feel good. Rather than having to explain, defend, or justify what we're experiencing, we feel listened to, accepted, and understood. This allows us to relax and become more receptive so that we can think more clearly, access our upstairs brain for reason and logic, think before we act, and better regulate our behavior. This translates into more sensible food choices.

Self-validation, like external validation, is comforting and soothing, and it helps lower emotional reactivity. It allows you to do for yourself what you have sought from others, and from food. The wisest part of you, your Inner Nurturer, comforts and reassures your *feeling self*, reminding her that all emotions and sensations are valid and okay to feel, and that there are no wrong feelings. She reminds you that feelings are precious messengers from within — street signs pointing you in the direction of your needs. She reassures you that it's okay to have needs, any needs, at any point in our lives. We're never too old to have needs. She comforts you by letting you know that all thoughts, even self-defeating thoughts, are acceptable and make sense in a given context. She meets you right where you are, in this moment, without judgment.

In this chapter, you'll learn how to validate your feelings. In subsequent chapters, you'll practice validating your needs as well as any self-defeating thoughts you may be recycling.

Practice Self-Validation

Using your Inner Nurturer voice, communicate with your *feeling self* and:

STEP 1. Express unconditional *acceptance* of internal experiences.

STEP 2. Offer *understanding* of internal experiences.

STEP 3. Notice any changes in your emotions and bodily sensations.

Step 1. Express Unconditional Acceptance of Internal Experiences

Unconditional self-acceptance is at the core of loving ourselves. When we receive consistent and sufficient parental love and care in our early years, we enter adulthood with a solidly internalized sense of value and worth. Loving ourselves and others comes easily. Years of experiencing external validation automatically translate into self-validation and kind and loving self-talk.

If our caregivers and family members devalue us, we learn to do it to ourselves. After years of experiencing unreasonable expectations, unfair comparisons, excessive criticism, judgment, or humiliation, we internalize a sense of shame and unworthiness. We learn to reject and diminish ourselves because we have experienced rejection in place of acknowledgment and loving-kindness.

Perhaps your caregivers told you not to feel the way you were feeling. I remember that whenever I started to cry, my mother would tell me not to feel sad. If I told her I was afraid, she would tell me there was no reason to be scared. While she meant well, her comments were invalidating and didn't help me process my sadness and fear, understand my needs, or learn skills for handling my emotions and needs. She was basically teaching me to disregard and disconnect from my internal world, as she had always done herself.

Self-validation is not the same as resignation. Many of us fear that accepting ourselves unconditionally translates into giving up and giving in to our own mediocrity, allowing ourselves to eat anything we want, anytime, and to stay on the couch watching our favorite movies all day. We fear that if we're too kind and accepting of ourselves, we'll just buy bigger clothes while the needle on the scale moves higher. We believe that our self-criticism and self-rejection are keeping us motivated.

Actually, the opposite is true. Self-rejection and self-criticism trigger both hopelessness and powerlessness. These states are not motivating: instead they lead to depression, isolation, resignation, apathy, and emotional eating. Self-acceptance does not represent resignation, because it is not a matter of *giving up*. Rather, it is an act of *giving*. You give yourself the gift of kindness and compassion, which is at the core of any loving relationship. You give yourself the acknowledgment and acceptance that you did not receive enough of as a child.

In this first step of self-validation, our Inner Nurturer uses kind, loving, compassionate phrases to reassure our *feeling self* that the feelings, needs, and thoughts we are experiencing are acceptable and valid. It's important that we remind ourselves every day that it's okay to feel all of our feelings, and that it's okay to have needs and to struggle with self-defeating thoughts.

Communicating Unconditional Acceptance

"It's okay to be upset."

"It's all right to have these feelings."

"All emotions are valid."

"It's okay to show your emotions."

"It's perfectly okay to feel this way."

"These feelings are real."

"Anything and everything you feel is okay."

"You have every right to be upset about this."

"All feelings are acceptable."

"Feelings convey important information."

"It's okay to be sad. It's okay to cry."

"It's all right to feel worried."

"It's okay to feel frustrated, lonely, ashamed, guilty, and so on."

"You're angry. It's okay to feel like you want to lash out."

"It's all right to be scared."

"It's okay to feel panicked about this."

"You just experienced a frightening event; it's okay to feel fear and for your heart to race."

"You're nervous. It's all right to have butterflies in your stomach."

"It's okay to feel tense and jittery after something like that."

"Yes, this situation is unsettling. It's all right to feel shaky."

"It's all right to be happy."

"It's okay to show your excitement."

"It's all right to need that."

"It's okay to have needs."

"It's all right to need comfort and soothing."

"It's okay to need ease and downtime."

"It's okay to think that way; you're upset."

"It's all right to be having that thought."

Step 2. Offer Understanding of Internal Experiences

It's natural for us, even as adults, to seek understanding from others. Life can be confusing and challenging at times. It feels comforting and calming to get feedback that what we're experiencing is normal and makes sense. Feeling understood is a powerful experience, and it strengthens our resilience and helps us access our willingness to persevere.

Offering Understanding

"It makes sense that you're feeling this way."

"I can understand feeling that."

"I get where you're coming from."

"I can see how you could feel that."

"I hear you."

"Given what you've been through, it's natural to feel this way."

"Anyone else would feel the same way in this situation."

"I don't blame you for feeling that — it makes perfect sense."

"It's totally understandable to feel that way."

"I understand how difficult this feels for you."

"I know this feels challenging and scary."

"I see you're worried, and it makes sense to be worried."

"This is a big deal — it's understandable that you feel concerned."

"It's natural for your heart to be racing after a confrontation."

"That news was shocking — of course you're feeling numb."

"Anger sounds appropriate when someone attacks you like that."

"It makes sense to feel relief now that it's all behind you."

"You're feeling proud of yourself, and that's understandable."

"Of course you're feeling excited. This is something to celebrate!"

"Feeling drained after a day like today sounds realistic."

"For sure you need a break after this."

"That need makes sense in this situation."

"It's completely understandable to need this."

"It makes sense to think that way about the situation."

"I can understand your thinking that."

We must also be capable of giving to ourselves the understanding that we seek from others. We may not always be able to receive understanding from other people when we need it. Other adults are busy meeting their own needs and obligations. We risk draining and depleting them if we regularly need them to attend to our emotions. The truth is, *you* are in the best position to offer yourself the understanding you yearn for — you know what you're going through and what you need better than anyone else. And you have a kind, loving, and wise voice within that is instantly available to offer you understanding.

In this second step, your Inner Nurturer reminds you that not only is it acceptable to feel any feeling, have any need, and think any thought, but that all of your feelings, needs, and thoughts are understandable as well.

Step 3. Notice Any Changes in Your Emotions and Bodily Sensations

Pay attention to how you feel when you offer yourself unconditional acceptance and understanding of your internal experiences. Keep in mind that when you're first practicing self-validation, it may not be all that comforting or soothing. You're new to using your Inner Nurturer voice, and it still feels awkward. Truth be told, you'd prefer to have someone else offer you acceptance and understanding, and that's understandable too! Keep up your practice. Over time, you'll find that your Inner Nurturer is your most trusted, accessible, and reliable source of validation. It's a powerful feeling to know that you can offer yourself the support and care you need without having to turn to external sources or substances.

When Should I Practice Self-Validation?

The best time to practice this skill is right after you pop the hood. Here are a few examples.

LIZ: OVERWHELMED AT WORK

Liz has been working long hours for months, and her boss just dumped another big project on her desk. When she pops the hood, she identifies her emotions as panicked, angry, annoyed, frustrated, overwhelmed, sad, inadequate, depressed, and powerless. She notices that her body feels energized, tingly, buzzy, frozen, tight, droopy, drained, slumping, and heavy.

Using her Inner Nurturer voice, she begins to practice self-validation by expressing unconditional acceptance of her internal experiences:

"It's okay to feel panicked and overwhelmed — this is a huge project, and you're already exhausted."

"It's all right to feel angry — she didn't even discuss this with you."

"It's certainly valid to feel depressed — it feels like the long days will never end."

"It's perfectly okay to feel all these feelings."

She offers herself understanding of these experiences:

"It's understandable that you're feeling this way."

"Of course you're feeling overwhelmed — you're not a machine."

"It makes sense to feel angry when someone is so insensitive."

"It's understandable that you're sad — you were looking forward to a break."

After practicing these steps, Liz notices that the panic is gone and that she feels less overwhelmed, angry, sad, and depressed. The energized bodily sensations have subsided, and the tightness in her jaw has decreased. The "droopy, drained" feeling has shifted to a mild state of relaxation. The slumping, heavy sensation is lighter. Now able to access her upstairs brain, she notices that the project has a long timeline, and she'll be able to pace herself. And she realizes that the department is understaffed and her boss is also overwhelmed.

JAN: HANDLING A DRAINING FAMILY VISIT

Jan had a difficult weekend visiting her depressed younger sister, Susan, who was recently passed over for a job promotion. Jan tried all weekend to be a good listener and offer support. Back at home, Jan pops the hood and notices that she feels drained, invisible, angry, frustrated, sad, lonely, down, and helpless. She notices that her body feels agitated, tight, constricted, braced, pressured, sinking, heavy, drained, and empty.

Using her Inner Nurturer voice, Jan practices self-validation and communicates unconditional acceptance of these internal experiences:

> "It's okay to feel drained and empty after being with someone
>   who is depressed."
> "It's all right to feel angry and frustrated."
> "It's valid to feel invisible — Sue is incredibly self-absorbed."

She offers understanding to her *feeling self*:

> "It's understandable that you're feeling drained and depleted."
> "Of course you're feeling helpless — Sue plays the victim."
> "It makes sense to feel angry and frustrated — Sue never sees her
>   role in anything."
> "It's understandable that you're sad — you care about and want
>   the best for her."

Once Jan feels seen and heard by her Inner Nurturer, her loneliness lessens, and she no longer feels invisible. As her frustration and anger recede, she notices that the agitation and tightness in her neck, jaw, and shoulders decrease, and she doesn't feel as heavy or tired. Her hands are relaxed, and she feels less pressure in her forehead and behind her eyes. The sadness and emptiness also diminish. As she accesses her rational, upstairs brain, she reminds herself that happiness is an inside job: she can't solve her sister's problems or make her happy.

LENNY: UPSET BY TALK OF WEIGHT AND EXERCISE

Lenny spent the afternoon with a colleague who talked nonstop about his recent weight loss and new exercise regimen. As Lenny pops the hood, he realizes that his colleague's endless talk of these successes has left him feeling jealous, angry, annoyed, frustrated, invisible, defeated, inadequate, and hopeless. He notes the following bodily sensations: electric, energized, hot, wiggly, clenched, churning, bracing, tight, sore, sinking, deflating, and weighed down.

Lenny accesses his Inner Nurturer and offers his *feeling self* unconditional acceptance of his emotions and sensations:

> "It's okay to feel angry and annoyed — he knows you're at your heaviest, and he still went on and on."
> "It's valid to feel jealous — he's lost a lot of weight and looks great."
> "It's all right to feel everything you're feeling."

Next, Lenny offers understanding to his *feeling self*:

> "It's understandable that you're feeling all these conflicting feelings."
> "It makes sense to feel angry when someone is inconsiderate."
> "Of course you feel invisible — he didn't even sense that you were uncomfortable."

After he practices these steps, Lenny notices that the energizing sensations in his shoulders, arms, and legs are subsiding, and the heat in his face has dissipated. His anger and annoyance have lessened, and his feet have stopped wiggling. The tight, bracing sensation in his upper body is barely noticeable. Calmer now, he acknowledges that he may have actually encouraged his colleague to continue talking by asking questions rather than changing the subject.

How Can I Practice Self-Validation When I'm Disappointed in Myself?

For sure, it's not easy to practice self-validation when you've just eaten an entire carton of ice cream and polished off a tray of brownies. Standing in front of the mirror, staring at that double chin and spare tire around your middle, you're furious with yourself. In a fit of frustration, you snap at your father on the phone, saying things you wish you could take back. In this situation, it's important to remember that what you're validating are the feelings behind the behaviors, not the behaviors themselves. You're not condoning wayward or unkind behavior: rather you're unconditionally accepting and understanding what motivates it.

You're validating that you felt intolerably lonely Friday evening, and that was why you ate the ice cream. You're validating that you were feeling depressed and hopeless about the prospects of finding a partner, and that was why you baked and ate an entire tray of brownies. You're validating that you've been feeling overwhelmed and exhausted from taking care of your sick father, and this is why you snapped at him. Cut yourself some slack.

Validation is a gift you give yourself, especially when you're feeling bad about your actions. By reminding yourself that all feelings and behaviors make sense in a given context, you make it okay to make mistakes. Self-validation is a compassionate act, and it leads to acceptance and forgiveness. Although it may be difficult to rein in your impulses at first, practicing popping the hood and self-validation before you act out your feelings offers you the best chance to feel good about yourself and make a dent in your emotional eating.

CHAPTER NINE

Skill 3. Reinforce the Alliance and Offer Love, Support, and Comfort

> Yes, I hurt. But I also feel care and concern. I am both the comforter and the one in need of comfort. There is more to me than the pain I am feeling right now, I am also the heartfelt response to that pain.
>
> — Kristin Neff, *Self-Compassion*

We could all use a best friend or kind family member to comfort us when we are upset or distressed: someone who accepts us unconditionally, who patiently listens to our concerns and fears, understands them, and doesn't rush to give advice or find solutions. Someone who consistently offers love, support, and comfort. If you have a person like this in your life, consider yourself blessed. If you've regularly experienced this kind of support, you probably have a kind voice in your head, however undeveloped it may be. This is the voice of your Inner Nurturer, your best friend forever. Your work here will be to strengthen this voice.

If you've had the misfortune of being raised by unkind, neglectful, or abusive caregivers and do not have close friends or family members to whom you can regularly or consistently turn for support and love, be gentle with yourself. It's okay. It's not your fault. I know it's not the way you want it to be, and it won't be this way forever. Your Inner Nurturer voice is going to be a lifesaver for you. Yes, it's there inside you, and it can be developed and strengthened.

Learning how to regulate your feelings and behaviors by comforting and soothing yourself is a major developmental milestone. As you strengthen this voice, you're also strengthening the self-regulation circuitry of your brain, making it that much easier to talk to yourself in a loving way and to manage your feelings and behaviors in the future.

In this chapter, I'll show you how to remind your *feeling self* that the wisest, kindest, most loving and supportive part of you is on the scene and ready to help.

Strengthening Your Inner Nurturer Voice

Most of us can access a supportive voice when we speak to small children or animals. What voice would you use if you were assisting a child lost in a department store? How would you speak to a stray dog or cat? You would want the distressed child or animal to feel comfortable while you tried to help. You would probably use a very soft, comforting voice. That's your Inner Nurturer voice! It may feel difficult to access if you haven't practiced it very often, but it's there.

If you have trouble accessing your own Inner Nurturer voice, you can model the voice of a caring relative, mentor, teacher, therapist, neighbor, peer, or colleague. You can use the voice of a public figure you admire, or a television or radio personality. One client of mine used the voice of his father, who had long ago passed away. Another used the voice of a nurturing church elder.

During my own journey as an emotional eater, I had difficulty routinely accessing a wise, mature, kind, nurturing internal voice. I knew this voice existed: I used it when I spoke to small children and animals and when I comforted friends and family members. But when I was upset or stressed, this voice was nowhere to be found. The adult voices in my head tended to be neutral or harsh. I regularly criticized, judged, and shamed myself. My Inner Critic was very overdeveloped.

THE INNER NURTURER'S JOB IS TO

+ help identify feelings, needs, and thoughts
+ validate feelings, needs, and thoughts
+ offer love and support
+ offer comfort and soothing
+ offer encouragement
+ help catch and reframe self-defeating thoughts
+ highlight resources
+ provide hope
+ provide guidance for meeting needs
+ set effective limits

THE INNER NURTURER MUST NOT BE

+ overly indulgent
+ overly permissive
+ childlike

The part of me that regularly turned to food for comfort, my *feeling self*, was very immature. When I attempted to set limits with myself, especially with food, that young part of me would rebel and demand that her needs be met. When I attempted to access a nurturing, limit-setting voice, saying things like "It's best if we stop eating now — we want to lose weight," my *feeling self* would respond with an adamant "I don't care. I want something now!"

At these times, my fledgling Inner Nurturer was more of an Inner Indulger, colluding with my *feeling self* and getting me into trouble with food. I'd hear my Inner Indulger voice say something like "Yeah, we had a really hard day. Let's stop for some cookies — we'll do better tomorrow." Sometimes my Inner Critic could act as a limit setter (more like a drill sergeant) and rein them both in, but more often than not, that young part of me had the last word.

You can learn to access and strengthen the voice of your Inner Nurturer through a simple, three-step process I call Reinforcing the Alliance. In step 1, your Inner Nurturer reminds and reassures your *feeling self* that she is on the scene and ready to help. Step 2 involves flooding your *feeling self* with loving and supportive phrases. Many of us haven't had enough exposure to kind, compassionate people, and we aren't familiar with the words that represent loving support. In step 3, you'll get crystal clear on how to comfort your *feeling self*.

Reinforce the Alliance

Using your Inner Nurturer voice:

STEP 1. *Remind and reassure:* Inform your *feeling self* that your Inner Nurturer is on the scene and ready to help.

STEP 2. *Offer love and support:* Flood your *feeling self* with loving and supportive phrases.

STEP 3. *Offer comfort:* Calm your *feeling self* with soothing words and gestures.

"I Am Here with You Always"

Step 1. *Remind and reassure:* Inform your *feeling self* that your Inner Nurturer is on the scene and ready to help.

Once you've popped the hood and validated your feelings, jot down a few sentences in your journal that convey to your *feeling self* that your Inner Nurturer is on the scene and available. Pick phrases that really resonate with you — ones you find particularly nurturing.

Remind and Reassure

"I am here with you now — everything will be all right."
"I am on the scene and ready to help."
"I am closer to you than your breath."
"You are never alone — I am always with you."
"I've got your back."
"I am here to help."
"You can count on me."
"I am by your side."

> "You are always safe with me."
> "We will get through this together."
> "Your feelings are very important to me."
> "I can and will take care of you and help you meet your needs."
> "Your needs are very important to me."
> "We'll take baby steps together — come on, hold my hand."

"Did I Tell You How Important You Are to Me?"

Step 2. *Offer love and support:* Flood your *feeling self* with loving and supportive phrases.

Take the time to write a couple of phrases of love and support to your *feeling self*. Select phrases that really call to you. Don't rush through this step. You deserve the same loving-kindness that you offer others. Try to *feel* the love and support you're giving yourself.

Offer Love and Support

"I love and care about you."
"You are very dear and special to me."
"Did I tell you today how much I love you?"
"Did I tell you how important you are to me?"
"I will always be here to love and support you."
"My love and care for you are unconditional."
"I love you just as you are."
"You can totally be yourself with me."
"You don't have to be perfect for me to love you."
"I love you even when you make mistakes."
"You can always count on me."
"I will never abandon you."
"I will never leave you."
"I will be here for you forever."
"You are safe here with me."
"I believe in you."
"I will always believe in you."
"You are incredible!"

Don't worry if it still feels awkward using this voice and talking to yourself in this way. It will take time for this voice to feel natural, and you may have to "fake it until you make it." You can think of this step as a mini self-lovefest.

"Everything Is Going to Be Okay"

Step 3. *Offer comfort:* Calm your *feeling self* with soothing words and gestures.

You know how to distract and pleasure yourself with your favorite foods and engaging pastimes. But do you know how to truly comfort yourself? In this step, you'll explore and practice new ways of comforting yourself and get clear on what feels most soothing. With this skill firmly under your belt, you'll be able to comfort and soothe yourself anytime, anywhere.

It's often easier to think of behaviors that are comforting, such as taking a bath or listening to music, than words and gestures. Many of us find it difficult to find the right words to comfort ourselves. And when our Inner Nurturer voice is still wobbly, its soothing words may not feel all that comforting.

Think about a time recently when you were upset. Perhaps it was an argument with someone. Maybe someone said something unkind to you. Perhaps you had negative thoughts about yourself; maybe you were feeling bad after comparing yourself to someone. Maybe you were worrying about your health, or perhaps you had a large, unexpected expense.

Whatever the situation, think about what someone else could say to you to comfort and soothe you. Take a moment and write down a few phrases of comfort. Using your Inner Nurturer voice, say these phrases out loud, as compassionately as you can.

How does it feel to say comforting, soothing phrases to yourself? Does it feel awkward and unnatural, like when you were first learning to ride a bicycle or speak a foreign language? Does your own voice feel the slightest bit soothing? If not, why is it that you don't consider your own voice soothing? What qualities do you attribute to others that you

Offer Comfort

Soothing Words

"I can understand being upset about this."

"Sometimes upsetting things like this happen."

"I'm sorry you're going through this."

"I know you're worried about this."

"I know how frustrated you are."

"I get how tired you are of struggling with this."

"This is a difficult time for you."

"I know how hard everything has been for you lately."

"Everyone makes mistakes; no one is perfect."

"Sometimes life throws a lot of curveballs."

"You don't deserve any more hardship."

"I know things are going to get better."

"Everything is going to be okay."

"This too shall pass."

"The tide will turn, and better days will come."

"Soon this will be behind us."

"We're going to make lemonade out of these lemons."

"You're going to see this differently over time."

"This isn't easy for you; over time you'll make sense of it."

"I know you are upset. I am here with you."

"The future doesn't have to be the same as the past."

"We'll get through this together. I'm right by your side."

Soothing Gestures

Gently stroke your face.

Stroke yourself from your shoulders to your elbows.

Hold or hug yourself.

Rock your body.

Place your hands on your heart.

Place your hands on the sites of uncomfortable bodily sensations.

Hug a pillow while lying in a fetal position.

Softly rub your hands together.

Massage your head and neck.

Gently massage different body parts.

Stretch your head from side to side.

don't attribute to yourself? How is it that you can soothe a friend, a small child, or a suffering animal but not yourself? It takes time to build and strengthen the voice of your Inner Nurturer. Your own voice can feel just as loving, supportive, and comforting as anyone else's. It's just a matter of practice.

One way to comfort and soothe yourself when you're alone and upset is to touch yourself. As previously discussed, physical touch releases the feel-good hormone oxytocin into your brain and body. As silly as this may sound, your body doesn't know the difference between your touch and someone else's. Start with a soothing gesture that conveys softness, care, and tenderness, like gently stroking your face or giving yourself a warm hug.

Try placing your hands on your heart. The warmth of your hands is soothing, especially when placed on uncomfortable bodily sensations. We all know how wonderfully soothing massage feels — why not try self-massage? Notice how you feel after you offer yourself soothing words and gestures. Are you feeling more calm and relaxed? Even a tiny bit? Jot down any noticeable changes in how you're feeling.

Here's an example of a client practicing the first three skills of inner nurturing.

CAROL: PRACTICING INNER NURTURING BEFORE A
DIFFICULT WORK ENCOUNTER

When Carol arrives at her office, her assistant informs her that John, her supervisor, wants to see her. Carol, a senior web developer for a media company, knows that this summons is most likely about the client complaint she received yesterday. She dreads heading into John's office: he isn't a very good listener, and he tends to micromanage everything. As her assistant leaves the room, Carol, frustrated and upset, her heart pounding, grabs a chocolate bar from her desk drawer. Catching herself, she decides to stop and practice inner nurturing before heading to John's office.

When she pops the hood, she identifies her emotions as dread, anxiety, fear, frustration, shame, worry, and powerlessness. Her bodily sensations are buzzy, tingly, racing, tight, tense, heavy, sinking, collapsing, paralyzed, warm, and droopy. She feels as if she wants to walk into his office with her head down.

Practicing self-validation, Carol accesses her Inner Nurturer and offers her *feeling self* unconditional acceptance of her internal experiences:

> "Honey, it's all right to feel fear and worry — you take pride in your work, and you don't want to lose your job."
> "It's normal to feel some shame when you've made a mistake."
> "It's okay to feel all of these uncomfortable sensations — you're scared."

She then offers her *feeling self* understanding of her internal experiences:

> "It's understandable that you're feeling anxious."
> "Of course you're feeling powerless — John rarely has your back."
> "It makes sense to feel frustrated — the client did not communicate her needs clearly, and you're not a mind reader."
> "It's understandable that you're feeling shame — the spotlight is on this mistake."

As she practices these first two skills, Carol notices that she feels less dread and anxiety, and the tension and tightness in her chest, shoulders, and neck is lighter. The racing feeling has subsided.

Carol then reinforces the alliance between her Inner Nurturer and *feeling self* with phrases that remind and reassure, offer love and support, and comfort through soothing words and gestures.

REMIND AND REASSURE

> "I am here with you right now, sweetie. Everything will be all right."
> "I've got your back."
> "We'll get through this together."

Offer love and support

"You can always count on me."
"I love you even when you make mistakes."
"I believe in you."

Offer comfort: soothing words

"I'm sorry you're going through this."
"I know you're worried."
"Everything is going to be okay."

Offer comfort: soothing gestures

Carol takes a deep breath, gives herself a gentle hug, and places her hands on her heart before she heads to John's office. She notices that she is feeling considerably calmer and more empowered. She no longer feels the sinking, collapsing, powerless, droopy sensations. The chocolate bar, unopened, is back in the drawer. She walks into John's office confidently, making eye contact and holding her head high.

Finding the Right Words or Phrases

When you are new to inner nurturing, your developing Inner Nurturer voice may not feel strong enough to soothe and comfort you. You can easily slip back to your old habit of disconnecting from yourself in an attempt to reduce the pain. You may grab something to eat or drink, pick up your phone and surf the web, turn on the television, or find some other distraction.

Sometimes a few small adjustments to the words or phrases of your Inner Nurturer can make all the difference in the world. Here's an example of an adjustment a client made that solved the disconnect she was feeling with her Inner Nurturer.

In a group therapy session, Tina, an anxious, stay-at-home mother of a five-year-old daughter, expressed the following concerns:

TINA: Late at night, I tend to obsess about my daughter's health or whether my husband will be safe when he travels for business. I can't fall asleep, because I ruminate on what might happen. I've been using my Inner Nurturer voice, but the voice doesn't feel very comforting — it feels kind of awkward, and I get frustrated. Then I get up in the middle of the night and eat. Because I don't sleep well, I'm tired the next day, and I turn to food for energy. It's maddening!

JULIE: It's great that you're working on establishing and reinforcing this loving alliance between your Inner Nurturer and your *feeling self*. I can understand how frustrating it feels when you're using this voice and it doesn't feel all that helpful *yet*. Can you share with me some of the phrases your Inner Nurturer says to your *feeling self*?

TINA: She says things like: "I'm here with you. I know you're scared. I know that you're worried about Jenny and Rod. I love you and care about you. But you don't need to be scared — you take good care of Jenny, and Rod is careful when he travels. You're going to be okay. Just try to put those thoughts out of your head."

JULIE: And does that feel supportive?

TINA: Yes, a little. But it feels kind of phony, and I don't feel like I get a lot out of it. I keep trying to say it, hoping I'll fall asleep before I go and get something to eat.

JULIE: It sounds like you're doing fine with step 1, Remind and Reassure, and with step 2, Offer Love and Support. But I can see that you quickly move on to giving advice to your *feeling self*. I think she could actually use more comfort and soothing. Does it feel more like a pep talk?

TINA: Yes. I can't really *feel* my Inner Nurturer's love and care. I think she really doesn't know how to connect with that young part of me. Or maybe she doesn't know how to love me. It's crazy — I think my Inner Nurturer gets frustrated, gives up, and abandons my *feeling self*. [*Laughs.*] Then we both head for the kitchen.

JULIE: That doesn't sound crazy. Your Inner Nurturer has to build her skill, her patience, and her own endurance and resilience. That will come in time, with continued practice. For now, I'd like you to make a few small adjustments that might help. First, I'd like you to write down more than two phrases for each step of this skill. I not only want you to remind and reassure your *feeling self* that your Inner Nurturer is on the scene, but I want you to *flood* your *feeling self* with phrases that offer love and support. I want you to go slow and really try to *feel* the love and support. Take your time in offering comfort — really try to pay attention to how different phrases feel, and notice which gestures are the most soothing.

Second, I think that your *feeling self* might feel more connection if, as often as possible, you use the word *we* or *let's* instead of *you*. Instead of "You're going to be okay," try "*We're* going to be okay." Instead of "Just try to put those thoughts out of your head," try "Let's see if *we* can quiet *our* mind right now." This gives your *feeling self* the sense that there is someone going through the experience with her. You can even suggest going to your safe space together.

And finally, I'd like you to avoid jumping to problem solving and advice giving. Generally, when we're upset, advice isn't very soothing. It takes us out of our feelings and into our thoughts. Just keep soothing and comforting your *feeling self*.

A few weeks later, Tina shared with the group that using *we* and *let's* was working really well, and she was beginning to feel the love and support of her Inner Nurturer. She discovered that lying in a fetal position and holding herself was very soothing. She was no longer getting out of bed to eat, and she was sleeping comfortably through the night. And without resorting to problem solving, Tina had addressed her needs. The youngest part of her needed soothing and comfort and to feel that she was not alone.

If practicing the first three skills of inner nurturing addresses your needs in any given situation, your work is complete. You popped the hood, connected with yourself in an intimate way, and allowed yourself to feel. You've met your developmentally critical needs for validation, reassurance, love, support, and comfort and headed your emotional eating off at the pass. But if comfort food is still calling because only some of your needs have been met, or you're unsure what you need, the next skill will help.

CHAPTER TEN

Skill 4. Get Clear on Needs

Some development of the capacity to be alone is necessary if the brain is to function at its best, and if the individual is to fulfil his highest potential. Human beings easily become alienated from their own deepest needs and feelings. Learning, thinking, innovation and maintaining contact with one's own inner world are all facilitated by solitude.

— Anthony Storr, *Solitude*

Everything changed for Clara at age forty-one, when lab work from a routine visit to her doctor showed that she had contracted the hepatitis C virus. She and her husband, Tim, loved to party; alcohol and marijuana were their drugs of choice. Clara suspected she had contracted the virus in her twenties, the one time when she and Tim tried harder drugs and shared a needle with a friend. Tim's test results came back the same.

Clara's physician recommended she quit drinking alcohol immediately because her liver was already compromised by the virus. This was shocking news for both Clara and Tim, and for the next five years, with their heads in the sand, they continued partying as if they had never received the diagnosis.

A visit to her doctor at age forty-six revealed more bad news: high blood pressure and high blood sugar. Her doctor, now concerned about heart disease and diabetes, suggested once again that Clara quit drinking. Clara had gained over forty pounds since her wedding day, and she could no longer pretend that her lifestyle wasn't having an effect on her health. Panicked and worried, she made a decision that day to quit drinking and smoking and to change her eating habits. Tim also decided to quit drugs and alcohol. Clara signed up for a popular online weight-loss program and felt good about taking charge of her health.

But her relationship with Tim began to deteriorate. Without alcohol and pot, he was moody and grumpy much of the time, and he began to bury himself in his work. He would come home late, say little during dinner, and then do more work or watch television until he fell asleep. Even though Tim also had gained weight over the years and was now consuming a pint of ice cream nearly every night, he wasn't interested in participating in the weight-loss program. He felt he could get his eating under control on his own.

Tim had little interest in throwing parties anymore, even the dinner parties he loved so much. He had little interest in intimacy with Clara. She had never seen him like this. He had always reassured her that he could control his alcohol and drug use if he wanted to, and she had never had any reason to question him. Now she wondered whether he could stay sober or if she was married to an addict. With all the tension at home, Clara found it difficult to stick to a healthy eating plan. She found herself dieting or "being good" one day and binge eating the next. In a state of utter frustration, she called me.

"I never expected my life to turn out this way," Clara told me dejectedly during our first session on a rainy January afternoon. "All I ever dreamed of was to be a dancer and a mother, and now I'm an overweight, middle-aged bookkeeper with no children, married to a workaholic addict. Where did I go wrong?"

As Clara recounted the story of her childhood, I began to understand her situation. As a girl, the middle child of seven, raised by working-class parents in a small East Coast town, Clara had learned early on to accommodate the needs of others and put her dreams and desires on hold. As a young girl, she hoped to become a dancer, traveling and performing in stage productions all over the world. She had taken many dance classes at school and had been cast as the lead dancer in a few local productions. But her parents discouraged her from pursuing dance as a career and insisted that she gain marketable skills by studying business and accounting in college. Working in an accounting office during summer breaks, she honed her full-charge bookkeeping skills.

At age nineteen, she packed up her belongings and drove from New Jersey to California to live with her older sister, Kira. Her plan was to finish college in Los Angeles while pursuing her passion for dance. Her parents weren't pleased with the idea of her moving so far away, but there was little they could do about it. At least Kira, three years her senior, was there to watch over her. Her bookkeeping skills came in handy when she arrived in Los Angeles. Short of money, she decided to put finishing college on hold and took a full-time bookkeeping job to cover her dance classes and living expenses.

Everything changed the following year, when Clara met Tim. A few years older, Tim was good-looking, outgoing, and funny, and he loved to have a good time. Clara, quiet and shy except when dancing, hadn't dated much and had had little exposure to life outside school and home. In her family, there was rarely enough money for anything more than the essentials. Her parents frowned on dating, and extracurricular activities like dance classes were only possible because she worked after school and during the summers.

Tim, who worked in his father's clothing manufacturing business, always seemed to have money. He was happy to spend it wining and dining Clara. Within a year of arriving in California, Clara moved in with Tim. Somewhere around that time, the weekend partying began. At first, it was just alcohol, but over time, Tim exposed her to marijuana and other drugs. Most of the people in their social circle smoked cigarettes as well, so Clara, wanting to fit in, picked up the habit.

Tim, Clara, and their friends often partied late into the night, with an abundance of food, alcohol, and drugs. Over the years, this lifestyle took a toll not only on Clara's figure and health but also on her motivation to finish college and pursue a career in dance. She couldn't remember exactly when she gave up on her dreams, but somewhere around age twenty-eight, she stopped taking dance classes.

While Tim always encouraged Clara to pursue her passion for dance, he was very driven and determined, and he had a way of putting his own ambitions first. His family's business was booming, and he wanted to get married and buy a home. While Clara would have been happy with a simple wedding, Tim insisted on a lavish affair and a European honeymoon. And Tim didn't want just any home: he wanted the biggest home they could afford. He found a five-bedroom home with ocean views in a nearby beach city, and by her thirty-second birthday, they were living a life Clara had never dreamed of.

At Tim's suggestion, she quit her bookkeeping job and started working with him part-time in the family business. This allowed her the extra time to take care of their home and the two dogs they had adopted along the way. Clara never questioned Tim's guidance — like her father, he was always so confident.

By her mid-thirties, Clara's biological clock was ticking loudly. For the next five years, they tried, unsuccessfully, to get pregnant. After multiple miscarriages and unsuccessful fertility treatments, they decided to take a break. Clara was heartbroken: while she enjoyed the luxury of a life without kids, her life felt empty, and she had a vague sense that something was missing. According to Clara, Tim was ambivalent: he liked the idea of fatherhood, but he felt that without kids, he and Clara could entertain regularly and travel whenever they wanted.

Needs — What Are Those?

Raised in a large family, Clara learned early in life to "go along to get along" and "not make waves." With so many siblings, it was easy to distract herself from her internal world by focusing on the needs of others. This is a common pattern for women everywhere and a valued practice in many cultures. And there is certainly nothing wrong with accommodating and being of service to one's family and community. But we can offer the best of ourselves to others only when we are taking good care of ourselves, and that means paying attention to our internal world. Being of service to those we love and care about and being in tune with our own feelings and needs are not mutually exclusive.

During our first sessions, Clara and I focused on the first few skills of inner nurturing. For homework, I asked her to practice these skills whenever she felt the urge to overeat or binge, or when she noticed that vague empty feeling. I suggested that she give herself permission to eat, if she needed to, *after* she practiced skill 3 — after she felt soothed and comforted by her Inner Nurturer.

Clara, always a good girl, did her homework diligently and reported that she was able to interrupt the urge to overeat or binge many times and that she was feeling more comforted by using her Inner Nurturer voice. She had identified and tracked the following emotional states: loneliness, emptiness, sadness, confusion, and a sense of being lost. After processing and discussing her emotions and corresponding bodily sensations, we moved on to exploring her needs.

JULIE: You're doing a wonderful job identifying and tracking your feelings, Clara. And it's clear from the reduction in your overeating that you're feeling more soothed by your Inner Nurturer. Beginning with the first emotions you mentioned today, I'm wondering, when do you find yourself feeling lonely or empty?

CLARA: Most of the time, especially now that Tim is more distant. But the times when I want to eat over it are at night, when he's working late or watching television, and I feel invisible.

JULIE: And when you're feeling lonely or empty and invisible, what do you need?

CLARA: The feeling part isn't so hard now. I love using my Inner Nurturer voice. I feel like I have a new friend. But I have such

a hard time figuring out what I need. I've spent so much of my
life pleasing others — my family, my husband, and our friends.
I haven't the faintest idea what I need most of the time.

Every phase of our development involves specific emotional needs
and particular kinds of nurturance. These needs are called *developmental dependency needs* because we rely, or depend on, direct caregivers and
extended family members, as well as on people like nannies, teachers,
mentors, and counselors, to meet these needs. At each stage of development, we have fairly specific emotional needs. Good mental health
depends on getting the majority of these needs met in the appropriate
period of life. Each phase builds on the successful completion of the previous phase.

If you were raised in a family where your emotional needs were consistently met, you probably have an easy time identifying your needs in
any given situation. But if your caregivers were unskilled or too preoccupied to be adequately attuned to your emotional state, your basic emotional needs were likely poorly met, and you may never have learned how
to identify and meet those needs. This sets up a lifelong pattern of trying,
often unconsciously, to get many of your dependency needs met from the
outside or of giving up on unmet needs. You may fail to develop the *trust*
that others can and will meet some of your needs.

We are starving to have our emotional needs met, even if we're
unaware of them or deny having them: the intense craving may feel like
physical hunger. Food is pleasurable and temporarily meets some of our
needs, but clearly it's not food we hunger for.

In this chapter, I'll show you how to get clear on your needs.

Identifying Your Needs

Any upset, agitation, or urge to disconnect from yourself and use distractions like food is the cue that you have unmet needs. After practicing
skill 3, Reinforce the Alliance, you're ready to access your *thinking self*

and identify your needs. You can begin addressing your unmet needs by first identifying what there isn't enough of, or what is lacking. Often you'll find that you can make a long list of what's missing, and this will point you toward your needs.

Identifying Your Needs

STEP 1. Ask yourself, "In this situation, what isn't there enough of?"

STEP 2. Ask yourself, "In this situation, what does the youngest part of me, my *feeling self*, need?"

STEP 3. Ask yourself, "In this situation, what does the adult part of me need?"

Step 1. Ask Yourself, "In This Situation, What Isn't There Enough Of?"

When we feel loved and nurtured by our caregivers, we grow up with a sense of sufficiency — we feel there is enough care, love, attention, interest, understanding, safety, warmth, encouragement, fun, excitement, opportunity, and hope. We venture out into the world trusting that our needs can and will be met.

When we have not had sufficient nurturance in our developing years, an exaggerated craving for nurturance persists into our adult lives. It may feel like an empty space that can't be filled. It shows up in our excesses as well as in our bouts of apathy, low motivation, and boredom. We crave attention, approval, validation, reassurance, soothing, comfort, guidance, safety, and security. Perhaps we hunger for tenderness and touch and long to be held and hugged. We may be yearning for protection and relief from distress.

We look outside ourselves to know if we are worthy and valuable. We regularly seek support and encouragement from others, even if it's merely in the form of a look or a nod. At the same time, we may try to hide these needs from others because we feel unworthy and ashamed of them.

The problem with relying on others too often to meet our needs is that we don't learn that we can meet the majority of our needs ourselves. Our expectations of others may be unrealistic. When we do get our needs met, it may not feel as if it's enough, and we may come across to others as overly needy or ungrateful.

If, like Clara, you've spent years disconnecting from your feelings, you're most likely unaware of your needs much of the time. After years of not getting many of your needs met, or focusing exclusively on the needs of others, you've become out of touch with them. When we identify needs that have gone unmet for a long time, they may feel more appropriate to an earlier phase of life — but it's perfectly okay to have any need at any stage of life.

Table 2, "Stage-of-Life Emotional Needs," gives a breakdown of our emotional needs from infancy to old age. Each stage represents the period when a particular need becomes predominant. Take a moment to review table 2. What does it feel like there isn't enough of? What's lacking in your life? Which needs call out to you? Which needs are you longing to have met? Jot them down. Be careful not to judge yourself during the process of identifying needs. *There are no wrong or right needs.*

When I asked Clara what there wasn't enough of most evenings when she felt lonely, empty, and invisible and found herself turning to food, she had no trouble responding.

CLARA: There isn't enough connection with my husband, or anyone. There isn't enough attention and good listening. There
isn't enough romance or affection. There isn't enough interest in me or my day. My husband shuts me out. My siblings
talk all about their kids. Oh, my God — I feel so selfish and
self-absorbed! It's all about me, right? As if my first-world
problems are so big and important. [*Clara sighs loudly, hangs
her head, and looks away.*]

Table 2
Stage-of-Life Emotional Needs

INFANCY (0–9 MOS.)	TODDLERHOOD (9 MOS.–30 MOS.)	PRESCHOOL AGE (30 MOS.–5 YRS.)	SCHOOL AGE (5 YRS.–12 YRS.)
Comfort	Acceptance	Acknowledgment	Adventure
Consistency	Attention	Approval	Affiliation
Echoing	Autonomy	Celebration	Awareness
Holding	Boundaries / limits	Clarification	Choice
Kindness	Empathy	Companionship	Competency
Love / care	Encouragement	Creativity	Connection
Mirroring	Exploration	Fairness	Cooperation
Patience	Fantasy / play	Fun	Counsel
Regulation of	Free expression	Growth	Honesty
emotional arousal	Idealization	Guidance	Industry
Relief of distress	Listening	Hope	Information
Safety	Mobility	Purpose	Mastery
Soothing	Nurturance	Respect	Mystery
Tenderness	Protection	Structure / order	Order
Touching	Reassurance	Validation	Role models
Trust	Support	Wonder	Separation
	Understanding	Worthiness	Stimulation

ADOLESCENCE (13 YRS.–18 YRS.)	YOUNG ADULTHOOD (19 YRS.–34 YRS.)	ADULTHOOD (35 YRS.–75 YRS.)	OLD AGE (76+ YRS.)
Authenticity	Commitment	Appreciation	Completion
Experimentation	Community	Beauty / aesthetics	Consideration
Fidelity	Efficacy	Consciousness	Contentment
Freedom	Humor	Contribution	Ease
Independence	Integrity	Expansion	Wholeness
Inspiration	Intimacy	Extension	
Justice	Joy	Forgiveness	
Sexual exploration	Meaning	Generativity	
Space	Passion	Harmony	
Spirituality	Peace	Significance	
Variety	Productivity	Silence	
	Recreation		

JULIE (as Clara's Inner Nurturer): Let's see if we can just notice what there isn't enough of, without judgment.

It's important to be gentle with yourself when you're identifying what you experience as lacking in your life. Needs that have gone unmet are clamoring for your attention. Remember to practice self-validation with your needs as well as your feelings. Try to view whatever comes up as a precious gift from within of information about yourself and your life.

Step 2. Ask Yourself, "In This Situation, What Does the Youngest Part of Me, My Feeling Self, Need?"

The best way to figure out which part of you is having a particular need is to ask yourself how old you feel when you identify the need. When it's an early developmental need, for things like attention, mirroring, reassurance, comfort, and soothing, you'll usually feel very young. Identifying these unmet early needs often leads us to our old pain and affords us further opportunity to grieve.

JULIE (as Clara's Inner Nurturer): Now that we're clear on what's missing, let's see if we can figure out exactly what we're needing.

CLARA: One thing is for sure — I want to feel close to my husband again.

Not yet used to identifying what the youngest part of her needs, Clara begins by identifying what her adult self is needing. As we'll see, this leads her to what the youngest part of her is needing. It's okay to start with whatever needs you can identify.

JULIE: What would closeness with Tim look like?

CLARA: I don't want our old party lifestyle back. I'm not sure I ever felt all that comfortable with it. I did it to please Tim. I really miss the times when we were alone together and he was in a good mood. We had fun when we first met — without drugs and alcohol. I guess I want him to reassure me and tell me that everything will be all right. I want him to comfort and soothe me and give me hope — that our life together will be good again. That I'm worth it; that I'm enough for him. That he finds me attractive. That he won't leave me. [*She starts to weep.*]

JULIE: It's okay to be sad, Clara. Allow yourself the time to experience all your feelings.

CLARA: I feel really sad. My chest aches, and my body feels heavy. And I feel so silly having all these needs. I sound like I'm a little girl rather than a grown woman.

JULIE: It's perfectly okay to have those needs, Clara. And it makes sense, even at age fifty, to yearn to have them met. You are getting clear on what the youngest part of you is needing.

In this exchange, Clara is moving away from her feelings, accessing her *thinking self*, invalidating her needs, and judging herself. She needs to have her Inner Nurturer validate her feelings and needs.

Step 3. Ask Yourself, "In This Situation, What Does the Adult Part of Me Need?"

The youngest part of you, your *feeling self*, and the more mature part of you can have the same needs. When you're having an adult need, you'll feel more grown-up. Don't worry too much about which stage of life your needs pertain to. The important part of this process is to get clear on your needs.

JULIE (as Clara's Inner Nurturer): Let's see if we can get clear on what the adult part of us needs in this situation.

CLARA: I think I need more joy and intimacy with my husband —
more good times, more happy times.

JULIE: What would joy and intimacy with Tim look like?

CLARA: Well, one thing we used to do together is go to the movies. We would hold hands and cuddle in the theater. Afterward, we would go out for a bite to eat and have time to talk
— about anything and everything. I miss those times. But
I'm not sure how I'm going to get these needs met by Tim.
He's lost in his own world now.

JULIE: Let's not worry about *how* to meet your needs just yet.
As you continue connecting with yourself and practicing the
new skills you're learning, I think you'll be pleasantly surprised at how many of your needs you can meet yourself. As
you're able to meet more of your needs by yourself, that sense
of emptiness and loneliness will lessen, and all of your relationships will feel different, including your relationship with
Tim and with food. Now that Tim is sober, it seems like he is
struggling to cope with his unmet needs as well.

CLARA: Yeah, I think Tim feels my neediness, and it pushes him
away. Not because he doesn't love me, but because he's in his
own pain. He can't rescue himself right now, and I'm looking
for him to rescue us both. But it feels so unfair that I have to
do this all by myself.

Feeling It's Not Fair

Perhaps, like Clara, you're feeling that it isn't fair that many of your emotional needs were unmet when you were a child and that now you have to
work to meet them yourself. It's natural to feel sad or angry about this.
You deserved, and still deserve, to be loved, nurtured, and properly cared
for. The sad reality is that in adulthood it's not possible to get all your
emotional needs routinely met by others.

Allow yourself to feel any feelings that might be surfacing when you read this — you're grieving the lack of a healthy, emotionally nourishing childhood. Grieving will help you release the pent-up emotion associated with loss or disappointment and prepare you for taking the best care of yourself today.

As an adult, you are best equipped to identify and meet your own needs. No one can do this for you. This doesn't mean you won't get *any* needs met by others. It just means you'll be able, more often than not, to meet many of your needs yourself. This will free up your adult relationships to focus on adult needs such as intimacy, companionship, and recreation.

Getting Clear on Multiple Needs

Whenever you find yourself turning to food for comfort, you may have many unmet needs. You may yearn to have specific needs met by particular people. Take the time to identify all of your unmet needs.

JULIE: You mentioned that some of the emptiness and loneliness you experience in the evenings is related to there not being enough connection with your siblings as well. What do you think your *feeling self* and adult self are needing in those relationships?

CLARA: The two siblings I'm closest to are very busy with their careers and their kids. I'd like to feel that they have an interest in my well-being and that I'm valued. But I'm realizing once again, as I'm saying this, that I feel really young, so these are my *feeling self's* needs. They are parents of teenagers, and I want them to pay attention to me like they do their kids. How crazy is that?

JULIE (as Clara's Inner Nurturer): You're not bad or wrong because you have unmet needs. It's all right to feel needy. And it's all right to want attention. You were the middle child

of seven children. It's easy to get derailed in the skill building required for self-care in such a large family. Your parents
were strict, and your childhood felt sheltered. It makes sense
that many of your needs went unmet. Let's try not to judge.

CLARA: You know, I'm not really being honest with myself. Two
of my older siblings actually try to take an interest in me, but I
shut them out. I don't share much because I'm not happy about
how my life has turned out. I feel ashamed. I have what seems
like a good life on the outside, but I feel empty on the inside. I
gave up on my desire to be a dancer long ago, and now it's too
late. We couldn't have kids, and that ship has sailed as well.
[*Sighs deeply. Tears flow again as she grieves these losses; her body
begins to relax.*] Ah, I know what's missing. I need purpose and
meaning in my life. That's what the adult part of me needs. I
need to feel like there is a reason to get out of bed every morning. I need to feel passionate about something.

JULIE: That's great! You've really gotten clear on your needs,
Clara.

Clara's need for attention from her siblings seemed to represent an
adult need. But as she processed her feelings further, she realized that
she actually wanted her siblings to pay attention to her the way they did
to their teenage children. It became clear that this was actually an early
developmental need that had never been properly met and that her shame
was keeping her from connecting in an intimate way with her siblings.
Grieving her losses helped her release some of this old pain. In a more
relaxed, receptive state, she was able to access her upstairs brain and get
clear on her adult needs.

Jumping to Meet Your Needs Too Quickly

Once we've identified our needs, we don't want to be told that it will
take time to address them. We all want immediate gratification of our

needs. But long-standing unmet needs generally don't get met overnight. In fact, you may not be equipped to meet them just yet.

First, you must believe that you truly deserve to have your needs met. If, like Clara, you don't feel inherently worthy, you'll need to strengthen the voice of your Inner Nurturer and firm up your entitlement muscle by learning to validate not only your feelings, but your needs as well.

You must also believe that you have the resources to meet your needs. Clara is still doubtful that she can meet her needs on her own. We'll revisit my sessions with her in the next chapter. As she learns to catch and reframe the self-defeating thoughts that fuel her doubts (skill 5), she'll feel more optimistic about meeting her needs.

Clara has many internal and external resources that she can draw on for assistance. We all do, and we need to regularly remind ourselves of these. I'll show you how to do just that in skill 6.

CHAPTER ELEVEN

Skill 5. Catch and Reframe Self-Defeating Thoughts

The deeper that sorrow carves into your being, the more joy you
can contain.
Is not the cup that holds your wine the very cup that was burned in
the potter's oven?

— Kahlil Gibran, *The Prophet*

How often does a thought or series of thoughts ruin a perfectly good day for you? Catching an unflattering view of yourself in a store window or photo can immediately trigger disappointment and hopeless thoughts such as "Oh, my God, I've gained so much weight — I don't even recognize myself." Or, "I look so old! I'll never find a partner." Then, later that day, even though you vowed to do better, you drown your frustration in a pint of Ben and Jerry's.

How often do you grab something to eat or drink to calm or soothe yourself because you're stressed out or overwhelmed and experiencing anxious, worrisome, or self-doubting thoughts? If you're like most emotional eaters, it happens more often than you care to admit. A misunderstanding with your best friend or partner might lead to agitated thoughts, neck and head tension, and an irritable mood. But a soda and an oversized bag of chips will fix it, right? Feeling as if you handled the new client meeting poorly can instantly create anxious feelings, a nervous stomach, and self-critical thoughts that are hard to shake. You immediately head to the break room for a flaky pastry and a hot chocolate to soothe yourself.

When your presentation to your peers at the monthly meeting doesn't go as planned, you attack yourself ruthlessly. You can't stop recycling critical, shaming thoughts like "No matter how much I prepare, I'm a terrible public speaker." And to make matters worse, you compare yourself to a colleague: "I'll never be as good as Sam — he can really captivate an audience." On your way home from the meeting, feeling exhausted and hopeless, you stop at the drive-through for a bacon burger and fries. Finally, it's quiet inside your head.

Researchers have demonstrated that the average person thinks more than twelve thousand thoughts per day. That's twelve thousand or more opportunities to feel good or bad. Positive experiences, such as receiving a loving note from your partner, a heartfelt thank-you from the new client, or praise for a well-received presentation, or seeing the needle on the scale finally moving in the right direction, can quickly create pleasant, optimistic thoughts. When the majority of our neural firings are positive and empowering, we feel good, "on top of the world," and capable of accomplishing anything. We're more likely to view difficult or challenging situations as opportunities, and we're hopeful about the future.

When our internal world is full of negative, critical, self-defeating thoughts, we feel bad — anxious, frustrated, depressed, hopeless, and powerless. These types of thoughts erode our self-esteem. We're likely to view difficult or challenging situations as obstacles or hardships, and we can easily feel overwhelmed and discouraged. The unpleasant feelings generated by our negative thoughts can quickly lead to an exaggerated desire for soothing, comfort, relief, and distraction. We are hungry for states such as inner peace, joy, hope, and fulfillment, but we lack the ability to shift our internal states. We may feel physically hungry at times like these.

Self-Defeating Thinking and Emotional Eating

Some of those twelve thousand thoughts we experience each day represent deeply held beliefs about ourselves, others, and the world. Aaron T. Beck, the author of *Cognitive Therapy and the Emotional Disorders*, suggests that when these core beliefs are critical and judgmental, they can predispose us to excessive sadness and depression. Negative core beliefs can be challenging to alter because they feel like truths embedded in the fibers of our being. They are responsible for our continual self-doubt, insecurity, low self-esteem, unpleasant moods, and a constant desire for external validation and approval. They can produce painful emotional states and unpleasant bodily sensations and lead to ineffective behavioral patterns such as avoidance, isolation, perfectionism, people pleasing, and emotional eating.

An important technique of cognitive therapy is to make these beliefs explicit (we are often unaware of them) and then decide whether they are effective or disempowering. In this chapter, you'll learn to identify your self-defeating thoughts and core beliefs, and the way they affect your body and your emotional state. You'll also learn to challenge and replace them with more affirming thoughts about yourself and others.

Meaning Making and Core Beliefs

As we grow, our brains assimilate a wide array of external and internal stimuli. When we experience something repeatedly, we assign a meaning to it, and over time this becomes the basis for a core belief. When a young child is frightened about going to the doctor, if her mother repeatedly comforts her and provides the support needed to address her fears, she learns to associate being frightened with the availability of someone to soothe and comfort her. She may then develop beliefs such as "When I'm scared, someone will be there to help me" and "I can rely on others for support." She also makes meaning, via her core beliefs, about herself and the world, such as "It's okay to be vulnerable and express my needs" or

"I'm worthy of time and attention." This type of early environment fosters positive, affirming core beliefs about herself and others. As she grows and learns to express herself, her body language (straight and sturdy posture, head held high, direct gaze) will communicate the core belief "I have a right to be here and express my needs and desires."

A young child who has had challenging or traumatic early-attachment experiences is more likely to form negative and pessimistic core beliefs. If his caregivers consistently fail to attend to his needs and comfort him, he may learn to detach himself, emotionally and physically, when he needs support. At these times, he may feel conflicting emotions — the desire for comfort and soothing and the fear of rejection, neglect, criticism, or shame.

If his caregivers are persistently unresponsive to his needs, he will likely make meaning of these experiences, in the form of negative core beliefs about himself such as "I'm too much to handle," "I'm not worthy of love and attention," or "I'm basically bad." He may also form negative core beliefs about others, such as "My mother doesn't have time for me" or "My father doesn't like me," or about the world, such as "It's not safe to count on anyone," "People will always let you down," or "The world is a dangerous place." When he attempts to assert himself, he may find that his body movements communicate something different. His muscles tighten, his shoulders slump, and he casts his eyes downward. This body language communicates anxiety, insecurity, and core beliefs such as "It's not safe to make requests," "It's shameful to admit I need help," or "I risk being perceived as difficult if I ask for too much."

Distorted Thought Patterns

The pioneers of cognitive therapy have identified many different kinds of distorted thought patterns. Our thought patterns depend on a number of factors, including our innate tendencies (shy or outgoing, fearful or adventurous), the thought patterns we were exposed to as children, and habitual patterns we've adopted as adults. My own adaptation of these patterns includes emotional thinking, black-and-white thinking, perfectionistic thinking, catastrophizing, personalizing, overgeneralizing, exaggerating and minimizing, should-ing, blaming, and ruminating and obsessing. In the following list, under each pattern, I've given examples of self-defeating thoughts and possible associated core beliefs.

Emotional Thinking

When we're flooded with emotion, we're unable to access the logic and reason of our upstairs brain. We get stuck in our lower, reactive, emotional brain, and whatever we're feeling and imagining seems to become reality. If we experience it and "feel" it, it must be the state of things.

SELF-DEFEATING THOUGHT:

"I won't be able to handle this situation."

POSSIBLE CORE BELIEFS:

"I can't cope with stress."
"I need someone to take care of me."
"I'm not good at handling things on my own."
"I'm too emotional."
"I'll never be a true grown-up."

SELF-DEFEATING THOUGHT:

"I can't believe I made such a stupid mistake."

POSSIBLE CORE BELIEFS:

"I'm basically stupid."
"I can't do anything right."
"I can't trust myself."
"I always get it wrong."

SELF-DEFEATING THOUGHT:

"I don't fit in with this crowd."

POSSIBLE CORE BELIEFS:

"I never fit in anywhere."
"I'm basically a misfit."

"There is something wrong with me."

"I have a boring personality."

"People are only drawn to stimulating, attractive people."

When we are stuck in our emotional brain, we need to remind ourselves that our thinking isn't clear and this is not the time to believe what we're thinking.

Black-and-White Thinking

Thinking in absolutes is an attempt to protect ourselves by controlling the uncertainty of the world around us. This type of distorted thinking pattern stems from difficulties in early childhood, often with an inconsistent and unpredictable caregiver. When our thinking becomes polarized in this way, our world is clearly divided into good and bad, right and wrong, with few gray areas. This can lead to rigid thinking and the perspective that "this is the way it is." With regard to our eating habits, we may see ourselves as either out of control (overeating) or in control (dieting).

SELF-DEFEATING THOUGHTS:

"I ate a chocolate bar after lunch; I've blown my diet for the day."

"One bite and I'm out of control."

POSSIBLE CORE BELIEFS:

"I can't trust myself."

"I have to follow my eating plan to the letter, or I'll lose control."

"I need strict rules to follow."

"I can't handle change, uncertainty, ambiguity, or imperfection."

SELF-DEFEATING THOUGHT:

"I've gained back a few pounds; I'll *never* reach my goals."

POSSIBLE CORE BELIEFS:

"I can't trust myself to follow through on things."

"I'm a failure at everything."

"I always fail."

"I have no control over anything."

"There is no use in setting goals — I can't stick to any plan."

This type of distorted thinking intensifies our shame and contributes to a rigid, restricted lifestyle. We need our Inner Nurturer to gently assist us in tolerating life's inevitable slipups and imperfections and the associated emotions. As we do so, we find ourselves experiencing more flexibility, spontaneity, and vitality.

Perfectionistic Thinking

Do you have a tendency to beat yourself up for perceived mistakes, failures, or flaws? Many emotional eaters are "good girls" and "good boys" who attempt to be perfect in all areas of their lives. By controlling their behavior, which includes eating, they hope to avoid experiencing any unpleasant emotions regarding their bodies and selves. Brené Brown, the author of *The Gifts of Imperfection*, writes: "Perfectionism is a self-destructive and addictive belief system that fuels this primary thought: If I look perfect, live perfectly, and do everything perfectly, I can avoid or minimize the painful feelings of shame, judgment, and blame."

The sad truth is that shame, judgment, and blame are an unavoidable part of the human experience. Perfectionism actually increases our risk of experiencing these painful emotions because it leads us to shame, judge, and blame ourselves.

SELF-DEFEATING THOUGHTS:

"I'm a horrible homemaker because my house is cluttered."

"My thighs have some cellulite and are disgusting."

"My nail polish is chipped — I look like a fool."

POSSIBLE CORE BELIEFS:

"If I'm perfect and do everything that pleases Mom (or Dad), then I'll get the love (or care, approval, or validation) I need."

"Unless everything I do is nearly perfect, I'll be perceived as a
failure."
"It's never safe to be authentic and let your guard down."

This type of thinking is a form of black-and-white thinking. It originates from a lack of unconditional acceptance early in life, and it often
develops in response to controlling and demanding caregivers. When you
are treated as if you are bad or wrong for not being perfect, you learn to
either strive for perfection or give up. The dominant voice in your head is
that of a harsh, shaming Inner Critic. Learning to challenge and reframe
your unrealistic expectations helps you replace these thoughts with more
realistic ones. Practicing the unconditionally accepting voice of your
Inner Nurturer helps you develop tolerance for and acceptance of your
inevitable errors and imperfections.

Catastrophizing

Do you expect or predict the worst outcome in challenging situations?
Do you worry about everything? Were you raised by worrywarts who
led you to believe that the world is an unsafe, scary place? Perhaps they
expressed catastrophic concerns about routine events like taking the bus
to school on a rainy day. Maybe they frightened you with fear-based
reminders, such as "Be extra careful" or "It's not safe to…" You were not
taught the skills needed to feel safe in the world, because your caregivers
lacked these skills. You learned to expect the worst and even look for it, a
state called *hypervigilance*.

SELF-DEFEATING THOUGHT:

"I'm experiencing some pelvic pain; I'm sure it's ovarian cancer."

POSSIBLE CORE BELIEFS:

"The worst will always happen."
"The outcome will be scary and painful."

"I won't be able to handle the pain. It will be terrible."

"I'll never feel safe and secure — it's impossible."

SELF-DEFEATING THOUGHT:

"When my boss finds out I made a mistake on the project, she'll probably fire me."

POSSIBLE CORE BELIEFS:

"Bad things will always happen to me."

"I'm powerless to change outcomes."

"One slip and you're out."

SELF-DEFEATING THOUGHT:

"My husband is traveling for business. I'm worried his plane will crash and I'll be a young widow."

POSSIBLE CORE BELIEFS:

"Something awful is going to happen, and I won't be able to handle it."

"I'm destined to endure unending pain and hardship."

"Other than brief moments of happiness, life is all pain and no pleasure."

Words like *awful* and *terrible* and phrases like "It's impossible" can create an attitude of fear and resistance. As we turn challenges and opportunities into catastrophes, we generate powerful negative emotions and unpleasant bodily sensations that dysregulate our nervous system.

Personalizing

It certainly *feels* personal when you experience rejection, exclusion, ridicule, neglect, or downright attack. But the truth is, it's often not really about you at all. The way another person or group treats you says more about them and their problems than about you. Let's say you join a new community organization, and you find some of the members unfriendly and uninviting. You can personalize the seeming rejection by saying to yourself, "I'm not interesting enough for these folks" or "I'm probably not attractive enough for this group." However, it may be that neither statement is true. Some members may have found you both interesting and attractive but may have felt intimidated by you. Some members may be worried about the group getting too big, and rather than taking up this concern with the powers that be, they projected it onto you by being cold. Clearly, their concerns are *not about you.*

This type of thinking pattern generally results from experiences of criticism, rejection, exclusion, favoritism, blame, shame, and attack in childhood. Children are inherently narcissistic and see themselves as the center of the universe. "If Dad is distant and cold, I must have done something to upset him." "Mom would spend more time with me if I were a better daughter."

My client Shana personalizes other people's bad behavior. If someone is rude to her, she wonders why the person doesn't like her or what she might have done to warrant rudeness. If a somewhat self-absorbed friend fails to return a phone call or invite her to join a social event, Shana concludes that she is not well liked.

POSSIBLE CORE BELIEFS:

"I'm responsible, in some way, for other people's behavior."
"If someone is angry or upset with me or rude to me, I must have done something to cause it."
"If someone rejects me in some way, there must be something undesirable about me."
"People should treat me in the same considerate manner I treat them."

Your Inner Nurturer is here to remind you that assumptions are not facts. By becoming aware of your tendency to personalize the behavior of others, you can stop judging, blaming, and shaming yourself. It's important to consider many possible interpretations of a situation before concluding that it's all about you or all your fault. Your tendency to personalize may highlight the need to adjust your expectations of others.

Overgeneralizing

You may find that you have a tendency to generalize about a variety of issues in your life. *Sometimes* becomes *every time*, *infrequently* becomes *never*, and *temporary* becomes *forever*. When you make sweeping generalizations based on a single event or a series of events, or use words that convey extremes, like *always, never, all, forever, no one,* and *everyone,* you are overgeneralizing.

SELF-DEFEATING THOUGHTS:

"I've tried to get pregnant for six months. I'm sure I will *never* conceive — I'm *always* the one who misses out."

"Every time I've tried to lose weight, I've failed. It will *always* be a struggle."

"I will *never* find the love of my life — *no one* wants an overweight partner."

"I'm no good at business. I'll *never* be able to build my practice and earn a consistent income."

POSSIBLE CORE BELIEFS:

"I don't deserve a happy life."

"I'm powerless to change the circumstances of my life."

"Patterns represent facts that are nearly impossible to change."

"There is some law or form of destiny that controls my chances for happiness."

Your thinking becomes distorted by the use of words that convey extremes. As with black-and-white thinking, this type of thinking tends to develop in households where caregivers overgeneralize and view a single negative event or series of events as a never-ending pattern of defeat. They fail to provide the hope necessary for coping with challenging situations.

Exaggerating and Minimizing

Do you exaggerate your flaws and shortcomings and minimize your strengths, abilities, and lovely qualities? Do you blow your mistakes out of proportion? This pattern represents a form of tunnel vision. As with other patterns, it often develops from experiences of being criticized and shamed in childhood. Deep down, we feel defective.

We often minimize the compliments we receive and exaggerate or magnify our flaws or any critical commentary. When someone comments how lovely you look in a new dress, you say: "Thanks, but it looked better when I weighed less." Or Someone tells you that they like your new haircut and color, and you say, "Thank you, but it's too short, and the color makes me look pale and old." Your employer writes in your annual evaluation that your performance overall has been very good, and she sees room for improvement in your managerial skills. You conclude, "I'm terrible at managing others; I'll never be promoted in this company." You're exaggerating the critical commentary and minimizing the overall positive tone of the evaluation.

You're also using this distorted and self-defeating thought pattern when, for example, you gain back a few pounds after a large weight loss and you're convinced that you will gain *all* the weight back and, once again, will fail at weight loss. When you do this, you are minimizing the wonderful effort you have made to lose weight, and you are forgetting to recognize your strengths and achievements.

POSSIBLE CORE BELIEFS:

"I'm basically defective."
"I'm unlovable, worthless, and bad unless I do everything right."
"Things are rarely perfect, and when they are, it never lasts."

These thinking patterns leave you feeling insecure, frustrated, and never good enough. Constantly magnifying your faults and errors can easily trigger an emotional appetite. You can learn to minimize this tendency by accessing your Inner Nurturer, who can remind you of your strengths and successes and give you credit where credit is due.

Should-ing

Most of us rarely check in with ourselves and examine what we expect in any given situation. If our life feels in balance, our expectations are most likely reasonable. It's generally when we feel a sense of frustration, disappointment, anger, or sadness that our unstated or unconscious expectations come to the fore. This is the best time to get clear on them and adjust them if necessary. Our expectations of ourselves can be too high, too low, or "just right" and reasonable.

Unrealistic expectations of yourself lead to what the psychiatrist Karen Horney calls "the tyranny of the shoulds." Even though your expectations may be rigid and unrealistically high, you still believe you can and *should* achieve this vision of your idealized self. Similarly, when you have low expectations of yourself, you believe you *should* be capable of more.

Horney suggests such thinking reflects a "disregard for feasibility": even when you see that you cannot achieve these goals and meet your expectations, you still believe you *should* be able to and that nothing should be impossible. The problem occurs because you perceive a gap between who you are and who you would like to be, and this gap highlights your sense of inadequacy. Rather than offering yourself the gift of unconditional self-acceptance while you work on achieving your goals, you deem yourself not good enough.

SELF-DEFEATING THOUGHTS:

"I should be able to control my food intake at all times."
"I should be able to get down to a size 6."

"I should be able to do the same amount of exercise I did years ago."
"I should never experience setbacks in my progress."
"I should not allow my frustration or anger to show."
"I should always be sweet, kind, and polite."

POSSIBLE CORE BELIEFS:

"I need to be perfect to love myself or to be loved."
"I'm a failure and a loser if I don't achieve my goals."

This distorted thinking pattern is another version of perfectionistic thinking, and it originates from a lack of unconditional acceptance early in life. Your Inner Critic is constantly on the scene, reminding you of where you fall short. Learning to challenge and reframe your *shoulds* will help you replace these thoughts with more realistic ones.

Blaming

Simply put, blaming is a way to avoid responsibility for your life. It distracts you from feeling the pain of your mistakes and shortcomings and shifts your focus elsewhere.

SELF-DEFEATING THOUGHTS:

"I can't lose weight because there's too much unhealthy food everywhere I go."
"I can't get ahead in my career because it's all about who you know."
"I'm unfulfilled in my marriage because my husband is a workaholic."

POSSIBLE CORE BELIEFS:

"I'm not responsible for my pain; I didn't cause it."
"I can't change the conditions of my life."
"I'm helpless and powerless to change my life."

This pattern often originates with caregivers who feel that their lives are, in many ways, controlled by external forces. If we feel victimized by circumstances, we look for someone or something else to blame. Stopping the blame game is the first step in becoming real with yourself and facing your own pain. You *can* change or accept the circumstances of your life, but first you must be willing to take full responsibility for your life.

Ruminating and Obsessing

Most of us have had the experience of thinking about something over and over in an attempt to figure out how to handle it or cope with it. Perhaps you've gained weight and you can't stop thinking about how full your face looks and how your thighs are rubbing together. Maybe your biological clock is ticking and you can't stop thinking about finding a partner and getting pregnant. Perhaps you're replaying a traumatizing incident over and over again, analyzing it and trying to sort out who did or said what and who was at fault.

When we think about something over and over, we call it *rumination*. The term comes from ruminant animals such as cows and sheep, which chew and rechew their partially digested, regurgitated food. Research suggests that women ruminate more than men, who are more likely to take action. There are certainly times when we need to replay a situation in order to assign responsibility and learn from it. But when ideas, images, or desires haunt us persistently, our thinking is considered obsessive.

You may have learned this type of thinking because your caregivers modeled it, or you may have developed it in an attempt to make sense out of a confusing or unpredictable environment. Some people have brain chemistry that makes them more prone to obsessive thinking.

SELF-DEFEATING THOUGHTS:

"I have to keep thinking about this until I figure it out."
"I'm unable to stop thinking about this situation."

POSSIBLE CORE BELIEFS:

"If I stop thinking about a problem, it will get worse."
"If I don't focus on a problem continually, I'll get lazy and never
    solve it."

There are many well-known techniques for handling obsessive
thoughts. There are thought-stopping techniques such as snapping a rub-
ber band worn on your wrist or ringing a loud bell every time you ruminate. You can also carry around a piece of paper with the word *STOP* on
it in big letters. Distracting techniques such as reading a book or playing
a musical instrument shift your attention and concentration elsewhere. A
more lasting solution, however, is to challenge and dispute these disturbing thoughts.

Replacing Self-Defeating Thoughts

Our self-defeating thoughts and beliefs are usually triggered by situations that cause distress: disappointment, loss, hurt, fear, rejection, criticism, shame, doubt, vulnerability, insecurity, and exposure. We're often
unaware of them, and when we are, we tend to treat them as facts. But
thoughts are not necessarily facts. If your thought patterns leave you feeling bad, then they are not working for you, and you would benefit from
learning to reframe them.

Change Begins with Mindful Awareness

There was a point during my emotional-eating days when I realized that
I had unwittingly become my own worst critic. I zeroed in on everything I perceived to be wrong with myself. I alone knew every one of my
weaknesses and inadequacies; I remembered my biggest mistakes, social
blunders, and most embarrassing moments. Only for fleeting moments
did I recognize what was right and good about myself. My insecurities,
self-doubts, and lack of self-control (primarily with food) made me easy
prey for self-abuse. My overdeveloped, perfectionistic Inner Critic was

constantly on the scene, ready to beat me up unmercifully. Perhaps you can relate.

I regularly recycled critical, judgmental, self-defeating thoughts about my body, my personality, my abilities, my relationships, the future, and the past. My mind chatter often began first thing in the morning:

"I can't believe I look so fat in this outfit."

"Nothing in this closet fits me."

"I'll never have a body I like."

"I hate my hair. It looks awful and has a mind of its own!"

"I didn't get enough sleep last night — I look like crap."

"I hate that I'm such a slug in the mornings."

If I ate something off my eating plan during the day — which was likely, since I was already in a bad mood and needing comfort — I'd flood myself with another stream of negative thoughts:

"I can't believe I blew my diet again."

"This day is shot. Might as well throw in the towel."

"I can't stick with *any* eating plan."

"I'll never lose this weight."

"It's not fair that some people can eat anything they want, and I have to watch everything I put in my mouth."

If I made the mistake of trying to seek comfort from my poorly attuned mother, I often ended up snapping at her, and, you guessed it, beating myself up with more self-critical thoughts:

"I'm such an idiot! Why did I turn to *her* for comfort?"

"When am I ever going to learn not to call her when I'm upset?"

"I hate myself for snapping at her when I know she's trying to help."

Days like these, when I felt utterly frustrated and hopeless, often ended in a binge. That triggered more negative thoughts about myself, filled with shame, guilt, and remorse. The following morning, before I opened my eyes, I quickly assessed the damage I'd done the night before. I might then spiral down and feel depressed for days or longer or binge for days on end. I call this "doing depression" because, unlike depression caused by a biochemical imbalance, it was actually within my control and caused by my own thinking.

It became clear to me that my overeating and recurring low moods were directly related to my thoughts. More specifically, they were a reaction by my *feeling self* to the negative evaluation and interpretation of situations and events made by my *thinking self*. I began to understand that although I would never be able to control all the stressful situations or events in my life, I could control the flood of self-defeating thoughts, which would allow me to regulate my emotional states and control my overeating. When I realized that it was within my power to change my thoughts, it gave me hope.

I knew that in order to change my thinking, I was going to have to be mindful of those thoughts. Because my self-defeating thoughts were automatic and insidious, I decided to back into them by writing down what I was *thinking*, in addition to what I was *feeling*, whenever I was upset — especially when I wanted to grab comfort foods or overeat.

I did this for an entire year. I know it sounds tedious, but it was incredibly enlightening. Not only was I able to see how critical and judgmental my thoughts were, but I also realized that my overeating wasn't just about soothing and comfort; it was a grand distraction from the powerlessness I felt in many areas of my life. It was easier to pleasure and comfort myself with food — and then obsess about my eating, weight, exercise habits, and low self-esteem — than to address the deeper, underlying issues.

Noticing the Language of Body Movements

Body movements include our postures and gestures, the way we hold tension, and the way we carry ourselves. Our bodies are continually responding to what is happening around us, how others are treating us, how we feel inside, and what we're thinking. My accounts of sessions with clients in earlier chapters include descriptions of their body movements, such as slumped shoulders or clenched fists.

In the *Emotional Eater's Repair Manual*, I introduced a two-step process, called Catch and Reframe, for addressing self-defeating thoughts and core beliefs. I've expanded this process to include the tracking of feelings and body movements so that you can notice the effect a change in your thinking has on your mood and body.

Catch and Reframe

STEP 1.   CATCH your thoughts about any situation causing distress. Write down what you're thinking and feeling. Pick the most troubling thought to work on.

STEP 2.   REFRAME this thought or belief with a calming or uplifting new thought that feels equally true. Notice how you feel when you say your new thought out loud. Notice your body movements.

Step 1. Catch your thoughts about any situation causing distress.
Write down what you're thinking and feeling.
Pick the most troubling thought to work on.

Stop for a moment when you're experiencing unpleasant feelings. Try to stop *before* you grab something to eat when you're not hungry, choose unhealthy comfort food when you are hungry, or eat beyond fullness. See if you can identify something that's bothering you and what you're thinking and feeling about it. If it isn't clear, take your best guess.

You'll need to be focused when you do this work. Don't shortchange yourself by trying to do this step in your head. Write down anything and everything you're thinking and feeling, including both emotions and bodily sensations. Try not to edit or censor yourself. Don't worry about whether a thought is a core belief. The core beliefs will become evident to you as you write them down: these are beliefs you have held for a long time.

Select the most painful thought about yourself or your life and how you feel, and focus on it. If the thought is about someone or something else, see if you can identify a related thought about yourself. For example, if you're thinking, "My husband will never be able to bring home a decent living," a related thought about yourself might be, "I'll never have the lifestyle I'd like to have."

Here are some examples of clients catching and reframing self-defeating thoughts:

JAN: TENSION WITH A COWORKER

Ever since Jan reprimanded a staff nurse recently, the nurse has been moody and cool around her. Jan catches herself thinking the following thoughts:

"I'm just not good at handling people."
"I'm powerless and ineffective when I deal with difficult people."
"I can't function well when there's tension in the workplace."
"I treat everyone with fairness; they should treat me the same way."

Jan notices that she feels hurt, disappointed, angry, frustrated, insecure, discouraged, powerless, and sad. Her body feels tight, tense, buzzy, wired, hyped, spinning, knotted, drained, and achy. Her body movements include her head dropping, shoulders and spine slumping, arms crossed. She walks heavily, clenching her fists and slamming cupboard doors.

The most painful thought she identifies is "I'm just not good at handling people."

Raised by a volatile father and a depressed, passive mother, Jan grew up with a sense of powerlessness regarding relationships. Nothing she ever said or did could please her father or lift her mother's spirits, and she was unable to protect her younger siblings from abuse. She had never been able to shake this core belief.

LENNY: ANXIOUS ABOUT A NEW RELATIONSHIP

Lenny has been dating Paula for six weeks. He's excited about the relationship but concerned that she is texting and calling him less frequently than she did during the first few weeks. He catches himself thinking the following thoughts:

> "Paula won't stick around because of my weight."
> "When someone gets to know me, they always find something
>   they don't like."
> "I'm unlovable as I am."
> "I won't be able to handle it if Paula bails."

Lenny notices that he feels anxious, worried, frustrated, insecure, inadequate, sad, discouraged, hurt, and angry. His body feels tingly, fuzzy, buzzy, prickly, tight, tense, blocked, weak, and heavy. His body movements include back and neck stiffening, shoulders and arms slumping, head dropping, and frowning.

The most painful thought he identifies is "I'm unlovable as I am."

This self-defeating thought represents a very painful, long-held core belief. Lenny's parents focused on his weight and took him to numerous diet doctors. His well-meaning grandmother often compared him to his slim older brother and reminded him when he took extra portions that "girls don't like fat boys." The shame he experienced has stuck with him, and he can still hear his grandmother's voice in his head.

CLARA: FEELING EMPTY AND UNFULFILLED

While spending time with her sister's family, Clara is reminded of what is missing in her life. She catches herself thinking the following thoughts:

"I wasted my life."

"I should have stopped partying with Tim long ago."

"I'll never feel complete without kids."

"It's too late for me to find purpose and meaning."

"I don't have enough determination to succeed at *anything*."

"I'll always feel bad about myself around my family."

Clara notices that she feels jealous, frustrated, defeated, inadequate, empty, invisible, sad, depressed, unfulfilled, and hopeless. Her body feels achy, sore, hot, tight, churning, fuzzy, foggy, dull, and wobbly. Her body movements include: hunched over, rocking from side to side, furrowed brow, legs and arms crossed, and wiggling feet.

The most painful thought she identifies is "I don't have enough determination to succeed at *anything*."

Clara begins to cry as she says this thought out loud. It symbolizes a lifetime's worth of insecurity and low self-esteem pushed down and numbed with food and alcohol. As a young girl, she dreamed of becoming a professional dancer. But without her parents' support and encouragement, she found it difficult to believe in herself. She had hoped that if she moved far away from her parents, she would be able to pursue her passion. But a combination of shyness, self-doubt, and pessimism had derailed her best intentions.

Step 2. Reframe this thought or belief with a calming or uplifting new thought that feels equally true. Notice how you feel when you say your new thought out loud. Notice your body movements.

Once you've identified your self-defeating thoughts and core beliefs, it's time to replace them with new thoughts. Start with any core beliefs you've identified, because once these have been reframed, it's often easier to work on associated negative thoughts.

Creating calming or uplifting replacement thoughts can be the most challenging (and exciting!) part of this process. You've been recycling some of your self-defeating thoughts for decades or longer. New thoughts don't feel comforting or true right away, even if, intellectually, you know they could be. Be patient with this process. Practice writing and verbalizing your reframed thoughts daily. It will pay off.

JAN

JAN'S MOST PAINFUL THOUGHT:

"I'm just not good at handling people."

JAN'S REFRAMES:

"I'm learning new people skills and getting better at them every day."

"When I slow down, breathe, and think before I act, I actually handle people fairly well."

"I am fair-minded and always consider what is best for everyone."

"I will never be able to please or be liked by everyone."

As Jan repeats these new thoughts, she feels calm, encouraged, confident, hopeful, and optimistic. She notes that the tightness in the back of her head, neck, and shoulders is less; her wired and aroused feeling has been replaced by a pleasant, energized feeling; her whole body feels calmer. She is holding her head high and her shoulders and spine upright. Her arms are uncrossed, her feet are quiet, and her hands are relaxed and resting on her thighs.

LENNY

LENNY'S MOST PAINFUL THOUGHT:

"I'm unlovable as I am."

LENNY'S REFRAMES:

"I am worthy of love."

"I do not have to be perfect to be loved."

"I am more than my excess weight; I have many wonderful attri-
butes."
"In this moment, I choose to love and accept myself as I am."
"My self-respect is attractive."

As Lenny repeats these new thoughts, he feels relieved, refreshed, calm, appreciative, encouraged, and hopeful. He notes that he is feeling warmth in his upper body and a clear head. The tension in his arms and hips is nearly gone; the pressure in his forehead is gone. His neck feels lighter, his back softer, and his stomach less knotted. He notices that he is sitting up straight, with his head up and looking forward, and beginning to smile.

CLARA

CLARA'S MOST PAINFUL THOUGHT:

"I don't have enough determination to succeed at *anything*."

CLARA'S REFRAMES:

"I actually do have determination and demonstrate it in many
areas of my life."
"I struggle with *believing* in my abilities — when I remind myself
to go slow and take baby steps, I feel more capable."
"As I practice patience with this process, I realize that I can be
successful."
"I can achieve my goals, one step at a time."

As Clara repeats these new thoughts, she feels encouraged, hopeful, optimistic, inspired, and grateful. Her upper body feels much lighter, and the pressure behind her eyes is gone. She feels a slight increase in energy, her brain is no longer foggy, and her stomach has relaxed. She notices that her hands are by her side; she is sitting comfortably and no longer rocking; her face and feet are relaxed, and her eyes are wide open.

It will take some dedicated time and attention to change deeply ingrained beliefs you've been repeating to yourself for years. But keep in mind that it takes a lot of time and energy each day to manage anxious, fearful, negative, judgmental, hopeless thoughts and the emotional states they produce. It would definitely be a better use of your time to work on shifting your thoughts.

Every time you reframe a self-defeating thought or core belief with a more calming or uplifting replacement thought, you're creating a new neural pattern. You're literally rewiring and changing the structure of your brain. As you continue to do this, catching and reframing will get a lot easier, and your new replacement thoughts will feel true and authentic.

Suggestions for Reframes

Replacing self-defeating thoughts with calming or uplifting thoughts is a surefire way to restore yourself to sane thinking and interrupt the urge to eat. Once you come up with new, reframed thoughts that work, wire them in by practicing them regularly. Here are some suggestions to help you get started:

1. Keep your reframed thoughts simple, short, and in the present tense. They are easier to practice when they are concise and to the point. Avoid statements about the future, such as "When I..." or "Someday I will..." You are living life in this moment, not waiting for your life to begin. This is not a dress rehearsal.

2. Make your statements unconditional. Avoid statements such as "If this happens, then..." Try on phrases like "I am...," "I can...," or "As I practice..."

3. Phrase your thoughts in a positive way, affirming what you are doing rather than what you are trying not to do. Rather than "I won't beat myself up anymore," try statements like "I choose to say only loving, supportive comments to myself."

4. If you can't think of a calming or uplifting thought, try on a neutral, nonjudgmental thought. "I look fat and disgusting in this dress" can be replaced by "I'm glad I chose to wear something comfortable today."

5. If you can't find any reframe that works, see if there is a core belief underneath the thought you are working on. Ask yourself, "What does this thought mean to me?" "I look fat and disgusting in this dress" may actually represent the core belief "I can't accept and love myself with excess weight." Work on creating a reframe for this core belief. For example: "I deserve love and acceptance no matter what size I am," and "Today, I choose to accept myself as I am."

6. Make reframes self- and life-affirming. Try on statements like "I'm proud of...," "I deserve...," I'm good at...," or I'm fortunate that..."

7. Think of something you would say to a friend or loved one to comfort or uplift her and help her see a challenging situation in a new light.

8. Pretend you are talking to a young child. Many of the critical things you've been saying to yourself are things you would never say to a young child.

9. Try gratitude statements to help you value what you have. "I hate my big thighs — they never fit in clothes" can be reframed into "I'm grateful that my legs are sturdy and get me where I want to go."

10. Act *as if* you believe these new thoughts until your feelings catch up with your wisdom. See if you can temporarily experience your new thought as a truth you'd *like* to believe. Try it on, suspend your "voice of reality," your doubts and "yes, buts," and allow yourself to experience the possibility. For a moment, adopt a childlike attitude that lets you believe anything is possible.

Practice your new thoughts often, using them whenever the old, familiar self-defeating thoughts or core beliefs surface. Calming and uplifting thoughts lead to hope, expanded possibilities, and healthier, more adaptive behaviors.

Here are a few more examples of calming reframes:

SELF-DEFEATING THOUGHT:

"I'm sure this pain is going to turn out to be something serious."

POSSIBLE CORE BELIEFS:

"Bad things always happen to me."

"I won't be able to cope with what comes my way."

CALMING REFRAMES:

"I don't have a diagnosis — it's best not to catastrophize."

"In this moment, I choose to believe it's nothing serious."

"There are many possible causes for this pain."

"Worrying nonstop is stressful and not good for my health."

"Whatever it is, there are resources I can rely on."

SELF-DEFEATING THOUGHT:

"I can't believe I made such a poor decision."

POSSIBLE CORE BELIEFS:

"I'm not smart enough to think things through properly."

"I don't have what it takes to make smart decisions."

CALMING REFRAMES:

"I'm human, and I'm bound to make mistakes at times."

"When I go slow and think things through, I can make smart decisions."

"I can learn from my mistakes and move on."

"In this moment, I choose to forgive myself for making an error."

"I'm lovable even when I make mistakes."

Here are a few more examples of uplifting reframes:

SELF-DEFEATING THOUGHT:

"It's going to take forever to make a new friend."

POSSIBLE CORE BELIEF:

"I don't have the patience or emotional endurance required to achieve my goals."

UPLIFTING REFRAMES:

"I can take the time I need to explore different activities."

"As I take part in new activities, I'm building my people skills."

"I can enjoy casual acquaintances while I build closer friendships."

"As I practice patience, I can lessen my expectations of quick results."

"I can tolerate the slow pace of change."

SELF-DEFEATING THOUGHT:

"I'm never going to find a partner — I'm sure I'll grow old alone."

POSSIBLE CORE BELIEFS:

"No one will ever love me."

"I have to be young, hot, beautiful, handsome, slim, and sexy for someone to want me."

UPLIFTING REFRAMES:

"I am worthy of love *as I am*."

"I do not have to be perfect to be loved."

"I have many wonderful attributes."

"In this moment, I choose to practice loving myself."

"My self-love is very attractive."

SELF-DEFEATING THOUGHT:

"I can't lose this weight because there isn't enough time to focus on myself, eat right, and exercise."

POSSIBLE CORE BELIEFS:

"I can't take care of so many things at once."

"It's impossible to have it all."

UPLIFTING REFRAMES:

"I'm worthy of time and attention."

"I'm capable of setting priorities and balancing the many demands of my life."

"I can make a few small dietary changes that support my health and well-being."

"I can easily add small amounts of movement into my day."

"Baby-step changes will make a dent."

SELF-DEFEATING THOUGHT:

"It's hopeless — I'll never have a small waist."

POSSIBLE CORE BELIEFS:

"I can't love myself as I am."

"No one else will love and accept me this way."

"I can't cope with not being able to change certain things."

UPLIFTING REFRAMES:

"My life is about so much more than the size of my waist."

"I have many wonderful attributes."

"Today, I choose to practice unconditionally accepting my body as it is."

"We all have body parts we would redesign if given the chance."

"I refuse to waste another precious moment on something so superficial."

SELF-DEFEATING THOUGHT:

"I have to stick to a rigid eating plan, or I'm out of control."

POSSIBLE CORE BELIEF:

"I can't trust myself and need to impose rigid limits."

"I have zero discipline."

"I can eat a small portion of foods that aren't part of my eating
plan and accept and tolerate the discomfort of wanting more."
"I take good care of my *feeling self* by allowing her to have treats
and by setting realistic limits."
"I am willing to be uncomfortable in order to reach my goals."
"I have discipline in many areas of my life."

You Have the Resources to Meet Your Needs

Catching and reframing your self-defeating thoughts is the first step in
addressing any doubts about being able to meet your own needs and cope
with what life throws your way. But before you're ready to create a game
plan for meeting your needs (skill 7), it's important that you truly believe
that they can be met and that you can meet them yourself. Perhaps you're
still not feeling very hopeful on this front.

Is it really possible to attract more nourishing people into your life
when you're working long hours and can't find the time? How can you
make new friends or find a love interest when you're shy and introverted
and suffer from social anxiety? Where will you find intimacy if your partner has shut down or isn't capable of it? What are the odds of finding
a partner at your current weight or stage in life? Could you really find
work you love when you didn't finish that college degree? How can you
leave your boring job when you can't think of anything else to do with
your life? Is it possible to meet your need to nurture little ones when your
biological clock has stopped ticking? Will you ever be able to find peace
or experience joy when your child has problems with day-to-day living?
How can you take care of your needs while meeting your family's needs
as well? Where will you find the motivation and drive to tackle all of these
unmet needs?

The answer to all of these questions lies in the realization that you
have many internal and external resources at your disposal: internal
strengths and capacities and external sources of support. You probably

don't focus on these very often, and you may have a tendency to minimize them. Research shows that the act of recognizing and acknowledging positive resources creates a sense of safety and security. It has a calming and regulating effect on your nervous system and reinforces your capacity for self-regulation. It shifts your attention away from negative self-judgments and distorted thinking and helps you hold hope that your needs can be met. And who better to highlight your resources and provide hope than your very best friend, your Inner Nurturer?

CHAPTER TWELVE

Skill 6. Highlight Resources and Provide Hope

Every difficulty in life presents us with an opportunity to turn inward and to invoke our own submerged inner resources. The trials we endure can and should introduce us to our strengths.

— Sharon Lebell, *The Art of Living*

Never in his wildest dreams did Matt, a fifty-one-year-old unemployed television writer, think that he would end up raising his daughter on his own. He and his wife, Sandra, a forty-seven-year-old corporate attorney, had been through the wringer in the previous two years. After celebrating their tenth wedding anniversary and their daughter Cloe's seventh birthday, Sandra received some bad news during a routine doctor's visit. The breast cancer she had survived years earlier had returned, and this time it had metastasized to her liver. The prognosis was not good. Determined to do everything they could, Matt and Sandra nearly depleted their savings pursuing both traditional and alternative treatments. On a dark, rainy winter's day, almost two years to the day after Sandra received the bad news, Matt and Cloe said their goodbyes to her.

I had begun working with Matt years earlier, when he was thirty-eight and single and had just started working as a writer for a popular television series. A self-professed underachiever, Matt had graduated with a degree in journalism and worked as a writer and editor for various local magazines and newspapers. He had wanted to write for television but couldn't motivate himself to finish and pitch scripts. When a writer friend had suggested he apply for an open position on a television show she was working on, he had jumped at the chance. He had been elated when they made him an offer.

Matt had loved his new position, but the combination of long days and an abundance of delectable food available around the clock at the studio had led to a fifty-pound weight gain in the first year. During our late-evening sessions, we had addressed his out-of-control eating, his difficulties with dating, the challenging relationship he had with his father, and his fear of losing his job.

Matt also had participated in my Twelve-Week Emotional Eating Recovery Program for skill building and extra support. As he had begun to pay attention to his hunger and fullness cues, he had stopped eating mindlessly at work and had started losing weight. As he had shifted to eating more whole, unprocessed foods, his energy level had increased, and he had started going to the gym early in the morning. He had started taking short breaks during the day to pop the hood and notice what he was feeling and to access his Inner Nurturer for validation, reassurance, and comfort. His ability to regulate his fear and anxiety had made him more confident about his future in television as well as the prospects of finding a girlfriend. He had met Sandra the next year.

Matt called me a month after Sandra's passing, his voice trembling. "Sandra was the best thing that ever happened to me. I'm not sure how I'll survive without her. The show ended five years ago, and I've been out of work ever since. I'm depressed, and my anxiety is through the roof. I'm eating compulsively again, and my weight has skyrocketed. I'm the heaviest I've ever been. I need to be strong for Cloe, but I don't feel very sturdy right now."

Internal and External Resources

During our childhood, with encouragement from our caregivers, we acquire capabilities — personal competencies and strengths — that support our development, bring relief from distress, and help us meet life's challenges and achieve our goals. These *internal resources* include a variety of capacities, such as the ability to identify, track, make meaning of, and express our feelings; recognize our needs; manage our thoughts; calm and soothe ourselves; ask for help; set limits with ourselves and boundaries with others; feel at ease in many situations; and explore our creativity. Internal resources also include our talents and aptitudes, such as playing a musical instrument or a sport, singing, reading, dancing, creating art, or being a computer whiz.

All of us possess a wide range of internal resources. Some resources, such as the ability to tolerate frustration or delay gratification, help us meet our goals. Others, like our capacity for empathy and the ability to see things from another's perspective, help us negotiate relationships. And still others, like a sense of humor, can help us shift perspective and increase joy.

Attunement and attachment difficulties and traumatic experiences can interfere with our ability to recognize, appreciate, and trust our internal resources. When poorly attuned caregivers fall short of meeting our needs, we are left with a diminished sense of our worth. We may perceive ourselves as incompetent, inadequate, untalented, unskilled, stupid, useless, or lazy.

Continual criticism, rejection, and shame condition us to focus on our mistakes and shortcomings and to ignore or disparage the many positive qualities we possess. We may tend to zero in on aspects of current situations and relationships we find unsatisfying or to ruminate on unpleasant memories. If our internal resources were insufficient to protect us from harm or bring us fulfillment when we were young, we may not even realize that we have resources for dealing with life.

Some internal resources, called *survival resources*, are psychological and physical adaptations that help us tolerate and survive challenging early experiences. Survival resources can be instinctive, as when we stand up to or run away from a bully. Others are developed over time, such as fine-tuning our radar for Dad's moods and pretending to be asleep or heading to the neighbors' house when he has an emotional outburst.

Some survival resources help us meet the approval and expectations of our caregivers and mentors. Being a good girl or boy, not making waves, going along to get along, emotionally withdrawing, smiling when we are upset, keeping our heads down around unkind elders, and adopting a subservient demeanor are all examples of survival resources. Getting good grades and becoming a high achiever can be a survival resource in a difficult family environment where achievement is valued. Acting angry or confrontational may be a survival resource we develop by observing a caregiver who models assertion in the form of aggression.

Survival resources also include the ways we attempt to regulate physical and emotional arousal and calm our nervous system, such as thumb sucking; rocking back and forth; escaping into our favorite books, movies, television programs, or games; using substances like food, alcohol, and drugs; cutting ourselves; and even ruminating on suicide. Other survival resources are adaptive strategies — like excessive exercising, shopping, masturbation, or gambling — for increasing arousal and energy in understimulating or depressing environments. These behaviors may help us to cope as children, but in our adult lives, they sabotage our growth.

In addition to our internal resources, we have *external resources* we can rely on. These include family, friends, mentors, neighbors, casual acquaintances, and companion animals; religious and spiritual affiliations and institutions; community organizations; work and colleagues; health practitioners and medical facilities; and material resources, such as a home, a car, food to eat, and money in the bank.

Becoming aware of our resources helps us navigate and cope with life's inevitable challenges and disappointments in a creative way. In this chapter, we'll work on getting clear on your internal and external resources and determine whether any of your early survival resources are still useful. You'll learn to use your Inner Nurturer voice to regularly highlight your resources and provide the hope necessary for you to believe that your needs and desires can be met.

Identifying Your Resources

We start with identifying and listing the three categories of resources:

Step 1. *List your internal resources.* Notice how you feel as you appreciate your strengths and capacities.

Step 2. *List your external resources.* Notice how you feel as you acknowledge the support all around you.

Step 3. *List your survival resources.* Identify the ones you still use today. Note whether they are useful. Notice how you feel as you recognize these resources.

Matt's parents were Holocaust survivors — penniless refugees who settled in New York after the war. They were grateful to be starting over on a new continent, yet fearful of the economic uncertainties that lay ahead. Matt was born the year after their arrival. His father, a hardworking, reserved man, worked two jobs to support the family while his mother stayed at home with him.

"In my family, our physical needs were met, for sure, but our emotional needs were often neglected. My father was always tired, and he was stern, critical, and unapproachable. My mother was a loving and affectionate woman, but she was extremely fearful and anxious. She never felt safe in this country, and I remember her crying a lot — she was sad and depressed about the loss of her family and having to leave her home in Europe," Matt said, crossing his arms and legs.

As a young boy, Matt coped with his father's coldness and his mother's moods by snacking and escaping into his favorite television programs. He was a slow learner, and without proper guidance, he did poorly in school. In elementary school, he often pretended to be sick so that he could stay home, watch movies with his mother, and eat the treats she baked. In high school, he discovered that he had a talent for writing, and his journalism teacher encouraged him to write articles for the school newspaper. "I think I would have flunked out of high school if Mr. Jimenez hadn't seen some potential in me."

Matt's brother, Sam, was three years younger. "Sam is killer smart, and he was always my father's favorite. He was athletic, outgoing, and good-looking, and he got straight As. He went on to medical school and became a physician. He definitely experienced a different version of my parents — he came along when they were more settled and feeling more hopeful about life in the States."

Matt feared that he wouldn't be able to find work again. Sandra had been the sole breadwinner for the past five years. Even though he had been taking care of their home, finances, and childcare, he was frightened by the prospect of going it alone. "I didn't want to appear pathetic in the group last night, but I wanted to tell you privately that I'm frightened that I won't be able to cope. I've been catching and reframing my self-defeating thoughts on a daily basis, but lately, I'm having a lot of doubt. My parents and my brother and his family live out of state, and I'm here all by myself with Cloe. I have a couple of close friends, but they have their own challenges."

As he rubbed and clasped his hands tightly together, I could see the panic in Matt's eyes, and I could feel him searching my eyes for comfort, soothing, and understanding. I reassured him that I was certain he already had everything he needed inside himself to cope with what he was facing. I reminded him that he also had external resources he could rely on (including me and the group), and I had no doubt that the skills he was learning would be lifesaving.

The following week, in our group session, when we worked on identifying resources, Matt began to realize that he actually had quite a few internal resources. He made a list of them, along with his external and survival resources, and noted his feelings as he completed each list. As he shared his lists with the group, he sighed loudly, and the relaxation in his face and entire body was visible and heartwarming.

Step 1. List your internal resources. Notice how you feel as you appreciate your strengths and capacities.

MATT'S INTERNAL RESOURCES

- EMOTIONAL: Access to my emotions; emotional endurance; awareness of my bodily sensations; some ability to regulate my emotions; ability to express my emotions; ability to perceive other's emotions; capacity for experiencing connecting emotions; a budding connection to my intuition
- COGNITIVE: Ability to read, focus, and pay attention; ability to solve problems; ability to store and retrieve memories; access to my intelligence
- RELATIONAL: Cooperative; accommodating; warm; friendly
- PSYCHOLOGICAL: Openness; flexibility; determination; curiosity; courage; sense of humor; access to my Inner Nurturer
- SPIRITUAL: Interest in revisiting birth religion; a sense of awe in nature
- CREATIVE: Writing; drawing; playing musical instruments; gardening; cooking; baking, learning to sew
- PHYSICAL: Okay health; ability to connect with my body; walking; hiking; swimming; enjoyment of sex

After making his list, Matt noticed that he felt more peaceful and calm. He also felt amazed and hopeful.

Examples of Internal Resources

EMOTIONAL

- Access to uplifting emotions (joy, excitement, inspiration, passion)
- Access to calming emotions (contentment, peacefulness, tranquility)
- Emotional endurance — the ability to tolerate unpleasant emotions and move through them
- Ability to identify how emotions present in your body as sensations
- Ability to regulate and manage emotions and sensations and allow them to guide you
- Access to gut senses and intuitive hunches
- Ability to communicate and express emotions
- Ability to perceive others' emotions and read their body language
- Capacity for experiencing connecting emotions (sympathy, empathy, compassion)

COGNITIVE

- Ability to focus and pay attention
- Ability to understand and comprehend
- Ability to read, study, and learn
- Ability to solve problems and work things out
- Ability to store and retrieve memories
- Capacity for thinking creatively
- Access to intellect and brilliance

RELATIONAL

- Ability to be a team player
- Ability to be cooperative and accommodating
- Ability to value relationships
- Feeling worthy of relationships
- Good conversationalist
- Friendliness
- Playfulness
- Warmth
- Caring
- Love of animals

PSYCHOLOGICAL

- Solid sense of self
- Good self-esteem; confidence
- Sense of competency and mastery
- Even-keeled nature
- Openness
- Flexibility

- Ability to hold hope; optimism
- Resilience
- Tenacity; persistence
- Determination; drive
- Ability to recognize needs
- Ability to assert and drive yourself
- Ability to envision goals; growth oriented
- Ability to delay gratification
- Willingness to be uncomfortable to meet goals
- Ability to set limits and boundaries
- Access to insight, wisdom, and a supportive inner voice
- Sense of humor
- Curiosity
- Courage

SPIRITUAL

- Ability to connect to "higher self" or any form of spiritual guide
- Enjoyment of spiritual or religious, faith-based practices and teachings
- Ability to connect to spiritual energy
- Ability to follow wisdom practices
- Uplifting sense of awe in nature
- Clairvoyance or transpersonal capacities

CREATIVE

- Access to the creative process through acting, beading, building, crafts, cooking, dance, decorating, design, drawing, gardening, making jewelry, knitting, music, needlepoint, poetry, quilting, sewing, sculpting, visual arts, writing, or any other creative pursuits

PHYSICAL

- Sturdy constitution
- Good health
- Productivity
- Industriousness
- High energy
- Good endurance
- Fitness — strong and toned muscles, strength, and flexibility
- Beauty or handsomeness
- Ability to connect with your body and pay attention to sensations and senses
- Enjoyment of sensual and sexual activities
- Capacities such as playing sports, dancing, running, walking, hiking, swimming, and climbing

Step 2. List your external resources. Notice how you feel as you acknowledge the support all around you.

MATT'S EXTERNAL RESOURCES

- EMOTIONAL: Family and close friends; movies; television; journaling; comfortable clothing
- COGNITIVE: Books; educational television; radio programs; podcasts; library visits with daughter
- RELATIONAL: Family and close friends; neighbors; accountant; mechanic; doctors; dentist; hairdresser; therapy group
- PSYCHOLOGICAL: Therapy (group and private); walking in the park or mountains
- SPIRITUAL: Synagogue; nature
- CREATIVE: Computers; classes; museums; helpful people at the garden store
- MATERIAL: My home; financial security (limited); car; appliances; stores

After making his list, Matt noticed that he felt uplifted, encouraged, and grateful.

Examples of External Resources

EMOTIONAL

- Family and friends
- Life partner
- Companion animals
- Journaling; therapy
- Movies, television, books, and music
- Podcasts and videos
- Hot baths
- Comfortable clothing
- Comfortable places

RELATIONAL

- Family and friends
- Life partner
- Companion animals
- Neighbors
- Colleagues
- Support groups
- Paid professionals
- Community members
- Group activities
- Activity buddies

COGNITIVE

- Classes, lessons
- Libraries
- Study groups
- Books and audio courses
- Online programs
- Games and puzzles
- Educational television
- Radio programs

PSYCHOLOGICAL

- Therapy, counseling, and coaching
- Seminars and workshops
- Books and workbooks
- Support groups
- Community programs
- Online programs
- Nature

MATERIAL

- Sources of income: job or investments
- Financial support
- A home
- Appliances and tools
- A car or alternative transportation
- Clothing
- Material goods
- Grocery stores and restaurants

SPIRITUAL

- Spiritual community and facilities
- Religious or spiritual mentors
- Spiritual instruction and guidance
- Ceremonies and rituals
- Spiritual books and recordings

CREATIVE

- Art and craft supplies and tools
- Cooking and baking supplies and tools
- Musical instruments
- Computers, MP3 and DVD players
- Classes, lessons, and groups
- Creative companions
- Community facilities
- Museums and galleries
- Theaters

Step 3. List your survival resources. Identify the ones you still use today. Note whether they are useful. Notice how you feel as you recognize these resources.

MATT'S SURVIVAL RESOURCES, STILL USED TODAY

- Attempting to please and accommodate others — useful, at times, but borders on codependent
- Taking care of others — useful, at times
- Hiding parts of myself — not useful anymore
- Escaping into movies and television — useful, at times
- Withdrawing or isolating — useful, at times, but not when I'm depressed
- Avoiding — not useful; keeping me stuck and not writing
- Cutting myself off from feelings — not useful
- Using food — definitely not useful
- Oversleeping — not useful
- Staying busy — not useful; draining
- Trying to be perfect — a waste of time

After making his list, Matt noticed that he felt enlightened, and sad but still encouraged.

Examples of Survival Resources

COPING WITH DIFFICULT CAREGIVERS

- Ability to predict caregivers' moods and behaviors
- Ability to discern caregivers' needs
- Ability to please and accommodate caregivers
- Ability to take care of caregivers and other family members
- Hypervigilance: looking out for abusive behavior
- Lashing out or acting out
- Throwing tantrums
- Getting into trouble

- Staying away
- Running away
- Using aggression and violence

SHUTTING DOWN

- Escaping into books, music, art, activities, fantasy, and so on
- Withdrawing or isolating
- Creating imaginary friends
- Avoiding contact
- Cutting off from feelings and needs
- Hiding aspects of yourself
- Using drugs or alcohol
- Overeating, undereating, or stopping eating
- Oversleeping
- Harming your body
- Disconnecting from yourself (dissociation)

EXCELLING AND OVERDOING

- Getting good grades
- Taking on leadership roles
- Being a superstar in the family
- Staying busy
- Trying to be perfect
- Being a know-it-all
- Taking on many extracurricular activities
- Driving yourself hard
- Focusing on externals: looks, things, money, accomplishments, and so on
- Getting attention for excelling at various activities
- Competing for attention

Although Matt was regularly reframing his self-defeating thoughts with more calming and uplifting thoughts, he was still riddled with doubt about his ability to take care of himself and Cloe. Together, we worked on reframes for some of his particularly troublesome, recurrent thoughts, as follows:

SELF-DEFEATING THOUGHT: "I won't be able to make it on my own."

CALMING REFRAME: "As I relax and breathe, I realize that I *am* making it on my own — one hour at a time, one day at a time."

SELF-DEFEATING THOUGHT: "I may be able to survive each day, but I'll never thrive."

UPLIFTING REFRAME: "I am building skills every day, and today I am stronger."

SELF-DEFEATING THOUGHT: "Something bad is going to happen, and I won't be able to handle it."

CALMING REFRAME: "I choose to focus on this moment. In this moment, I'm okay."

SELF-DEFEATING THOUGHT: "I lost the love of my life, and I'll never find anyone as incredible as Sandra."

UPLIFTING REFRAMES: "I've been blessed to have had twelve glorious years with an incredible soul mate. Together we created a beautiful daughter. Sandra lives on in Cloe. Today I choose to focus on that. I don't know what the future holds."

SELF-DEFEATING THOUGHT: "I'll be stuck grieving this forever."

UPLIFTING REFRAMES: "It's okay to grieve a big loss for as long as I need to. Grief generally lessens over time. I can grieve *and* move forward with my life."

Combating Self-Doubt and Pessimism

After practicing the first five skills, you may still be wondering if it's really possible to make the changes necessary to meet your needs. Like Matt, you may be doubting that you have what it takes. You're not used to thinking so positively about your abilities or your future, and you're finding it challenging to hold on to those positive reframed thoughts. It's time to access your Inner Nurturer for a reminder of all your resources and to provide hope that you can, and will, meet your needs.

Highlight Resources and Provide Hope

Using your Inner Nurturer voice:

STEP 1. Remind your *feeling self* of a few internal and external resources at your disposal. Notice how you feel when you highlight your resources.

STEP 2. Flood your *feeling self* with hopeful thoughts. Notice how you feel when you practice optimism.

Step 1. Remind your feeling self of a few internal and external resources at your disposal. Notice how you feel when you highlight your resources.

Make your list of resources right now. Keep it handy so that you can refer to it regularly. Add more resources as you become aware of them or as they show up in your life. When you're experiencing distress, or a strong urge to snack or overeat, take time to practice the first five skills and then begin your practice of this skill by reminding yourself of a few of your resources. You are reinforcing and strengthening the neural association between your Inner Nurturer's kind and loving voice and your relaxed mind and body. Down the road, a quick reminder of your resources will be all you'll need to calm down and shift gears.

After reframing his self-defeating thoughts, I asked Matt to practice step 1 and have his Inner Nurturer remind his very young and scared *feeling self* of the resources at his disposal.

Matt's Inner Nurturer: "I know you're afraid and worried that you won't be able to handle what life throws your way. It's okay to feel this way, and it's understandable, given that you're out of work and have a young child to raise." Here Matt is practicing self-validation (skill 2), which is a wonderful way to begin calming and soothing himself when he feels panicky. He went on:

> I want to remind you of all of your resources: first and foremost is your determination — you're determined to make it, and that's why you've joined this group. You're open to learning how to better manage your emotions. You're intelligent, funny, caring, and kind. You have a great sense of humor. You're good at problem solving and taking care of all of the household affairs and Cloe's needs. You know how to reach out and ask for help when you need it. You have Mom, Dad, and Sam to talk to daily. Your close friends are always around, and they have reassured you that they are here for you.

Matt always felt relief when he highlighted his resources. His anxiety lessened, and as he began to relax, he felt grounded in his body once again. But he was concerned about his tendency to quickly backslide and reignite his anxiety by minimizing his resources with thoughts like "So what if I'm warm and funny? My social anxiety holds me back. And, yes, I have a brother and aging parents, but they live too far away to be there for me if I really need them." Matt needed to learn how to hold more hopeful thoughts.

The Power of Hope

The *Random House College Dictionary* defines hope as "the feeling that what is desired is also possible or that events may turn out for the best." Hope allows us to approach problems with a mind-set that increases our chances of succeeding and a set of strategies that will help us accomplish our goals.

The eminent positive psychologist Charles R. Snyder and his colleagues suggest that hope involves the will to get where you want to go and the ability to generate strategies to get there. Hope can be conceptualized as a way to motivate yourself. Hopeful thoughts lead to a positive mental state, a calm or uplifted bodily state, and a willingness to take action.

It's easy to have hope when everything is going your way — like when you just landed a great job, lost a lot of weight, or met the partner of your dreams. But how do you hold on to hope when things aren't running so smoothly — when you've been out of work for a long while, you've gained a significant amount of weight, you or a loved one has been diagnosed with a serious illness, or you're coping with a significant loss? The answer lies in developing or strengthening your hope-generating capabilities.

If you were raised by caregivers capable of providing hope when you felt disappointed or discouraged, you most likely believe that events will turn out for the best and your needs can and will be met — that outlook is wired into your brain. During trying times, a quick reminder that things will be all right may be all you need to reactivate these neural connections and motivate yourself to get back on the horse or to keep on trucking.

But if, like Matt, you were raised by depressed, anxious, pessimistic caregivers who modeled fear-based, hopeless thinking, you may never have developed the neural-firing patterns associated with optimism. It's natural to experience self-doubt when you've had a history of difficulty moving forward in particular areas of your life. It feels phony to tell yourself everything will be okay when you don't believe it will be. You're not sure that you can make the changes you need to make to create the kind of future you desire. You may have little tolerance for frustration, and quit prematurely when you don't experience immediate progress on your goals. How could you ever really know that you'll succeed?

Unable to generate or hold on to hopeful thoughts, you've learned to minimize your expectations to avoid disappointment. Perhaps you believe that the future will be a replay of the past, and you give up hope before you commit completely to anything. You may act helpless at times because you feel a lack of control over your environment. Maybe, like Matt, you've developed convenient excuses to cover up the hopelessness and protect yourself from experiencing any more discomfort, discouragement, and loss:

> "It's impossible to lose all of this excess weight with all the stress I'm under."

"It's just too difficult to find work as a writer in television at my
   age. Today they only hire millennials."
"There's no point in dating — no one is going to want to date a
   guy who has a young child."

Without hope, you may be living a life of quiet desperation. Perhaps
you've given up on your dreams and goals. You're using food, alcohol,
shopping, working, and other distractions to fill up the emptiness. Sure,
these activities provide some degree of pleasure, comfort, and soothing.
But, unfortunately, none of these distractions teach you how to hold hopeful thoughts. And none of them address those pessimistic neural tendencies.

In my childhood, I had to fight to hold on to hope. My parents were
fearful and often said things couldn't be done or pooh-poohed things I
wanted to do. They'd say, "You won't be able to do that," or "It's impossible." In my teens, I rebelled against their pessimism with a defensive
brand of optimism: "Oh, yes, I can," or "You'll see." But in my twenties,
I found myself ill-equipped to deal with life's inevitable ups and downs.
As long as things went my way, I was able to remain optimistic and hopeful. And even when they didn't, I could sometimes resort to that defensive
optimism that had previously worked. But when I began to encounter
more challenging adult disappointments, like relationship breakups and
job dissatisfaction, I sank into depression and, at times, despair. There it
was: the hopelessness of my childhood home, the hopelessness I fought
so hard to guard against. Bingeing on comfort foods became my way of
coping, but it always came at a high price — more hopelessness.

Step 2. Flood your feeling self with hopeful thoughts.
Notice how you feel when you practice optimism.

What do you do when positive, hopeful thoughts don't *feel* true? How
do you go about developing or strengthening your capacity for hope?
You suspend your sobering, perhaps pessimistic, voice of reality for a
moment and think about a particular issue *as if* you had hope. You try
on a childlike mind-set in which anything is possible (without the "yes,
buts"), and, using your Inner Nurturer voice, you flood your *feeling self*

with as many hopeful statements as you can think of. Keep them simple and short. Write these down. Yes, you'll have to fake it until you make it. The key is to practice more optimistic thinking. Over time, these statements will actually help you feel more hopeful, and the whole process will get easier. Use a mixture of the *I* and *we* forms so that the youngest part of you feels that someone else is there with you. Notice which form feels better to you.

Providing Hope

"Everything will be all right."

"I know you're going to be okay."

"I am sure that things are going to work out just fine."

"You're talented and skilled."

"Where there's a will, there's a way."

"You're doing everything you can. It will all work out."

"You can do this, one baby step at a time."

"You're building the skills you need to succeed."

"You have lots of resources at your disposal."

"Help is available."

"Unforeseen assistance is all around you."

"There are skilled professionals that can help."

"You never know what can happen."

"Miracles can and do happen."

"Anything is possible."

"Sometimes scary things like this happen — you'll be all right."

"We're going to get through this together."

"We've been through things like this before, and everything turned out okay."

"Together we'll find a way."

"Brighter days are ahead."

"This will be behind us soon."

"Let's take it one day at a time."

"Let's keep up the faith."

"Let's stay positive."

"I believe in you."

"You're incredible."

Accessing his Inner Nurturer, Matt wrote down the following hopeful thoughts:

"I have no doubt that you can manage your anxiety, move through this grief, and create a meaningful life once again."

"I believe in you — you are a skilled and talented writer."

"There are lots of people in the writers' community for us to network with."

"Where there's a will, there's a way."

"You can replace your pessimistic thoughts with more hopeful thoughts."

"You can reach your goals, one step at a time."

"You have many more years ahead to work in this field."

"Let's choose to focus on progress, not perfection."

"Even a glimmer of hope feels better than the depth of hopelessness we've been living with."

Matt noticed that he felt more positive and confident when he tried on hopeful thoughts. He noticed that he held himself up straighter and described a "tingly, energized, upbeat" feeling in his whole body and an "exciting sense of possibility" that he remembered feeling when he landed his first writing job. And even though this sense was fragile and fleeting, it gave him hope. He was now ready, and *willing*, to develop an action plan for meeting his needs.

A Little Bit of Hope Goes a Long Way

One weekend afternoon, Matt picked Cloe up from a playdate. Her friend's father, Jeff, was a well-connected writer who was working on a long-running television series. Jeff was usually working when Matt came by to get Cloe, and the few times Matt had run into Jeff, he felt too depressed and ashamed to discuss his lack of work. But this time, he mustered his courage and asked Jeff if he knew of any shows hiring writers. Jeff responded positively, and Matt was sorry he hadn't asked sooner. "Matt, you are one of the most talented writers I know. And you've been through such a terrible ordeal these past few years. I'm sure I can help you find something. Let me make a few calls."

Matt shared in the group session that week that his outlook on everything, including his eating and weight challenges, was rosier. And he had two resources to add to his list: Jeff, who was an external resource he hadn't previously considered; and the ability to hold hope, a brand-new internal resource.

CHAPTER THIRTEEN

Skill 7. Address Needs
and Set Nurturing Limits

Whatever you can do, or dream you can, begin it.
Boldness has genius, power and magic in it.

— Johann Wolfgang von Goethe, *Couplets*

Finally, it's time to make an action plan and address your unmet needs. You've pulled yourself away from a situation that has been causing distress, interrupted the urge to grab comfort food, and popped the hood. You've validated your feelings, reinforced the alliance with the kindest and wisest part of yourself, and flooded your *feeling self* with love, support, and comfort. You've gotten clear on your needs, and with your Inner Nurturer's help, you've reframed any self-defeating thoughts and highlighted your resources. Now, with a calm mind and body, you're feeling hopeful that your needs can be met. You've diligently practiced the first six skills, and you're ready for solutions.

Hopefully you've come to understand the importance and value of feeling first and thinking and solving later. We just don't do our best thinking when our emotional brain is sending out alarm messages and our nervous system is on overdrive. First come feeling, validating, calming, and soothing; then come clear thinking, problem solving, and action plans.

Meeting Your Needs

With skill 4, you learned how to get clear on your needs. First you identify what there isn't enough of, or what's missing, in any given situation. Then you identify what the youngest part of you, your *feeling self*, is needing and what the adult part of you is needing. These needs will, at times, be the same.

Many clients tell me that they don't feel equipped to meet their own needs. Without realizing it, they're secretly hoping to receive from other adults what they didn't receive as a child. They want *someone else* to be responsible for meeting many of their needs. Like Clara from chapter 10, they want another person (in Clara's case, her husband) to validate them and make them feel special, cared for, and safe. Like Liz from chapter 2, they want someone else (in Liz's case, her mother) to tell them that they're okay and that everything will be just fine. They figure that if they get enough of their needs met from the outside, they'll finally feel complete and whole. Intellectually, their *thinking self* understands that it's best for them to learn to meet their needs themselves, but their *feeling self* isn't happy about it and is kicking and screaming.

If you experienced poor attunement in your early years, you may find that many of your current needs are needs that were not adequately met long ago. The key to meeting these most basic needs and getting your emotional development back on track is the alliance formed between your Inner Nurturer and your *feeling self*. You strengthen this alliance and the voice of your Inner Nurturer every time you practice the skills outlined in this book. Over time, as you rewire the circuitry in your brain and meet these most basic needs yourself, you'll find that your needs grow up and become more age appropriate.

Whenever you slip back into thinking that you need someone else to meet your needs, remind yourself that everything you need in order to feel whole, complete, and satisfied is already inside you. You'll begin to experience this wholeness by regularly practicing the loving, supportive connection between your Inner Nurturer and your *feeling self*. The strong desire to seek comfort and reassurance from others, or from food, will subside.

Being Specific about Your Needs

When you identify a need, see if you can break it down further into an even more specific need. Perhaps you've identified a need to feel more connected to the people in your life. What would meeting this need look like? Would you have frequent telephone conversations with specific family members? Who, and how frequent? Would you spend more time with your best friend? How much time, and doing what? Would you receive more physical and verbal affection from your husband? What would this look like? A kiss when he arrives home? Saying "I love you" more often? What *exactly* does "more connected" mean to you? The more specific you are, the easier it will be to meet your needs.

Meeting Your Needs

✦ IDENTIFY A NEED and be as specific about it as you can. "I need attention" can be rephrased more specifically as "I need someone to ask me how I'm feeling." "I need support" can be rephrased as "I need someone to fold the laundry and dry the dishes."

✦ LIST TWO OR THREE WAYS TO MEET THIS NEED, being as flexible and creative as you can. Try to suspend those "yes, buts."

✦ SET YOUR INTENTION and access your willingness to be uncomfortable in order to meet this need. Write down your intention. Notice how you feel when you set your intention.

✦ COMMIT TO TAKING ACTION and monitor your progress. Notice how you feel when you make a commitment. Access your Inner Nurturer for reassurance and support. Follow through until you succeed.

When Clara reflected on the loneliness and emptiness she experienced every evening when her husband distanced himself and either worked late or watched television alone, she identified the following needs:

I need reassurance that everything will be all right and that my
    husband won't leave me.
I need comfort, soothing, and hope that our life will be good again.
I need to feel that I'm worthy of my husband's love — that I'm
    enough for him.

As she wrote down her needs, Clara realized that these were the needs
of the youngest part of her, her *feeling self,* and that she had spent a good
portion of her life trying to get these needs met by those closest to her.
The situation had changed — she had transitioned from being a lonely
young girl in her parent's home to an insecure young woman living with
her sister to Tim's wife — but the desire to have these early developmental needs met by someone else had remained the same.

At age fifty, it was unrealistic for Clara to expect that her husband and
family members were going to meet these basic needs. This was a job for
her Inner Nurturer. Every time she was aware of these particular needs,
Clara accessed her Inner Nurturer for validation, reassurance, comfort,
soothing, and hope, saying things like:

"It's okay to have these needs at this stage of life, sweetie. It
    makes sense that you're still longing to have them met. They
    weren't properly met when you were young."
"You are worthy of love."
"I am here with you, and I love you."
"I'm closer to you than your breath."
"I can and will take care of you."
"I will never abandon you."
"You already have everything you need inside yourself to feel
    whole."
"We can't predict or control what anyone else will do, but
    together we can make sure our needs are met."

Clara also identified a few adult needs:

I need more joy and intimacy with my husband — more good
times, more happy times.
I need purpose and meaning in my life. I need to feel passionate
about something.
I need to grieve the many disappointments and losses I've experienced.

Being as Flexible and Creative as You Can

Once you identify an adult need, it may take some flexibility and creativity to meet it. It's generally easier to meet physical needs than emotional
needs. Access your *thinking self* and come up with a few ways to meet
each need. See if you can let go of yes-buts, rigid expectations, and black-
and-white thinking. The more creative you get, the easier it will be to find
a satisfying solution. Choose baby steps that allow you to move in the
direction of meeting a need. Big, lofty plans can leave you feeling like a
failure, concluding that the need can't be met or that you're not equipped
to meet your own needs.

Let's say you identify the need for more physical affection in your
life, but you lack a friend or partner who might provide this. Snuggling
with a furry companion or getting a regular massage could temporarily
meet this need while you focus on ways to bring affectionate people into
your life. Maybe you've identified the need to calm down and relax on the
stressful drive home from work so that you can avoid the drive-through
burger joint. Listening to soothing spa music or Gregorian chants might
help. Maybe you've identified the need for stimulation and adventure and
would love to take an action-oriented vacation, but you don't have the
time or budget to do so. A bus or train ride to a new location or a hike in
an unexplored area could partially meet this need.

To address Clara's need for joy and intimacy, she came up with two possible solutions:

I could join my husband when he watches television and hold his hand. He likes it when I do this, but I generally don't join him, because I don't like the shows he watches.

I could ask my husband to go to the movies with me one time per month. We used to do this, and we enjoyed it.

To address her need for purpose and meaning in her life, she came up with these ideas:

I'm passionate about animals — I could volunteer with an animal rescue group.

I could volunteer to teach dance to kids at the recreation center. This would get me dancing again and spending time with children.

To address her need to grieve her many losses and disappointments, she concluded, "I could journal about not becoming a dancer or a mother. I could take the time to process my sadness and grief."

There will be times when your needs cannot easily be met, and you'll have to delay their gratification. If you are newly divorced or out of a relationship, your need for an intimate partnership may go unmet for a long period. When you're handling a family member's health crisis, you may not be able to get out and meet your need for stimulation and recreation. If you've moved to a new city and your closest friends live far away, your need for local companionship will be on hold until you can form new friendships.

These are times when a strong, soothing connection with your Inner Nurturer is crucial. This will carry you through the rough times when you can't get your relational needs met. With your Inner Nurturer by your side, you'll be better equipped to handle any sadness, disappointment, or frustration that arises.

Setting Your Intention

When you've identified one, two, or even three possible ways to meet a need, it's time to set your intention to take action. This means stating that you intend to focus on this need *and* take action. It's not enough to just think about ways you could meet your needs. Intention involves accessing your willingness to be uncomfortable as you move forward. When we try on new behaviors, we often shift from one set of unpleasant emotions to another. For example, perhaps you feel lonely, sad, and depressed when you're alone most evenings. But when you push out socially, even though you feel less lonely and down, you feel more anxious and insecure. If you're not prepared for these different emotions, you might easily slip back into your old ways. See if you can embrace these emotions and view them as a sign of growth. Write down your intention to take a particular action and your willingness to be uncomfortable. Notice how you feel when you set your intention. Sharing your intention with someone close to you is a great way to hold yourself accountable.

Clara wrote down the following intentions:

I intend to join my husband at least once this week to watch television, cuddle, and hold hands. I am willing to be uncomfortable if he's moody or rejects my affection.

I intend to ask my husband to go to the movies with me once this month. I am willing to be uncomfortable if I get a negative response.

I intend to investigate volunteer opportunities with the rescue group and recreation center. I am willing to be uncomfortable and push past my shyness when I make telephone calls or meet the coordinators in person.

I intend to journal about my losses and grieve once or twice this week. I am willing to be uncomfortable as I revisit some of the pain I've been pushing away for years.

Clara noticed that when she set her intention to join her husband, she felt a fluttery feeling in her chest and head that she described as a mix of anxiety and excitement. It felt exciting to imagine snuggling and touching each other again, and these sensations were pleasurable.

When she set her intention to investigate volunteer opportunities, she felt a surge of dread, which she described as a heavy, solid, bracing, and freezing sensation. And she caught a self-defeating thought: "I hope I don't get so shy and insecure that I hang up." She quickly reframed this with the calming thought, "I don't feel shy when I call repairmen to come to the house — this doesn't need to be different from those calls. I'm not signing a contract — I'm just researching possibilities."

When she set her intention to carve out time to grieve, she noticed a calm, relaxed feeling in her entire body. She had been stuffing down her sadness and pretending everything was all right for too long. It felt comforting to give herself permission to cry about her losses.

Committing to Taking Action

Many emotional eaters have a love-hate relationship with the word *commitment*. They love to commit to things that are pleasurable, like a good movie, a delectable meal, or an exciting vacation. But they hate to commit to anything that increases their level of discomfort, such as a healthier eating plan or an exercise regimen.

If the notion of committing to things that create discomfort makes you want to put this book down and grab a donut, hold on. You're reading this book because you are already uncomfortable *and stuck*. You'd like to improve your relationship with yourself and food. Remind yourself that you can break down any commitment into teeny, tiny, doable baby steps. Start with a baby step you can say yes to. Write down your commitment.

Commitment requires surrender: letting go of hesitation and the chance to change your mind and turn back. The exciting part is that once you commit, all sorts of things occur to help you move forward. It's as if the clouds part and Providence moves as unforeseen incidents, encounters, and sources of support come out of the woodwork to help you.

Commitment also requires persistence — the willingness to keep at something until you reach your goal. It may take several attempts or additional time to meet certain needs. Follow-through is important, and you'll need a way to monitor your progress. Marking a date on your calendar when you'll check back in with yourself, or maintaining a log of needs and progress toward meeting them, can be helpful.

Here are Clara's commitments:

I commit to joining my husband this Thursday evening at 8 PM when he watches his favorite program. I will snuggle up next to him and hold his hand.

I commit to asking my husband after our cuddle session, or the next day, if he'll go to see a movie with me this month.

I commit to calling the rescue group on Monday and the recreation center on Wednesday to discuss volunteer opportunities.

I commit to buying a new journal and to writing in it two evenings this week when I'm alone and in the mood.

Clara felt excited and hopeful as she wrote out her commitments regarding connecting with her husband. Her body felt energized, and she could feel herself smiling. It felt good to be moving forward with her relationship. As she wrote out her detailed commitments regarding the volunteer opportunities, she felt slight tension in her neck and shoulders and a queasy feeling in her stomach. She accessed her Inner Nurturer for reassurance and comfort: "I know you're feeling anxious about making those calls. It's okay to feel that way, and it makes sense. You're stepping out of your comfort zone. I love you, and I'll be right here with you when you make the calls. I believe in you, and I know you'll be glad you did it. You're going to feel more purpose in your life when you start volunteering. You are very warm and friendly, and people are always drawn to you." As Clara highlighted her resources, she felt buoyed up and hopeful that she could meet these commitments.

As she wrote down her commitment regarding grieving her losses, she felt a warm, fuzzy feeling come over her. She could envision herself journaling and feeling cozy on the couch with a blanket and a cup of tea.

Expressing Your Needs

Even though you can meet many of your needs on your own, there are times when you'll want to ask others for support. Expressing your needs and asking for them to be met requires courage and the ability to assert yourself. It is not without risk. You may experience rejection, anger, resentment, abandonment, judgment, shame, blame, and even unwanted expectations of reciprocation. You might feel guilty when you ask for something, as if you're burdening others. It may feel more comfortable to stay in control by giving more than you receive.

Perhaps expressing your needs makes you feel selfish. Remind yourself that expressing your needs is a way you take care of yourself, no more selfish than eating healthy foods or brushing and flossing. It's a way of letting others know that you feel worthy of asking for their support and worthy of receiving it. You're letting them know that you trust them enough to ask for their help and rely on them, and that you don't expect them to read your mind. You do, however, need to be respectful and recognize that others may not be able or willing to meet your stated needs. This doesn't mean you're unworthy or that your needs are not valid.

In order for your requests to be effective, you need to be considerate of the feelings and needs of others and deliver your requests with kindness, appreciation, compassion, and empathy. If you've denied your needs or disconnected from them for a long time, your initial attempts at expressing them and making requests may come off as demanding or ungracious. If you've been passive about getting your needs met, and secretly resentful that they haven't been met, when you finally do make requests, they may lack warmth and sound aggressive and angry.

Perhaps you deliver the request in a condescending or attacking way: "I am so tired of you giving me advice every time I share my feelings with you — you're a terrible listener." Or "You could express appreciation once in a while — you are so self-absorbed." Others are not likely to want to meet your needs when you express them in this way. You're likely to be met with confusion and defensiveness. It can be helpful to practice expressing your needs and making requests by writing them in your journal before sharing them with others.

We begin expressing our needs by sharing how we feel, utilizing "I feel..." statements. We express our needs with "I need..." statements, being as specific as we can about our needs. Next, we express our respect and concern for the other person's needs with an empathic "I realize that..." or "I understand that..." statement that lets them know we've taken their needs as well as our own into consideration. We end by asking for support in meeting our needs with an "It would be great if you could..." or "I would appreciate it if you would..." statement.

Expressing Your Needs

✦ BEGIN BY SHARING HOW YOU FEEL with an "*I feel...*" statement.

✦ STATE WHAT YOU NEED with an "*I need...*" statement. Be as specific as you can.

✦ EXPRESS YOUR RESPECT AND CONCERN for the other person's needs with an empathic "*I realize that...*" or "*I understand that...*" statement.

✦ MAKE A REQUEST with an "*It would be great if you could...*" or "*I would appreciate it if you would...*" statement.

✦ NOTICE HOW YOU FEEL when you express your needs.

Clara practiced expressing her emotions and needs before sharing them with her husband. She wrote:

Tim, I feel lonely when you watch television alone every night.
I need more physical affection and conversation with you.
I realize that you miss our old lifestyle and are struggling with your sobriety.
I understand that you care for me and are not intentionally shutting me out.
I would appreciate it if you would allow me to join you tomorrow night. You can pick the program. It would be great if we could cuddle and hold hands like we used to.

Clara noticed that she felt nervous and fearful when she practiced expressing her needs. She felt a fluttery, tingly, racing feeling, and she noticed that she was clenching her jaw slightly. She accessed her Inner Nurturer for reassurance that she wasn't asking for too much and that most likely Tim would respond favorably. She began to calm down and relax as she remembered the kind soul she had fallen in love with so many years ago.

Clara mustered up her courage the following week and expressed her need for more physical affection and conversation with her husband. Here's how it went:

TIM: Honey, I'd be happy to watch television together. And *you* can pick the program. When I get home from work, you're usually talking on the phone. I didn't realize that you wanted to connect.

CLARA: You always seem so tired when you come home — I thought you wanted to be alone.

TIM: When we first stopped drinking and smoking, I was really struggling and not in a good mood most nights. I know I was pushing you away. But I'd like to connect more now.

Clara was pleasantly surprised by Tim's reaction and realized that each of them had been misinterpreting the other's behaviors and needs.

Timing is Everything

Remember Liz, the social worker from chapter 2 who had an argument with her mother regarding her fortieth birthday celebration? Liz had learned that it wasn't always in her best interests to share her fears and insecurities with her mother. But there were times when she really wanted to share what she was going through, and she needed understanding and patient listening. Liz practiced expressing her emotions and needs in her journal:

Mom, I feel inadequate and ashamed when you criticize me and
tell me what to do.

I need understanding and patient listening from you, not opinions
and advice.

I realize that you love me very much and are always trying to
help.

I would appreciate it if you would allow me to find my own
answers and have some faith in me that, at age forty, I can and
will figure out what is right for me.

Liz noticed that she felt anxious when she practiced expressing her
needs. She felt a buzzy, hyped-up feeling, her breathing was shallow, and
she could feel her heart beating faster. She accessed her Inner Nurturer
for soothing and reassurance that it was okay to ask her mother for better listening. She reminded herself that there was no rush in having this
conversation and that she could find a time to express her needs when
her mother was in a receptive mood. She felt her body calm down as she
recalled times in the past when she and her mother had been able to have
heart-to-heart talks.

Setting Nurturing Limits with Yourself

Once you've begun to address your needs, you may find that you're still
eating when you're not hungry. Perhaps you're choosing unhealthy comfort foods more often than you'd like, snacking mindlessly, or continuing to eat beyond fullness. Or maybe you're doing great with food, but
you're drinking, smoking, or shopping too much; surfing the internet
excessively; watching more television than you used to; and procrastinating on your to-do list.

Maybe there still isn't *enough* attention, good listening, care, affection,
and support. Perhaps you aren't experiencing *enough* joy, meaning, passion, purpose, and inspiration. You may be longing for more downtime,

relief from pressures, and ease, or more stimulation and excitement. The problem may be that you haven't yet experienced enough of the right kind of fulfillment in your life. You may need more time to grieve disappointments and losses before you're ready to work on meeting your needs. You're settling for second best: feeling full and pleasured by food or distractions rather than being fulfilled by your life.

Clearly, getting your needs met will require some patience on your part: it won't happen overnight. But that doesn't mean that you can't rein in your wayward behaviors. Now that you've been practicing inner nurturing, your internal world is likely feeling more like the sanctuary it was meant to be. You're ready to strengthen your Inner Nurturer's capacity to set nurturing limits.

Setting Limits Means Delaying Gratification

Many emotional eaters bristle at the mere suggestion of delaying their gratification. To them it means enduring deprivation and tolerating uncomfortable cravings and impulses. Setting limits feels restrictive, and it can easily lead to black-and-white thinking, such as "There will be nothing left to eat: I'll have to live on lettuce leaves and never enjoy my food." It reminds us of a chronic experience of lack and limitation.

When we contemplate setting limits with food, we're reminded of past failures and the associated frustration and shame. Attempts at setting limits can trigger a "last meal" mentality and a desire to eat everything that isn't nailed down. We are not about to give up gratification in the present moment for some goal in the future. The future is unknown and unpredictable. Eating is a guaranteed good time. What guarantee is there that delaying our gratification now will lead to fulfillment down the road? We may lose some weight or improve our health, but at what price? Will we really achieve our goals? Will we really be any happier?

The truth is, you're already delaying gratification in many areas of your life. You routinely forgo activities so that you can meet the needs of those closest to you. You skipped the dinner out with the girls so you could attend your son's soccer game. You put off buying a new computer so your daughter could get braces. You haven't bought a new car because you're saving for a home. Your inability to apply the skill of delaying gratification to meeting your own long-term needs is a sign that your life is still lacking fulfillment in too many areas and that the self-regulation circuits of your brain still need some strengthening.

The Ten-Minute Pause

Learning to delay gratification in more areas of your life requires practice and patience. Your impulsive *feeling self* can wear you down and get you into trouble. Guiding her toward a more disciplined life has immense rewards. Each snack, meal, purchase, or urge to procrastinate is a new opportunity to practice self-discipline.

You can learn to pause when you want to eat and you're not hungry; when you're hungry and want to eat unhealthy comfort foods; when you want to keep eating beyond fullness; when you want to use alcohol or drugs, impulsively spend money, or use other distractions; or when you want to procrastinate.

Here's how: *stop*, slow down, and make the conscious choice to delay gratification for ten minutes. Say to yourself, "I am willing to be uncomfortable for ten minutes so that I can reach my goals." Remind yourself, "I *can* endure discomfort for a short while. It's not a root canal or childbirth!"

Acknowledge and praise yourself for any success you have in delaying gratification. Even the smallest steps are worthy of praise. The road to overeating recovery consists of many tiny steps. By regularly taking the time to connect with yourself in this way, you are creating new neural pathways and a nurturing inner world. When your inner world feels consistently loving, safe, and secure, you'll be able to delay gratification whenever you need to, confident that whatever you're desiring will still be available later.

Strengthening the Voice of the Inner Limit Setter

When it's time to set limits with yourself, your Inner Nurturer must morph into an Inner Limit Setter. Just like a kind but firm parent, she gently sets and enforces an effective limit. It may seem challenging to set limits with your *feeling self* when she is demanding and impulsive. In the beginning, she may win out more often than you would like. Your current attempts at limit setting may sound like this:

FEELING SELF: I'd really like to have some ice cream.

INNER NURTURER (as Inner Limit Setter): Better not; we had a big dinner, and we already ate too many sweets this weekend. Let's just have some fruit for dessert.

FEELING SELF: No, I want ice cream! I don't want fruit! Can't we just have some?

INNER NURTURER (as Inner Indulger): All right, we do have a really hard week ahead. We'll do better starting tomorrow. But just one scoop.

FEELING SELF: Wow, I love that purse. It would go great with my new blue shoes. I want it.

INNER NURTURER (as Inner Limit Setter): It's really expensive and not in our budget. It's best if we don't buy that purse; we'll find something else within our price range.

FEELING SELF: No, we won't. It will be hard to find a purse to match those shoes. I want this one!

INNER NURTURER (as Inner Indulger): Well that's true — it's a difficult blue to match, and we can put it on a credit card. Okay, just this one time.

The best time to work on strengthening the limit-setting capabilities of your Inner Nurturer is when your *feeling self* is attempting to run the show. You'll need to become mindful of these times. Your Inner Nurturer must do her job as an Inner Limit Setter and set an effective limit. When your *feeling self* resists, your Inner Nurturer steps in and finds out what she is truly longing for or what she feels there is not enough of. Your Inner Nurturer also reassures your *feeling self* that her needs can be met.

Your new, effective limit-setting inner conversations will sound like this:

FEELING SELF: I'd really like to have some ice cream.

INNER NURTURER (as Inner Limit Setter): Better not; we had a big dinner, and we already ate too many sweets this weekend. Let's just have some fruit for dessert.

FEELING SELF: No, I want ice cream! I don't want fruit! Can't we just have some?

INNER NURTURER: I know you're not hungry, so tell me what you're feeling; what are you truly longing for right now, other than ice cream?

FEELING SELF: I feel empty and unsatisfied. It wasn't very fun visiting Mom this weekend. I want more fun, and ice cream sounds really good right now.

INNER NURTURER: I know it was kind of boring visiting Mom, and the weekend was hectic. What else would be fun tonight besides ice cream?

FEELING SELF: Watching a movie would be fun. *With ice cream.*

INNER NURTURER (as Inner Limit Setter: Well, we do have time to watch a movie tonight. But we're not going to have ice cream. We can have some fruit, but that's all.

FEELING SELF: Okay, a movie sounds good. What about popcorn or cookies instead of fruit?

INNER NURTURER (as Inner Limit Setter): A movie it is! But we can't improve our health and lose weight if we eat those kinds of foods every night.

FEELING SELF: I don't care about health or weight. I want something yummy now!

INNER NURTURER (as Inner Limit Setter): Well, I care. As I said, we can have fruit. We're not having anything else tonight.

FEELING SELF: Wow, I love that purse. It would go great with my new blue shoes. I want it.

INNER NURTURER (as Inner Limit Setter): It's really expensive and not in our budget. It's best if we don't buy that purse — we'll find something within our price range.

FEELING SELF: No, we won't. It will be hard to find a purse to match those shoes. I want this one!

INNER NURTURER: Well that may be true, but we do need to stick to our budget. I'm sure we'll find something similar when we can afford it. What does it feel like there isn't enough of?

FEELING SELF: Feeling good about myself. I don't feel very attractive lately, and having a purse that matches those shoes would make me feel better.

INNER NURTURER: You are always beautiful and attractive to me. I love you just the way you are. We don't need a new purse to feel attractive. Our beauty radiates from the inside out.

INNER NURTURER (as Inner Limit Setter): We're going to stick to our budget and not buy the purse.

FEELING SELF: No! I want it! It will give me something to feel good about.

INNER NURTURER: We're not going to buy it. Let's find something nurturing and uplifting to do that doesn't involve spending money or eating.

FEELING SELF: I can't think of anything.

INNER NURTURER: How about we go home and take a nice warm bubble bath? Then we can curl up with the cats and read some spiritual passages you like.

FEELING SELF: Okay, but I'd still like to have the purse.

Limit-Setting Inner Conversations

STEP 1.   Pay attention to what your *feeling self* desires.

Feeling Self: I want the cheesy pasta dish and the garlic bread.

STEP 2.   Have your Inner Nurturer (as Inner Limit Setter) set a loving, nurturing, and effective limit with your *feeling self.*

Inner Nurturer (as Inner Limit Setter): Our body doesn't do well on those particular foods. We're trying to reduce our intake of flour, gluten, and dairy, so let's select something without these ingredients.

STEP 3.   If this limit feels overly restrictive, and your *feeling self* isn't on board with the plan, have your Inner Nurturer explore further.

Inner Nurturer: "I know you really want to have pasta and garlic bread. What are you feeling? What are you truly longing for? What isn't there enough of?

Feeling Self: I feel tired and lonely. I want something comforting and exciting.

STEP 4.   Have your Inner Nurturer reinforce the limit and reassure your *feeling self* that she is always there to take care of her and help meet her needs.

Inner Nurturer (as Inner Limit Setter): We're *not* going to order the pasta and garlic bread. It's not flour and cheese that you're longing for; it's comfort and excitement. I'm here to comfort you, and I will help you find something exciting to do. When we get home, we can change into comfortable clothes and plan our next vacation.

Setting Realistic Limits

It's best not to start setting limits with an all-or-nothing mentality; for example, resolving that starting tomorrow, you're going to totally stop drinking diet sodas, eating chips, and surfing the internet before bed. This is the quickest way to set up a *feeling self* rebellion. We all want change immediately. But realistically, changing ingrained habits is a gradual process that requires patience and perseverance. Master the ten-minute pause first and work on strengthening the voice of your Inner Limit Setter.

Practice setting limits gradually. Try tapering off diet sodas and chips and perhaps not bringing them into the house. Try limiting your web surfing to a few evenings per week for a certain length of time. Taking it slowly will help you adjust your black-and-white thinking and ensure follow-through. Notice how you feel when you set a limit with yourself. If you feel anxiety or panic about a limit you're setting, or if the new limit represents an extreme change from what you've been doing, it's probably not realistic.

If you're struggling with addiction to certain foods, rather than starting with very restrictive limits, such as complete abstinence and the notion that this is forever and you can never eat this food again, try starting with a partial abstinence. For example, get your feet wet with a few days off of diet sodas, or a week without sugar or flour. This gives you the opportunity to see that you can go without this particular substance. If you're feeling good after the specified time period and it feels right to extend your abstinence, go for it. If not, perhaps you're ready to set some limits with this substance instead.

When setting limits, you don't ever have to use the word *forever*, unless it feels right for you. Some overeaters are so exquisitely sensitive to particular substances that eating just a small amount triggers cravings and compulsive eating. The problem is that complete restriction can also trigger compulsive eating or rebound eating. The key is to find a happy medium that works for you *right now*. Don't worry about what you'll do in the future.

"I Can't Believe How Easy That Was"

Clara was encouraged by Tim's favorable response to her request to watch television together, and she was looking forward to reconnecting with him. But she feared that she would not be strong enough to resist joining him in his nightly snack of ice cream and cookies. She decided to set a limit with herself ahead of time — she would fill up on what she truly wanted and needed, which was physical affection and conversation, and if she wanted ice cream and cookies, she could have them some other time.

Clara made a few important discoveries that first night as she and Tim held hands, snuggled, and talked about the day. She realized that it was okay to have needs, that it was okay to express them, that they could be met, that things weren't always the way they seemed, and that it was easy to stick with limits when she felt nourished and fulfilled by her life.

PART THREE

Creating Nurturing
Connections

CHAPTER FOURTEEN

Taking It to the Street

No man is an island.

— John Donne, *Devotions upon Emergent Occasions*

O nce you're consistently practicing the seven skills of inner nurturing and feeling more nourished on the inside, you'll begin to notice that you're less attracted to food as a source of comfort. You'll also discover that you're feeling more self-sufficient and turning to others less often to meet your needs. Perhaps you're thinking, "Geez, it would be great if everyone was practicing these seven skills." You may notice that those closest to you are missing many of the skills you have just learned and are unskilled at nurturing *you*. A new hunger or craving may surface, representing a yearning or desire for more truly nourishing connections.

Many emotional eaters have never experienced consistent, sufficient nurturance from an external source and may feel unsure about how to attract nurturing others into their lives. When we're young, we unconsciously adopt interpersonal patterns of relating. Some of these patterns, modeled by our caregivers and other mentors, are maladaptive. As we grow and mature, these patterns can keep us stuck attracting the same types of people. We tend to gravitate toward similarly disconnected, non-nourishing souls. They may be overeaters, people pleasers, codependents, worrywarts, hypochondriacs, workaholics, alcoholics, gamblers, addicts, or narcissists. And the list goes on.

While you may be aware that you've been attracting these non-nourishing types of people into your life, you may be unaware of the relational patterns that you engage in that cause you to do so. Becoming aware of these patterns is the first step in consciously transforming them. Then you can begin practicing new, healthier behaviors that help you increase the odds of attracting nurturing people. And even if you have lots of close, nurturing friends, you may still find that you are guilty of slipping into some of these unhealthy patterns.

The regular practice of inner nurturing may also make you painfully aware that you haven't been as nurturing as you could be to those you care most about. It's impossible for us to give something to another if we don't have it ourselves. People learning inner nurturing often lament how poorly attuned they have been to their children, partners, siblings, parents, and friends.

If you want to nurture those closest to you, you need to offer them the same compassion and loving-kindness you've now learned to give to yourself. Nurturing our relationships requires attentive listening and empathy. We must refrain from problem solving and giving advice too quickly. It's important to get clear on what others want and need from us and to be capable of setting firm yet flexible boundaries so that we can take good care of ourselves as well as others. These are all habits you can learn and practice.

In this section of the book, you'll discover

- how to attract nurturing others into your life;
- how to break free from the grip of loneliness;
- the importance of making your inner "house" a home;
- the top six sabotaging interpersonal behavior patterns;
- six empowering strategies for transforming these patterns;

- the importance of self-connection as a prerequisite for nurturing others;
- how the circuitry in your brain helps you relate to others;
- how to strengthen your empathy muscle;
- four habits you must practice; and
- that nurturing others nurtures you.

If you can change yourself, you can change your world. If you don't already have close, nurturing friends, try to imagine what your life will be like when you do. Because whether you suffer from shyness, social anxiety, or a lack of motivation, you're going to be able to attract other nourishing souls. How can I be so sure of this? Because self-connection and self-nurturance are very, very attractive. Just keep practicing the seven skills covered in part 2. You may have to pass on the non-nourishing souls drawn toward your light, but keep an eye peeled for the other bright lights hovering nearby.

Please try not to be too hard on yourself if you've discovered that you haven't been all that attuned and nurturing to those closest to you. The practice of inner nurturing is all about self-compassion, self-acceptance, and self-forgiveness. Marshall Rosenberg, the author of *Nonviolent Communication*, writes: "An important aspect of self-compassion is to be able to empathically hold both parts of ourselves — the self that regrets a past action and the self that took the action in the first place."

It's never too late to improve your nurturing of others: they will always appreciate your efforts.

CHAPTER FIFTEEN

Attracting Nurturing Others

We all need to find a way to become individuals, by finding our own depths and even our own darkness, without cutting ourselves off from the maternal guidance within ourselves that keeps us in life and in community.

— Thomas Moore, *Care of the Soul*

For most of her career, Dee, a dedicated and ambitious speech pathologist, was employed by a large university, and she was well liked and respected in her professional community. Personable, friendly, and possessing a disarming sense of humor, she had relationships with her clients as well as her colleagues that were, on the whole, fulfilling. But working for a university had its drawbacks, and Dee longed to control her schedule and to earn enough to buy a home.

At age forty-one, she decided to leave the university and start a private practice. Because of her reputation, building her practice was easy, and she soon had a full-time clientele. She was thrilled that she could set her own fees and schedule. But there was a downside to private practice that she hadn't fully accounted for: she felt lonely. Renting space in a suite shared by many different types of practitioners, she felt isolated and had little contact with colleagues. Scheduling lunches with her colleagues on campus had always been easy, but now the extra travel time made it more challenging. At the university, there was always someone she could get together with to grab dinner, take a walk, or catch a movie after work. Now Dee felt she was really on her own.

At the university, she often used to walk across campus a couple of times daily, and this moderate exercise kept her weight down. Now her weight was climbing, and her plan to join a gym hadn't panned out. Getting up early to work out was difficult, and after work she was too tired. She called me after a doctor's visit revealed that she was prediabetic and forty-five pounds over her ideal weight.

Dee's struggles with weight had begun in adolescence and continued through college. Studying late into the night and eating dormitory food, she gained fifteen pounds her freshman year. During graduate school, she packed on an additional fifteen, grabbing food on the run and exercising infrequently because of classes, schoolwork, and a part-time job. She stopped gaining weight once she began working at the university.

When I asked her why she felt she was unable to manage her food intake, Dee explained:

> My mom's a nurse, and she raised me by herself. She always stressed the importance of having a career and not depending on anyone. I'm passionate about my work, and I've put a lot of time and energy into building my career.
>
> Unfortunately, I never put that much energy into taking care of my body. My eating habits have been pretty bad since college. I eat whatever I want, and while I don't binge, I make poor food choices and overeat at meals. I enjoy exercising, but I don't make the time for it — something always seems to get in the way.
>
> While I've been bothered about the extra weight I'm carrying around, I thought that if I paid closer attention to my food intake and exercised regularly, I'd be able to lose the weight. But now I'm

wondering if I've just been fooling myself. And I think there are a couple of other things that I've been in denial about.

As Dee spoke, her body sank into the chair.

Breaking Free from the Grip of Loneliness

Dee's satisfying professional life was a far cry from her personal life. Her evenings were lonely, and she was facing a reality that she had not been willing to deal with until now — that she actually had few close friends. Her friendships at the university tended to be superficial. She had two friends from high school, but she had put little energy into maintaining these relationships and saw both of them infrequently. "Tara and I go back as far as grade school — I love her, but she's draining. Carrie and I met in middle school — she's married with two kids, so I don't see her as much as I used to. When I do see her, it's all about Carrie."

Dee had never married, and, turning forty-two, she wondered if she would ever find a partner. "Dating and sexuality — that's a whole other issue," she declared. "Over the past ten years, I've gone on dates here and there, but in general, I've felt too big and unattractive to date. While I've dated men in the past, I'm also attracted to women, and I'd like to explore this further. But my poor mother, a devout Catholic, would have heart failure if she found out I was bisexual — or, God forbid, gay — and I think my father, who I've just recently reconnected with, would disown me."

Dee was an only child with a large extended family. While she enjoyed spending time with family members one on one, she felt invisible at large family gatherings and experienced an overwhelmingly painful and at times paralyzing sense of loneliness and shame with no partner, siblings, or children to accompany her. Even though no one mentioned her weight, she sensed they were all focusing on it. She felt guilty when she declined invitations, but she rationalized that she never forgot a birthday or a special occasion.

Make Your House a Home

Dee continued: "My mother came from a generation of hardworking women who put their emotions and needs on hold. While she was loving and she made sure that all of my physical needs were met, she worked long days and was disconnected from herself in many ways." Following in the footsteps of her mother, Dee was also out of touch with her feelings and needs.

The painful sense of loneliness Dee was experiencing was not due solely to her lack of close friends and a partner. The voice she heard most often in her head was the voice of her Inner Critic, judging and shaming her for her lack of self-control as well as her lack of close connections with others. Work and food had become her main sources of pleasure, fulfillment, and distraction. Although she did not realize it, her internal "house" was not a home.

As she began to feel more connected to herself by practicing the first few skills of inner nurturing, Dee had an "aha" moment:

> I'm experiencing a new relationship with myself — one I never knew was possible. When I take the time to pop the hood, self-validate, and reinforce the alliance, the loneliness that I've lived with for so long seems to lessen, and I feel more peace, maybe even joy, within. As strange as this may sound, even though I'm still alone most of the time, I don't *feel* as lonely. Even though it's counter-intuitive, I realize that whenever I feel that intense loneliness, I need to "go home" rather than look outside myself for connection. And I've discovered an important side benefit — I'm not grabbing food the minute I feel lonely — I'm able to tolerate those feelings long enough to navigate through them.

Releasing Interpersonal Patterns That No Longer Serve You

Ready to work on attracting nurturing people into her life, Dee was concerned about her ability to pick the right people.

I think my mother modeled quite a few behaviors that aren't healthy or adaptive. She was always rescuing and taking care of others and making friends with people who were down on their luck. I guess it's the nurse in her, and I'm sure it boosted her self-esteem, but I don't think these people contributed much to her life or well-being. I've attracted non-nurturing types also, like my high-school friends, who have little to give because they also feel empty. I'd like to find friends, and a life partner, who are more connected to themselves and who have something to give. I'm feeling more hopeful about this now.

As she spoke, she sat up straight, reflecting a new level of optimism.

Dee had developed a number of interpersonal behavioral patterns that helped her survive a dysfunctional family environment. While she was aware of the types of people she attracted as friends (women who were self-absorbed, strong, and demanding) and lovers (men who were emotionally unavailable), she was unaware of the patterns that she herself engaged in that sustained these dynamics.

Sabotaging Patterns and Empowering Strategies

While there is no simple formula for attracting nurturing people into your life, below I've listed the top six sabotaging interpersonal behavior patterns that emotional eaters engage in, plus six empowering strategies for transforming these patterns. As you read through each pattern, see whether any of the statements apply to you. It isn't necessary that they all apply or that they apply all of the time. You may find that you engage in a particular pattern only around certain people, or only at particular times. Some patterns may reflect your behavior more closely than others.

If, like Dee, you would like to attract nurturing folks into your life, you need to become aware of your relational patterns and consciously work to transform them. Whenever you make changes to longstanding patterns, you will experience different feelings that may make you uncomfortable. Jot down these feelings in your journal and access your Inner Nurturer for soothing and reassurance that this is a sure sign that you're on the right track. You'll grow more comfortable over time.

Sabotaging Pattern 1. Taking Whoever Will Take You

- I'm not good at figuring out what I want in a relationship.
- I have a hard time reading others and perceiving their intentions.
- My anxiety and insecurity cloud my vision when I first meet someone.
- I often confuse attention with caring.
- Most of my friends and lovers have chosen me.
- It's difficult for me to assert myself and pursue someone's friendship.
- I'm afraid that I might be rejected or humiliated if I approach someone.
- I wait for people to pick me.
- I find it easier to go with whoever chooses me.
- I'm afraid that I might upset someone if I don't accept their friendship.
- I don't always feel safe expressing how I feel.
- When I'm unhappy in a friendship, I avoid dealing with it.

This type of pattern generally begins early in life. Anything that makes it difficult for a child to fit in, connect with others, and make friends may be a contributing factor, including shyness, introversion, social anxiety, passivity, awkwardness, low self-esteem, inappropriate clothing, excess weight, ethnicity, religious affiliation, attention or behavioral problems, and learning disabilities.

The above statements resonated with Dee. She reflected:

It wasn't easy for me to make friends when I was young. In grade school, I was chubby and awkward; my hair was frizzy, and I wore thick glasses. I never fit in with the thin, pretty girls. Tara picked me as her partner on a science project, and that's how we became friends. In middle school, Carrie invited me to her birthday party, and I think I won her over with my sense of humor. As an adult, I've never been good at figuring out what I want in my relationships — I guess I don't put that much thought into it. I do put a lot of thought into what I want from my career, so I need to apply the same energy and attention to my personal life. I'm sad to say that I go with whoever chooses me — I'm not very proactive about friendships. But I think I can learn to be more selective. I have nothing to lose, since I don't have many close friends. And I never feel like I'm in the driver's seat in terms of picking love interests — the men I've been attracted to haven't been attracted to me. Maybe I'll have better luck with women.

Empowering Strategy 1: Envision Your New Friend or Lover

When you think about attracting a new friend or lover, what qualities or traits are you looking for? Take the time to get clear on what is most important to you by writing your vision in your journal. Be as specific as you can.

Dee wrote:

I'd like to meet a female friend, around my age, who is

- warm and caring;
- a professional;
- capable of taking an interest in my welfare;
- nonjudgmental;
- not self-absorbed;
- playful and fun to be with; and
- interested in some of the activities I'm interested in.

I'd like to meet a male or female lover who is all of the above plus physically attractive to me.

You can increase your odds of connection by taking part in activities where you have repeated contact with others and an opportunity to interact. This gives you time to get to know people and determine if they fit your vision list. Community involvement, whether it is professional, social, or spiritual, brings you into contact with others who share your interests. Select activities you enjoy; it's easier to connect with others when you have similar interests and feel engaged.

When you're out socially, muster your courage and strike up a conversation with someone who seems to embody the attributes on your vision list. Give yourself permission to do the picking and to pass on those who don't fit your list. Be careful not to give up on the whole project if the other person isn't interested. Access your Inner Nurturer for encouragement that over time, you'll be able to attract just the right people into your life.

Dee decided to start with the gay and lesbian center near her home. "I'm uneasy walking in there since I'm not really 'out' anywhere in my life yet, but I know I have to start somewhere. Right now, I'm not looking for a love interest. I'm just wanting to explore this community and consciously connect with nice, kind women — the ones that fit my vision list. I'm a bit uncomfortable with people taking an interest in me, but I'll get used to it. I definitely feel more nourished by the company of the few women I've met so far, so that's a good sign."

Sabotaging Pattern 2: Attracting Emotionally Unavailable People

- I gravitate toward people who seem strong and confident.
- I sometimes confuse arrogance and grandiosity with confidence.
- If someone I get to know pulls away, I try harder to get them to like me.
- I find it intriguing when someone plays hard to get.
- I find it mysterious when people put up walls.
- I often overlook bad behaviors like rudeness or chronic lateness.
- If someone gets close to me quickly and then pulls away, I assume there is something wrong with me.
- I have a tendency to get bored with relationships.
- I'm attracted to people who have "sharp edges."

- Kind, warm, available people seem soft, weak, and mushy to me.
- I'm uncomfortable when someone takes a deeper interest in me.
- I'm comfortable in relationships that are superficial and lacking in intimacy.

Emotionally unavailable doesn't necessarily mean that people don't express or share their emotions. An emotionally unavailable person might easily share particular emotions with you and complain about her problems or other people. The determining factor is whether she is open to processing her emotions and yours. Emotionally unavailable types tend to avoid deeper discussions. They also tend to avoid taking responsibility for their part in problems. And because they lack empathy, they generally show limited interest in other people's emotions and challenges.

This type of pattern generally results from a childhood in which caregivers were emotionally unavailable. Whether they were kind and loving or unkind, neglectful, or abusive, they lacked the skills for processing emotions — theirs or anyone else's. People who experience this sort of childhood learn to gravitate toward emotionally unavailable people, because their energy feels familiar, or family-like.

Many of these sabotaging interpersonal patterns go hand in hand. You may find not only that you take whoever takes you but that you have an affinity for people who are emotionally unavailable. When Dee read the above statements, she gasped. "Oh, my God — that list describes my father, and all of the men I've ever dated, to a tee. My father was always preoccupied whenever I spent time with him. I felt like I had to perform to get his attention, and even then I never really felt that he was interested in me."

Dee had infrequent contact with her father from age three until her teenage years. When she was sixteen, he moved out of state, and she lost contact with him for the next twenty years. "When I started dating, I gravitated toward men just like him. I was aware of the pattern, but men without those edges felt boring and not masculine enough. I'm not sure how to change this pattern, but I want to. I can't believe that I left this off my list. I definitely want to attract people — men and women — who are emotionally available. Can I redo my list?" she asked jokingly. I reassured Dee that her vision list would evolve continuously as she honed her inner nurturing skills.

Empowering Strategy 2: Gravitate toward the Warmth

If, like Dee, you've attracted or accepted as friends or lovers certain non-nourishing types, consider this a great opportunity to pay attention to how you feel in your body when you're around these types. You're not about to disconnect from everyone in your life who isn't nurturing, but noticing how you feel around them will help you get clear on your needs. Your body is your best guide as to what does or doesn't feel comfortable. Pay particular attention to both arousing and deflating emotions and bodily sensations. Notice your body movements. With more clarity, you'll be able to express your needs and request that those closest to you make small adjustments in how they relate to you.

The repeated experience of trying and failing to get her father's attention had been encoded in arousing neural patterns in Dee's brain and nervous system from an early age. When she first met someone who was emotionally unavailable, she felt stimulated and excited by the drama of the chase, and she experienced this as a "whole-body tingly, surge of energy." But within a few weeks, she usually felt invisible, abandoned, lonely, sad, hurt, agitated, and angry, and she experienced "heavy, achy, drained, and tight" sensations. These feelings, and the corresponding sense of not being good enough, were too uncomfortable to tolerate. Chasing the person's attention was the only way to stop the pain and feel uplifted again. Like Pavlov's dogs, as long as Dee received intermittent reinforcement for her efforts, she would keep up the chase. She had become somewhat addicted to this kind of stimulation and arousal. If that didn't work, there were always French fries.

Work on breaking old patterns by moving toward people who are kind and welcoming. Seek out people who are friendly and supportive, people who don't have a need to dominate or to pull you in and push you away. Even though you may not immediately find your new best friend or life partner, the experience of warmth and acceptance will provide the positive reinforcement needed to motivate you to keep working on attracting the right people.

If you feel uncomfortable around people with available, welcoming energy, you may feel a strong urge to pull away. It's easy to conclude that it just doesn't feel right or that you have nothing in common. Try a different approach: *look for the similarities*. This will help you feel more comfortable. Notice how you feel in your body when you're around kind, warm people and you focus on commonalities rather than differences. Notice what feels good about being with caring others. Give yourself time to experience the shift.

Sabotaging Pattern 3: People Pleasing

- I'm not always clear on what I feel or need in any given situation.
- I seek approval and validation from others.
- It's difficult for me to express my feelings or opinions when some- one feels or thinks differently.
- I can't handle conflict or confrontation.
- I avoid the disapproval of people I'm close to.
- I'm more concerned with being liked than with liking others.
- I don't speak up about things that bother me.
- It's hard for me to say no to someone.
- I have difficulty defining and expressing personal boundaries.
- I'm attracted to strong, take-charge people I can depend on.
- I'm not comfortable asserting myself and taking the initiative.
- I sometimes act out my feelings of anger or resentment in a passive-aggressive way.

It's natural for us to try to please our parents and other caregivers when we're young. If we can please them, we can avoid their disapproval and the associated experience of shame. If we get kindness and care only when we are compliant, we may learn that this is the best way to get their love and approval. If we are raised by parents who are preoccupied or neglectful, we may adopt this pattern in an attempt to avoid being ignored or abandoned. If we have a caregiver who easily flies off the handle, people pleasing may be a way to avoid attack. If we've been rejected and treated as unworthy, we may perceive our value and experience a corresponding lift in self-esteem only when we cater to other people's needs.

Many cultures and societal institutions encourage compliant behavior, especially from girls and women. Dee's grandparents were devout Catholics who emigrated from South America. "My mother's father was a stern, controlling, macho man, and my grandmother was always trying to please him. This behavior has been passed down generationally. The women of my culture are people pleasers. These messages were reinforced by the nuns at the Catholic schools I attended. It was basically all around me."

Empowering Strategy 3: Practice Self-Assertion

Before you're ready to transform your people-pleasing pattern, you'll need to become aware of the people and situations that trigger it. Dee noticed that she engaged in this pattern when she was around emotionally unavailable people and authority figures, both men and women. She noticed this pattern with a prior supervisor from the university, whom she described as "icy"; with a couple of strong women colleagues; with her father; and with men she had dated.

Next, you'll want to get clear on what form your people pleasing takes. What exactly do you do when you're being compliant? Do you have a tendency to agree with whatever the other person says or does? Do you get quiet when you disagree? Do you accommodate their needs before your own? Do you give too much, for example, running errands for them or buying them things you think they'll enjoy? Do you say yes when you really want to say no? See if you can become aware of your people-pleasing behavior right when it happens and notice how you feel when you act this way.

Dee's people pleasing took many different forms. With the cold supervisor, she clammed up and did whatever was demanded of her, whether or not she thought it made sense. With her two strong female colleagues, she expressed support for anything they said and did, even though sometimes she was secretly judging them. She observed their preferences and regularly offered to do favors for them, such as pick up coffee or lunch from their favorite place. With her father, she rearranged her plans to see him when he was available. She made sure she expressed an interest in whatever he shared, and she tried to be entertaining. With men she had dated, she accommodated their needs and desires by asking about their preferences and rarely sharing her own. She noticed that she felt better about herself when she acted this way: "I feel energized and like I'm a good person."

Next, in each situation, figure out what you're seeking from the other person and what you're afraid will happen if you stop trying to please them and start expressing your desires. Dee was clear that with her supervisor, she had been seeking approval, and her biggest fear was that there would be conflict and her job would be on the line. It was a little less clear what she was seeking with her work colleagues, but after some thought, she blurted out, "I know — I'm looking for acceptance and closeness with them. I want to fit in and be included. I'm afraid if I share my true feelings or disagree sometimes, they'd kick me to the curb. I feel like I need them more than they need me. The same with my father and the men I've dated. I guess I fear rejection, abandonment, and humiliation."

Finally, in each situation, decide on a baby step you can take to start breaking your people-pleasing pattern. Access your willingness and take a risk by expressing how you feel and what you truly need. If someone pushes back, try standing your ground, even though it may make you uncomfortable. Access your Inner Nurturer for a reminder that taking the best care of yourself sometimes means displeasing others. People worthy of being in your life will allow you to make these changes.

Dee had regular contact with her colleague Sue from the university, so she decided to focus on this relationship. Sue always expected Dee to drive to campus to meet for lunch, and Dee always did. The next time Sue called, Dee took a chance and asked if Sue could drive to meet her, explaining that she had little spare time in a very packed day. Worried about repercussions, Dee could feel her heart pound and her muscles tighten as she braced herself for Sue's response. She was shocked, and pleasantly surprised, when Sue replied, "Of course I can. I'd be happy to drive over to your office. You know, I've never seen it."

With some success under her belt, Dee was ready to try breaking her people-pleasing pattern with her father. First, rather than rearranging her schedule as she usually did, she scheduled her next visit with him at a mutually convenient time. Then she coached herself to take a chance and share with him something about her life, rather than listen to him nonstop. With tears in her eyes, she reported, "Wow. I think he actually wanted to get closer to me too, but didn't know how. Even though he wasn't the greatest listener, he did his best, and for the first time since I was a little girl, I felt close to my Dad. All this time I've been pleasing and performing, I've been missing out on *connecting* with the people in my life."

Sabotaging Pattern 4: Caretaking

- I'm good at anticipating other people's needs.
- I enjoy helping people solve their problems.
- I've always gravitated toward people who need help.
- I feel best about myself when I have met someone else's needs.
- I've been known to drop everything to help someone.
- I'm so busy taking care of others that I put my needs and wants on hold.
- I'm not always clear on my needs and desires.
- It feels safer to give than to receive.
- When someone gives to me, I feel like I owe them something in return.
- Sometimes I feel bored and empty when there isn't a problem to solve.
- I often feel angry when someone doesn't appreciate my assistance.
- I never feel that anyone takes care of me the way I take care of them.

Caring about and giving to others are desirable qualities and aspects of any nurturing relationship. Caretaking becomes maladaptive, however, when you have a strong desire or need to help or rescue others at the expense of your own needs and desires. This may involve supporting and caring for others, or it can take the form of trying to control others because you feel you know what is best for them.

Giving to or helping others elicits positive physiological sensations called the "helper's high." These positive feelings can be energizing and addictive and may be part of the reason you attract people who become dependent on you.

This pattern generally develops early in life and can be traced back to unmet needs for attention, acceptance, connection, comfort, appreciation, and unconditional love from parents or caregivers. Low self-worth is often at the heart of the caretaking pattern. Children who don't feel good about themselves often feel compelled to prove how good they are.

In families where members suffer from a physical or mental illness or have difficulty caring for themselves, a child may erroneously form a belief that she is responsible for taking care of others in need. Unable to tolerate other people's pain, she learns to extend her personal boundaries and take care of or rescue others. The child may fear that others — including parents, grandparents, siblings, and friends of the family — will not be able to take care of themselves. She may also be afraid of being judged or abandoned by others for failing to perform caretaking duties.

Caretakers are often people pleasers, and these two patterns overlap. The main difference between the two is how you view yourself and others. If you're a caretaker, you view yourself as strong and capable and tend to see others as needy and unable to care for themselves. If you're a people pleaser, you tend to see others as strong and powerful and yourself as weak and small.

"You'll be pleased to know that this is *not* one of my patterns," Dee declared emphatically, grinning from ear to ear.

My mother is the caretaker, not me. I made sure *not* to follow in her footsteps on this one. While I do have a tendency to give more than I receive, I don't think it's because I'm a caretaker — I think it's because I'm a people pleaser.

My mother has been taking care of everyone — me, her parents, our extended family, the neighbors, stray dogs and cats, her patients and coworkers, the hospital staff, you name it — for as long as I can remember. I don't think she is capable of saying no to anyone, ever. Sometimes, her caretaking borders on enabling — for example, when she continues to give money to an alcoholic family member. But everyone loves her and thinks highly of her. The problem is that she doesn't take very good care of herself. She has high blood pressure, serious digestive issues, and arthritis, and she is very overweight. I think, deep down inside, she'd love to have someone take care of her.

Empowering Strategy 4: Practice Self-Connection

In order to transform this pattern, you'll need to gather some information about your caretaking habit. First, you'll want to become aware of who and what triggers your caretaking behavior. Do you tend to take care of certain people and not others? Do you do it only when you are asked for help or when there's no alternative? Do you seek out caretaking opportunities? Do you push your support on others?

Dee's mother, Maria, joined us for a few therapy sessions, and we had a chance to explore this pattern with her. At age sixty-eight, Maria was still taking care of everyone, everywhere. "If anyone expresses any need, I just automatically step up to the plate to assist them. I offer help even when they don't ask. Sometimes I do push it on others — especially if I think they can't take care of themselves properly, like my cousin who drinks too much. I know I need to work on this, because I'm exhausted all the time, and my body is suffering," she said.

Next, you'll want to get clear on the form of your caretaking. What exactly do you do when you're taking care of others? Do you try to quickly solve their problems? Do you offer assistance prematurely? Do you push solutions on them? Do you run errands for them or drive them places? Do you do things for them that they could do for themselves? Do you shame or judge them if they don't accept your help?

"I'm the oldest of four children, and my mother had severe back and hip problems when we were small," Maria said. "I was required to take care of her and the other kids. Because there was so much to do, I just took care of everything. It was easier to do things myself than to ask for help. My siblings still turn to me for advice. I tend to do this at the hospital — rather than ask a coworker for help, I'll do everything myself. My daughter tells me that I do things for others that they can do for themselves. I'm sure she's right, but this pattern is so ingrained, I'm not sure if I can change it."

In each caretaking situation, what are you afraid will happen if you don't offer assistance? What will you gain if you refrain from caretaking? Maria had a good amount of insight into her caretaking behaviors, and she was clear about her fear that her siblings and parents wouldn't be able to care for themselves. Dee chimed in: "Mom, they can *all* take care of themselves. It may not be the way *you* would care for them, but they'll be fine." With her coworkers, patients, and neighbors, her caretaking was a way of connecting with others and seeking their validation and approval.

Maria had her own lightbulb moment during our discussion. "I think if I were to slow down and pay attention to what I'm doing, I could stop some of the caretaking. But I'm so used to being busy, I don't know what I'd do with myself if I wasn't taking care of everyone. I'd gain free time, but maybe I'm afraid of having that much time to myself."

Dee grabbed her mother's hand and lovingly said, "Mom, I think you suffer from that same inner loneliness and emptiness that I have. Grandma has it, you have it, and so do I. But I'm really learning how to address it. I think you would benefit from practicing inner nurturing."

Caretakers are generally out of touch with their internal world of feelings, needs, and thoughts. For Maria, interrupting the caretaking urge and popping the hood will be the first steps in connecting to herself. Practicing self-validation will help lessen her dependency on others for her self-esteem and sense of self-worth. As she builds a nourishing connection with her Inner Nurturer, she'll learn firsthand that caretaking is not necessarily the same as nurturing.

As she gets clear on her needs, Maria can define baby steps toward stopping her caretaking pattern and firming up her loose boundaries. By embracing the empty space within her that she fears and has filled with busyness, she can create the space needed to allow nurturing others to step forward. Fritz Perls, the father of Gestalt therapy, suggested that "the feared empty space is a fertile void. Exploring it is a turning point towards therapeutic change."

Sabotaging Pattern 5: Being Overly Judgmental

- I feel dissatisfied with many of my relationships.
- I regularly judge others, even though I don't share my thoughts.
- I form opinions quickly about the character of others.
- I tend to notice and focus on the things I don't like in people.
- I'm not very tolerant of the shortcomings of those closest to me.
- I sometimes confuse warmth and kindness in others with weakness.
- I get disappointed in people when I don't get my needs met.
- I find it difficult to feel compassion for someone who disappoints me.
- I'm annoyed that others don't treat me the way I treat them.
- I think most people could and should behave better than they do.
- When I'm upset with someone, I recycle their crimes, and I can't let go.
- I often stay angry or hurt for a long time.

This pattern of relating generally stems from a lack of empathy and unconditional acceptance in childhood. Modeled by judgmental, intolerant caregivers, the dominant voice in your head is that of a harsh, shaming Inner Critic. Those who suffer from this pattern do to others what was done to them: they constantly evaluate others in a black-and-white fashion. "I hate to admit it, but I'm guilty of almost every statement on this list," Dee exclaimed, sighing loudly. "I think this is why I have few close friends. I don't express my judgments, but I distance myself from others because I'm so disappointed in them."

Dee's grandparents were the source of this imprinting. "I remember from a very early age listening to them put my father down, and everyone else as well. After large family gatherings, we would sit around the dining room table and pick everyone apart. Everything was fair game — personality, body size, hairstyle, skin tone, clothing, career, choice of partner, aging, you name it. My mother didn't participate much; when she did, she usually stood up for the underdog. But I think I've always seen her as weak because of this — oops, there I go judging her!"

If you regularly engage in this pattern, you're probably aware of it. You've developed a keen eye for people's weaknesses, flaws, and shortcomings. Your judgments of others probably feel like truths to you. And since water seeks its own level, you've most likely gravitated toward similarly judgmental people.

We're all guilty of judging. In fact, it appears that we're hard-wired to notice the negative in any given situation. Rick Hanson, the author of *Hardwiring Happiness*, suggests that to help our ancestors survive and pay attention to dangerous situations, the brain evolved a negativity bias. This bias makes the brain less adept at learning from positive experiences but efficient at learning from the negative ones.

The problem isn't so much that you notice other people's inadequacies and flaws — it's that you choose to zero in on them and fail to compassionately highlight their strengths. Everyone has shortcomings, and everyone has redeeming qualities and strengths. We can choose what we want to focus on. You've acquired the bad habit of focusing on the negative.

Judging others harshly serves no purpose other than to make you feel superior and give your self-esteem a temporary boost. It makes you want to distance yourself from others. When you paint with a broad, critical brush, you'll end up pushing away the nurturing types (deemed weak and mushy) as well as the non-nurturing types.

If you're hard on others, you will be just as hard on yourself. You already know that self-judgment doesn't feel good. Research studies demonstrate that judgment and criticism are not motivating. If you'd like to attract nurturing people into your life, you'll need to cultivate kindness and compassion. The compassion you cultivate for others will ultimately translate into self-compassion and improved self-esteem.

Empowering Strategy 5: Focus on Strengths

Altering and transforming any sabotaging pattern begins with aware-ness — start with observing your behavior. Set an intention to notice the content of your judgments, *without judging yourself.* Do you judge character flaws more harshly than physical aspects such as body weight or hairstyle? Is every characteristic of another person fair game? Are there certain things that you never judge, such as a chubby child or a disabled person? Are there aspects of a person that you tend to go easy on? Are you more forgiving of certain mistakes? Are you more critical of women than men, weight than height, older people than younger people?

Pay attention to how often you engage in this pattern and what, if anything, triggers you to start judging. Do you usually start judging when you see or experience something you don't like, such as someone cutting you off in traffic or saying something unkind to you? Do you judge when you're disappointed about something or when you're in a bad mood? Or do your judgments represent a kind of live-streaming com-mentary running in your head all day? Notice how you feel when you're judging.

Dee realized that she was carrying on the legacy of her family's dining-room table tradition. There wasn't a day that went by when she failed to make a snap judgment about another person. "It's unbelievable how much judging I do. I was never really aware of this. When I'm driv-ing, I'm judging other drivers. At the market, I judge how quickly the cashier moves and the efficiency of the bagger. At the bank, I judge the teller for being too slow, and the bank itself for cutting costs and not hav-ing enough tellers. I judge my dental hygienist if she rushes me through a cleaning. When I walk down the street, I evaluate everyone's hairstyle, clothing, fitness level, and so on. I make judgments about my client's progress or lack thereof. And that's only half of it. I'm judging myself all day as well. No wonder I'm so drained at the end of the day and in need of comfort food."

In order to transform this pattern, you'll need to be mindful of your judgmental thoughts and catch and reframe them with more compassionate ones. Write down some of your judgments and see if there is another way to view the situation or the person's behavior. If you've focused on a character flaw or inadequacy, see if you can find a strength the other person possesses. For example, if you notice that your friend always prefers to go to inexpensive restaurants, rather than labeling him as "cheap" or "a tightwad," perhaps you can admire his financial discipline or his frugality and respect your differences regarding spending and saving money.

There is always a reason why people act the way they do. If you've judged someone for the way they dress, see if there is another way to view this. Try to think of a compliment versus a criticism. For example, "That oversized necklace Jane is wearing is gaudy and unattractive" can be replaced with "Jane likes to express her creativity with wearable art. Good for her." Notice how you feel when you think kind thoughts.

You can gradually put an end to those negative neural firings by routinely catching and reframing your judgmental thoughts. Practicing the unconditionally accepting voice of your Inner Nurturer will help you develop tolerance for and acceptance of other people's imperfections and shortcomings. As you radiate more nurturing energy, nurturing others will be drawn to you.

Sabotaging Pattern 6: Impatience

- It's difficult for me to delay my gratification.
- I'm frustrated if I don't see results quickly.
- I struggle to control my impulses at times.
- I have a low tolerance for frustration.
- I get anxious when I can't figure something out right away.
- I avoid projects that I find overwhelming.
- I have a tendency to procrastinate.
- I often quit things before I succeed.
- I feel annoyed and bored when people don't get to the point.
- I make poor decisions because I don't do the necessary research.
- I've ended relationships prematurely.
- I have a hard time setting and enforcing boundaries with others.

The *Random House College Dictionary* defines *patience* as "an ability or willingness to suppress annoyance when confronted with delay; the bearing of annoyance without complaint, loss of temper, or irritation." Impatience is the response of annoyance, anger, or upset at not getting what you want when you want it.

We all struggle with impatience. We don't like to wait for anything. Whether we're downloading a video, checking out at the grocery store, or waiting for a red light to turn green, we want everything to happen faster than it does. We know that patience is a virtue, but it seems to be in short supply.

When we observe infants, we can see innate differences in their tolerance for frustration. Our preference for instant gratification appears to be hard-wired. Environmental factors such as early deprivations and trauma also play a role, as does the presence of patient, soothing, and comforting caregivers.

But even if you weren't born with the patience gene or raised by patient elders, you *can* learn to practice patience. And since the process of attracting nurturing others won't happen overnight, you'll need lots of patience to continue your efforts, month in and month out, until you succeed.

Empowering Strategy 6: Adjust Your Expectations

"Bingo! This is another pattern that fits me. I've scored a whopping 5 out of 6 on these patterns. Do I win a prize? And how quickly can I transform this pattern? The sooner the better," Dee kidded, laughing out loud. Dee's sense of humor, one of her many strengths, was going to be a valuable resource for her efforts to attract others.

You can begin transforming this pattern by making a list of all the situations that trigger your impatience. Next to each item, list your typical response, ranging from slight annoyance to rage. See if you can identify an unstated expectation underlying your impatience.

Here's Dee's list:

- *Waiting in line anywhere.* My response: agitation and annoyance. My expectation: cashiers won't make small talk, and they'll open up another register.
- *Being placed on hold on the phone.* My response: annoyance and anger. My expectation: that I shouldn't have to wait for more than five minutes.
- *Waiting longer than fifteen minutes for a doctor.* My response: disappointment and outrage. My expectation: that the practice will respect my time, hire assistants, and not overbook.
- *Solving computer problems.* My response: intense, paralyzing, sense of overwhelm and frustration. My expectation: that these things shouldn't eat up my time.
- *Assembling furniture.* My response: mild frustration to anger and throwing things when I can't figure out the poorly written instructions. My expectation: that they'll write these inserts for the tech impaired.
- *Following a clean eating plan and not losing weight.* My response: frustration and hopelessness. My expectation: that I should lose weight immediately when I reduce my intake.
- *Exercising and not seeing results.* My response: frustration and powerlessness and a "what's the use" attitude. My expectation: that I will instantly have toned muscles.
- *Investing time and effort in something (dating, making friends) without quick payoffs.* My response: frustration and hopelessness bordering on despair. My expectation: that it should happen quickly and effortlessly.

The next step is to adjust the expectations that trigger your impatience and make them more reasonable. The last item on Dee's list was directly related to her desire to attract nurturing others into her life, so we focused on this trigger. The question was: how could she motivate herself to continue to push out of her comfort zone to build connections if there wasn't a quick payoff?

I reminded Dee that getting a four-year college degree and a gradu-ate degree was evidence that she could delay her gratification in order to achieve her goals. She responded: "You're right. I guess the trick is to focus on what I'm gaining during the process rather than the end result. If I get myself out to more social and professional events, I can focus on the fact that I'm working on my patterns and gaining social skills, and that's the quick payoff. That will work for me. Truthfully, I need time to get to know people and see if they fit my vision list."

The final step in transforming this pattern is to notice how you feel when you adjust your expectations. Impatience is a stressful mental state, but it may actually feel more energizing than the quiet, and perhaps dull, mental state of patience. Huffing and puffing at the grocery checkout is more energizing than quietly reading a magazine article or repeating a mantra. Adjusting your expectations by lowering them a bit may leave you feeling restless or unproductive. Tolerating these uncomfortable feeling states will help you transform this maladaptive pattern. Access your Inner Nurturer for the encouragement and hope needed to stay the course.

"It's Easier Than I Expected"

Over the many months of Dee's inner work, she noticed that she was attracting a different kind of female friend. "I'm becoming a magnet for nurturers," she joked. "But seriously, I never realized how I was attract-ing the wrong types and keeping the right ones at a distance. And I didn't know how much this had to do with my overeating. When I allow the good to flow in and I feel more nourished by the company of others, it feels effortless to make better food selections." She continued:

> Now that I'm feeling less lonely and more connected to myself, I've decided to put a toe in the water and reconnect with my extended family. I've been saying yes to their invitations more often. Rather than focusing on what I don't have in common with them, I've been looking for the similarities. And you know what? There are many. I think I always judged them because I felt so different from them.

I was ashamed of my weight and of always being the single one. I realize now that judging them was a way of pushing them away and keeping myself away from *my* pain. I was throwing the baby out with the bathwater. A few of my cousins are really nurturing, and I don't think I ever gave them credit. I viewed their kindness as weakness and a sign that they felt sorry for me. The problem was with me, not them.

I still feel some vulnerability and shame around them, especially the ones who are thin and seem to have it all together. But I'm able to check in with myself and get clear on what *I'm* feeling and what *I* need. Sometimes I'm really sad about getting older and not having a partner or a perfect body. At times like this, I know I need to "go home" and have a good cry and nurture myself without food. The good news is that I'm not stuffing down these feelings anymore. With my Inner Nurturer by my side, I'm more willing to feel the unpleasant stuff and more able to hold hope that I can create the future I desire. I'm so excited about all of the progress I'm making. I thought it would be much harder. It's amazing — a little bit of inner nurturing goes a long way.

CHAPTER SIXTEEN

Nurturing Our Relationships

The foundation of love is understanding, and that means first of all understanding suffering.

— Thich Nhat Hanh, *The Art of Communicating*

Once we know what sufficient nurturance is all about and, more importantly, what it feels like, it's natural to want to offer it to others. Many clients, especially those who are parents and caregivers, tell me that their practice of inner nurturing has highlighted a painful awareness — that they haven't done a very good job of nurturing those closest to them. And this makes sense. Self-connection is a prerequisite for connecting to others in a nurturing way.

We must be capable of looking inward and understanding our own internal world before we can understand the internal state of those closest to us. In fact, our awareness of another person's internal world depends on how well we know our own. As we develop our capacity to know ourselves, we become more receptive to knowing, and nurturing, others.

Jack, a fifty-three-year-old CEO of a women's clothing manufacturing firm, looked agitated while practicing self-validation (skill 2) during a group coaching session.

I'm validating my feelings of sadness and guilt regarding my relationship with my daughter Lindsay. I traveled a lot for business
when she was little. When I was home, I wasn't very patient with
her. She was our first child, and she was always anxious and fearful.
I was young, new to parenting, and chronically overwhelmed. My
wife worked part-time, and she's a good mother, but she also had
difficulty handling Lindsay's moods. Believe it or not, I'm the more
touchy-feely one. I don't think either of us did a very good job of
attuning to Lindsay's emotions and needs. No wonder we've had
such a troubled relationship with her and she has so many emotional
challenges today. She's twenty now and off at college, but I hope
it's not too late to heal our relationship, offer her the nurturance she
needs, and help rewire her brain.

Barbara, a sixty-two-year-old art history professor, had an "aha"
moment during the same group-coaching session. While working on getting clear on her needs (skill 4), she exclaimed:

I get really frustrated trying to figure out what I need. I'm wondering: if I don't know what I need most of the time, how could I possibly know what my husband, mom, sister, son, and grandson need?
Even though I'm often focusing on their needs, I'm realizing that I
don't actually know *what* they need. I just decide what I think they
need, and this is probably why they don't always feel nurtured by
me. I struggle the most with the relationship with my sister Karen.
I know how effective inner nurturing is, and I'm wondering how
I can offer her the same kind of nurturance I'm learning to offer
myself, without being pulled into all of her drama.

Strengthening Your Empathy Muscle

Crucial to our understanding of another person is our ability to register
and feel their internal state. In the mid-1990s, a group of Italian neuro-
scientists identified specialized cells in the cortex of the brain that came

to be known as the *mirror neuron system*. These brain-to-brain links begin functioning as soon as we're born, allowing us to mirror the emotions and behaviors of caregivers. Using our eyes and ears, as well as our intuition and senses of touch and smell, we can assess the emotional state and behavioral intentions of another. Researchers have postulated that this system is the source of our capacity for empathy, enabling us to unconsciously map the internal world of another person.

Clearly the internal states of others affect our own internal states. Consider how you feel, for example, when you're watching the evening news and you observe a mother grieving uncontrollably for her young child, who has just been killed by a drunk driver. You think for a moment about the loss she's experiencing, and perhaps you reflect on the devastation you might feel if this were your child. Your throat gets tight, and tears well up in your eyes as you register her pain. Your mirror neurons and the empathy circuit in your brain are allowing you to imagine what this woman might be feeling and thinking.

Our empathy circuit allows us to feel not only the pain and suffering of others but also their excitement and joy. At any sporting event, you'll observe both ends of the empathy spectrum as you listen to the cheers, and jeers, of adoring fans. Think about how you feel when someone close to you lands that new job, passes the licensing exam, or announces that she is pregnant after years of trying. You feel her joy.

When we nurture those closest to us, we promote their continuing development by providing attentive listening, validation, loving-kindness, support, and encouragement. Nurturing our relationships begins with increasing our capacity for empathy. Empathy is not a personality trait but rather a cognitive attribute that can be developed and strengthened. The best way to do this is to practice the habits of highly empathic people.

Four Habits You Must Develop

Habit 1. Convey interest and availability
Habit 2. Listen reflectively

Habit 3. Ask how you can help
Habit 4. Clarify your boundaries

Habit 1. Convey Interest and Availability

When someone you care about is experiencing a difficulty, you can begin the nurturing process by letting them know that you are both interested and available to listen and help, either immediately or at an agreed time in the future. "I'm sorry you're going through this — would you like to talk about it?" and "I know you're upset — I'd be happy to listen if you want to get together after work" are examples of ways you can communicate interest and availability.

Good nurturance involves not only listening to problems but also supporting, educating, and mentoring others. "I can help you with that" and "If you need support, please don't hesitate to ask" are examples of ways you can communicate support. When it comes to nurturance, you can never go wrong with a gentle approach. Rather than push your support on someone, let them accept your offer when they're ready.

The setting or environment you choose should support good communication. Choose a space that ensures privacy and undisturbed conversation. If you talk on the phone, limit interruptions. Having the television or stereo on in the background or answering other calls during a conversation sends the wrong message.

If you're face to face, make good eye contact and use facial expressions that communicate care. Let the speaker determine the appropriate physical distance between the two of you. While some people prefer to sit face to face with full eye contact, others may find eye contact too intimate or distracting and may prefer to sit side by side.

Give the speaker time to experience and explore feelings on a deeper level. Active, attentive silence on your part allows the speaker to think, reflect, and proceed at their own pace, without fear of interruption. Silence is especially useful in helping another person open up about a difficult problem, or in situations of loss or grief.

Be conscious of your body language. Glancing at your phone or watch while listening, sneaking glances at others passing by, crossing your arms, tapping your fingers, and fidgeting convey a lack of interest in the other person. Try quieting your mind before listening for an extended period. While much of this is common sense, it's surprising how easily many of us slip into these bad habits.

Jack lamented, "I have definitely not been the best listener with my daughter. She is *very* emotional and long-winded, and she gets angry if I interject a comment. I don't know how to help her when she's upset; it seems that whatever I say is the wrong thing. These days, she clams up and doesn't share much with me. I think she would shut me out even if I told her I was interested and available." As he spoke, his head drooped.

It's not uncommon for young adults, who are separating from their parents and asserting their own identities, to establish rigid boundaries and withhold information. But I was fairly certain that the wall Jack's daughter had erected was a means of protecting herself from attunement misses and further disappointment. In cases like this, where there is a long-standing pattern of communication difficulties, it takes time for the other person to develop trust, because it requires a willingness to be vulnerable. To nurture the relationship with his daughter, Jack needs to go beyond merely conveying his interest and availability; he needs to communicate to her his desire and intention to do better at listening than he has done in the past. But before he does this, he'll need to make sure he's practicing the next habit.

Habit 2. Listen Reflectively

This is one of the most valuable personal-growth skills you can learn and practice. Reflective listening is a special type of listening that involves paying attention not only to what another person says but also to their feelings and body language. In order for your listening to be effective and nurturing, you need to be able to perceive accurately what the other person is experiencing and trying to communicate. This means you must keep your attention focused completely on the speaker.

When someone you care about feels truly heard and understood, an emotional burden is lifted. They feel comforted, and as they calm down, they can more easily explore their feelings. With better access to their upstairs brain, they can clarify thoughts and needs and decide on a course of action.

Reflective listening involves hearing and understanding what the other person is trying to communicate and then reflecting back to them, in your own words, the feelings and content you heard. This is an especially powerful form of listening to use when someone you care about is experiencing a difficulty or problem.

This type of listening is not the easiest skill to master, because most of us would rather talk and give advice than listen and mirror what we hear. It's more difficult than basic listening, because we don't necessarily like to accompany people into their sadness and pain. And while this empathic form of listening will benefit everyone you offer it to, it will also stretch you to become more attentive and patient.

It's easiest to attend to the essence of both the content and the feelings a speaker is sharing if you listen and reflect back short segments of the communication. This also allows you to check the accuracy of what you're hearing and make sure you're understanding what is being communicated. Some people, like Jack's daughter, talk nonstop, and it becomes difficult to get a word in edgewise. It's best to gently break in to the other's communication by saying something like "Excuse me for a moment — I want to make sure I understand what you're saying" or "I need to interrupt you for a second so I know I'm hearing you accurately." It's okay to take charge of the communication in this way, especially when you are trying to be of service.

When you reflect back the essence of a bite-size portion of the communication, pay careful attention to both verbal and nonverbal reactions. This way, you can immediately discern whether you are on or off target. If you're right on, the speaker may continue without hesitation, or say something like "Yes, exactly." Your interruption has served as a form of validation and may help to reduce repetition on the part of the speaker. Your feedback also informs the speaker as to how she is coming across, and this often allows for new insights. If your reflection is off base, a courageous speaker may verbally correct you. But since not everyone is comfortable asserting themselves, you may need to read their body language to figure out that you're not in sync.

When you reflect feelings, you name the emotional state of the other person, in your own words. In this way, you can help the speaker get clear on her feelings and own them. In addition to noting strong, obvious feelings, look for hidden feelings and highlight these to the speaker. Sometimes you sense someone is feeling something but isn't expressing it or isn't aware of the feeling. As you notice physical signs such as facial expressions and posture shifts, as well as verbal signs such as tone and volume, you can reflect back with statements such as "You feel..." or "You're sounding like..." or "You look..." Try to be as accurate as you can when reflecting feelings and behavior. Rather than saying something vague like "I see you're upset," try to pinpoint the emotion with comments like "I see that you're feeling sad" or "You sound angry." This type of observation can also serve as a door opener, communicating your interest and availability for listening.

After you feel you have a good grasp of the speaker's feelings and the content of the communication, you can pull it all together by reflecting the meaning of this bite-size portion of the message. Statements such as "You feel _____ about _____ " or "You feel _____ when _____" help inform the speaker that you've listened accurately. You can also use statements such as "What I'm hearing is..." or "I'm sensing that you're feeling...," but keep in mind that these expressions can make some folks feel as if they're being analyzed. At the end of the entire communication, if appropriate, you can summarize the overall essence of what you've heard, and close out the communication.

Don't forget to check in with yourself and notice how *you're* feeling after you practice reflective listening. Are you feeling satisfied, calm, energized, bored, impatient, or drained? Getting clear on how you're feeling will help you make any necessary adjustments in the future.

RESPONSES THAT DO NOT CONSTITUTE REFLECTIVE LISTENING

Sometimes we think we're offering good listening, but we're actually responding in a way that actually derails the conversation. These types of responses typically fall into three categories:

EVALUATING

With this type of response, we shift the focus of the conversation from the other person's feelings and concerns to our own interpretation, assessment, analysis, diagnosis, or judgment of their message. We share our opinion and let them know whether we agree or disagree with their thoughts. Perhaps we praise or criticize them. This is not an effective way to listen reflectively, because we are not maintaining the focus on the other person's feelings and thoughts. This type of response is likely to negatively affect the other person's self-esteem and may cause resentment or defensiveness. We're sending a subtle message that we know best. We're creating an environment that is not conducive to increased vulnerability and safety, and we risk diminishing the other person's motivation and initiative.

Trust the other person to be responsible for his or her own life. Of course, there may be times when you feel someone may be in danger and that it's best to intervene. When your eleven-year-old tells you she's afraid to walk to school because she's being bullied, or your nineteen-year-old tells you his mood swings are worsening and he hasn't left his dorm room in two days, it's time to evaluate and take action.

SOLVING AND FIXING

Have you ever noticed that when you're upset about something, those closest to you offer opinions or advice at the drop of a hat? You tell your mother that you're worried about finding another partner after your spouse of twenty years passes away, and she says matter-of-factly, "There are plenty of online dating sites — I'm sure you'll find someone." She's been alone since your father passed away, and her comments feel more dismissive than helpful. Newly single, you feel like a fish out of water, and you can't shake your fears of being rejected and deemed undesirable at your age. You need her to listen to your fears and concerns and allow you to feel. You need gentle understanding, reassurance, comfort, and soothing, not opinions or advice.

You tell your father that you're worried about the political backlash of quitting as chair of a committee at work. You've been mulling it over for weeks when you finally share it with him. The first thing your father says is "I wouldn't quit that committee. It looks good on your résumé." No exploration of how you're feeling, why you're wanting to quit, what your gut tells you to do, or what you need. Telling you what to do doesn't address your concerns or how you feel; in fact, it increases your confusion and anxiety. And his advice, though well intended, adds guilt to the situation, because now you're worried about disappointing him. You need good listening, patient exploration of your feelings, understanding, encouragement to trust your instincts, and wise counsel, not a quick fix.

Another way that caring others try to help is by asking questions before giving advice. You tear up when you tell your walking buddy that you had to put your dog down, and she says, "Are you going to get a new puppy? The shelter has some cute ones." You shift gears and answer her question. But her comment, meant to be supportive, has shifted you right out of your emotional brain and your grieving *feeling self* into your prefrontal cortex and your logical *thinking self*. It's only been two days since you lost your pal of twelve years. You need to grieve, and you need good listening, comfort, and time to process the loss. She has unintentionally robbed you of an opportunity to grieve and you both of an opportunity for increased intimacy and bonding.

In our fast-paced Western culture, we've learned to cut to the chase. We all do it. We want to solve the problem, take away the pain, and move on. We value quick action and productivity. No one wants to get stuck in messy emotions. There's a time and a place for advice, and sometimes that's all we want and need. But more often than not, patient listening and attention to our feelings and thoughts can offer a more expansive solution to the problem.

What do most people in your life do when you share your problems and concerns? Do they quickly offer advice, opinions, and solutions, or do they stop and offer patient listening and help you explore your feelings? Do they allow you time to process all your conflicting emotions and thoughts? Do they offer comfort, soothing, encouragement, and hope?

Do they help you get clear on your needs? Consider yourself lucky if the majority of people in your life are skilled at reflective listening.

I hope I convinced you in part 2 of this book that jumping to problem solving before exploring feelings, needs, and thoughts is not an effective way to nurture yourself or anyone else. When you move too quickly to offering solutions, you interfere with the natural process of self-exploration. You send an overt message of impatience and a covert message that you don't believe the other person can figure out their own problems.

Don't assume that you know what is best for the other person. When you listen reflectively, you empower others and help them increase their self-awareness and self-esteem as they make sense of and solve their own problems. Give others the space and time they need — they will get to the heart of the matter, in their own time.

DIVERTING

Trying to talk someone out of their feelings, deny the strength of their feelings, make them laugh, or distract them is a subtle way of lessening the intensity of the conversation. Presenting facts and logical information or arguing and debating feelings limits self-exploration. Asking too many questions distracts the other person from their process, as does trying to cheer them up. Quickly reassuring the other person that everything will be all right may be a way of withdrawing from the conversation. It sends the subtle message that you are uninterested in or uncomfortable with their problems. This is a surefire way to derail or divert the conversation; it blocks the other person from processing their feelings with you. If the issue is disturbing to you or you are unable to listen reflectively for another reason, it's best to just say so and take responsibility for your discomfort.

When we reviewed these pitfalls of reflective listening, Jack spoke up enthusiastically, his head held high. "I've made all of these mistakes with my daughter. And with my employees. And with my wife! She and I are practicing this habit with each other so that we can do a better job with our daughter."

While his heart was in the right place, Jack had a habit of interrupting and derailing group members by asking questions, telling stories, and giving advice. He enlisted the support of a couple of group members to give him a thumbs-down signal whenever he engaged in these behaviors. Over time, he began to catch himself, and as he did, he gained insight into what triggered these behaviors.

Jack was raised by a father who, like his daughter, talked *at* him nonstop. As a young child, he discovered that interrupting and diverting his dad with storytelling could stop the barrage of words. "I'm realizing that when anyone talks for an extended period of time, I feel overwhelmed and my body feels restless, and that's why I start interrupting. Now that I'm aware of this, I can take a few deep breaths, calm myself down, and relax into listening. And with this new technique, I'm learning how to play an active role in listening, so I feel less antsy."

Habit 3. Ask How You Can Help

This is a very simple habit to practice, but one that is often overlooked. If you want to nurture another person, you must find out what they need. Sometimes that is simply reflective listening. You assist them in processing their feelings and finding their own solutions. And maybe they aren't even looking for solutions; they just need to vent or get something off their chest. Reflective listening is nurturing in and of itself.

At other times, those closest to us need more than good listening. Like Jack's daughter, they may talk incessantly because their needs aren't being met. They may not even be aware of what they need, which makes everything more complicated. Perhaps they need help identifying their feelings and needs. Maybe they need validation, comfort, and soothing. They may be seeking reassurance, encouragement, and hope. Or they might like some feedback or advice.

Most of us don't feel comfortable simply listening. To avoid the natural tendency to start solving someone's problems after you have listened, or to cut off the conversation abruptly because you're nearing your limit, ask the other person how you can help or what they need from you. This serves two functions: first, it directs their focus to their needs, and second, it helps them clarify what they need from you so you can attempt to provide it and complete the interaction.

Try asking an open-ended question such as "Now that you're clear on how you're feeling, what do you need in this situation?" If the other person has difficulty clarifying needs, you can help with comments such as "It seems like you might be needing..." or "If I were in your shoes, I might need..." You can find out what they need from you specifically with a question such as "I'm wondering how I can help?" or "Is there something more you need from me?"

Barbara was hesitant to try reflective listening with her sister Karen, fearful that she wouldn't be able to extricate herself once Karen got started. "I can't shut my sister up. If I were to tell her that I was available and interested, it would open up an emotional floodgate. She goes on and on, and I feel like the life is being sucked out of me. When I need to go, no matter how long I've listened or how gently I say I need to stop, she always seems empty and unsatisfied."

But Barbara soon discovered that reflecting back bite-size chunks of the conversation actually calmed her sister and slowed down the flow. Helping Karen clarify her needs regulated Karen's nervous system even further. "I'm realizing that I've always launched into giving advice as a way to stop her from flooding me with her problems. All she really needed from me was good listening, empathy, and a space to process it all. Our conversations are less overwhelming now, but I'd still like to learn how to cut down the amount of time I spend on the phone with her. I'm still feeling drained, and sometimes I eat compulsively after our phone call."

Be careful not to rush through the listening process to get to the other person's needs and close out the conversation. If you are out of time or are feeling drained, gently set a boundary. You can always schedule another time to talk further.

Habit 4. Clarify Your Boundaries

Just as we must learn to set limits with ourselves, we need to learn to set limits, or boundaries, with others. Personal boundaries are protective.

They are physical and psychological edges or limits that define where we end and the world, or another person, begins. They must be firm yet flexible, not too loose and not too rigid. When they are effective, they keep us from feeling overwhelmed, drained, or used by others while still allowing us to take in the connection, closeness, warmth, safety, and intimacy we need and desire.

If our caregivers model healthy, appropriate boundaries and encourage our growing autonomy, we feel entitled to have boundaries and comfortable asserting them. Caregivers with poor boundaries raise children with poor boundaries.

If our boundaries are too loose, like Jack's or Barbara's, we have little sense of our own separate self, and we tend to get overinvolved in other people's lives. When we're unclear on our own feelings and needs, we're unable to express them, and we risk being swept away by the emotions and needs of others. Unable to tolerate the uncomfortable feelings others are experiencing, or our own sense of helplessness, we may try to fix or control others with our demands, opinions, judgments, and advice.

Loose boundaries often represent an attempt to avoid the unpleasant feelings we associate with separateness and aloneness. Merging with others provides us with a sense of connection, purpose, and perhaps safety, but it tends to disconnect us from ourselves. This disconnection leads us right back to eating, which is soothing and comforting and provides, if only temporarily, a blissful and undemanding experience of merging or oneness.

Rigid boundaries represent an attempt to avoid the uncomfortable and often terrifying anxiety we associate with vulnerability and closeness. We may avoid the deeper sharing and processing that intimacy requires, because too much closeness brings on a feeling of being suffocated or engulfed. Eating, which is soothing and nurturing, provides the nourishment and deliciousness of intimacy without the risk of hurt, suffocation, or loss of self.

We often partner with people whose boundary challenges are the opposite of our own. Jack's wife, Sarah, was well aware that her boundaries were rigid. She had been raised by cold and distant parents who had rejected her desire for closeness. She had rarely experienced warmth, empathy, or compassion from them. She learned early in life that it was best not to want anything from others and to disconnect from her emotions and needs. When she met Jack, his warmth and emotional availability won her over.

Sarah has few friends because she often loses her sense of separateness and independence around other people. She craves a closer relationship with others, including her husband and daughter, but she often can't relate to their emotions. While her rigid boundaries protect her, they also leave her feeling disconnected and frustrated with the lack of nourishing relationships in her life. Like Jack, she turns to food for comfort.

Noticing how you feel when you listen reflectively will help you get clear on *your* needs. Practicing expressing your needs will make setting and enforcing boundaries easier. If you tend to have loose boundaries, remind yourself that setting boundaries is not selfish; it's an important form of self-care and a great way to model self-care to others. If your boundaries tend to be rigid, remind yourself that you can redefine them and express yourself if others get too close or intrusive.

You must try to remain reasonably separate and objective when you listen reflectively. You need to avoid becoming so personally involved in what the other person is saying that *your* emotions are hijacked by the other person's emotions and trigger a defensive response in you. That's easier said than done, for sure.

It's important that you get clear on your boundaries before you commit to making yourself available to someone. Check in with yourself and assess whether you're up for reflective listening and how much time you have. You can clarify your boundaries up front with a statement like "I'd love to hear about that, but I only have twenty minutes," or "I'm so sorry you're going through that — I don't have time to listen now, but how about this afternoon?"

If someone close to you has loose boundaries and doesn't heed those you have set, interrupt with a gentle "I just need to let you know that I have to get off the phone in ten minutes." Access your Inner Nurturer and nourish yourself with loving, supportive phrases as you make boundary adjustments. This will help you tolerate any unpleasant emotions and thoughts that surface.

"I FEEL A BURDEN HAS BEEN LIFTED"

Barbara's boundaries were loose, and they needed firming up. She was merging with the emotions and needs of everyone, especially her sister, whose boundaries were practically nonexistent. The two sisters had been raised by an alcoholic father and a "people-pleasing, codependent" mother with very poor boundaries.

Barbara realized that she rarely set a boundary up front during telephone calls with her sister, and as a result, she felt rushed and impatient. Setting a limit to the conversations was a simple change that made all the difference in the world. "Reflectively listening to my sister and helping her identify her feelings and needs has dramatically changed our relationship. I can tell that she feels nurtured by me now, and she moves through everything faster. I'm realizing that she is capable of solving her own problems. I let her know up front how much time I have, and she's getting better at respecting my boundaries. In fact, this week, for the first time ever, she said, 'I'll let you go — I know you only had twenty minutes to talk.' It was absolutely amazing," Barbara said, wiping away tears. "In an odd way, I feel like we're helping each other grow and build the skills we missed out on in childhood. And the icing on the cake — drum roll, please: I'm actually beginning to feel nurtured by *her* company, and I'm not grabbing food after our conversations."

"I'M GETTING BETTER AT STAYING WITH MY DAUGHTER'S EMOTIONS"

After practicing the four habits in the group and at home for a few months, Jack was ready to give reflective listening a try with Lindsay. He waited until she was home for summer break, and driving home from a day at the beach together, he told her about the new skills he was learning and expressed his desire to work on being a better listener.

> Lindsay was upset about an incident with a boy she liked, so I asked her if she wanted to talk about it. I thought she might be receptive since we'd had a nice time at the beach, playing around and laughing like we did when she was younger. I know she was leery of her old advice-giving, storytelling Dad, but she gave it a try. I reflected her feelings back to her, and as she began to open up further, she started to cry. I stayed with her, touched her hand, and validated her emotions as she processed them. I helped her get clear on her needs, and that was it. She was done. No drama, and no screaming at me that I never understand her. We were both shocked at the results. She even gave me a kiss and a hug afterward and said, "Thanks, Dad. I really appreciate you."
>
> After we finished the conversation, she asked me if we could grab something to eat. I took her to her favorite pizza joint, and you know what? Lindsay ordered a slice of pizza, and I ordered a salad! I *rarely* order salads. I guess that because I felt so good about myself and our relationship, I didn't feel the need to stuff anything down.

Jack was beaming when he shared this story. Creating a close relationship with his daughter meant the world to him. He had worked hard on building new skills, and he had just experienced a huge breakthrough in his communication with Lindsay. His hard work was paying off.

A regular practice of inner nurturing builds and strengthens neural pathways that help you connect in a loving and joyful way to yourself first, and then to everyone and everything else. As you nurture those closest to you, you nourish yourself with the good feelings generated by caring for others and connecting in an intimate way. As you pay empathic and respectful attention to others, you come to know your own deepest desires and needs.

CONCLUSION

Our most challenging relationships, including the ones we have with ourselves, offer us the greatest opportunity for personal growth. If you're an emotional eater, your relationship with food has served many purposes in your life beyond simple sustenance. It has brought you pleasure, it has helped you cope, and it is truly a blessing in disguise. It highlights a disconnection that has been robbing years from your life. A constant focus on food, body image, calorie counting, and weight loss has crowded out joy and vitality and replaced them with vigilance, anxiety, and frustration. The approach I've outlined in this book offers you the chance for an improved relationship with yourself, a once-and-for-all resolution to your emotional eating and a way out of dieting.

The causes of your overeating or imbalanced eating have most likely existed for a very long time. Chronic stress, the easy availability of high-calorie and nutrient-deficient foods, a history of restrictive dieting, and inherited body and brain imbalances have certainly all played a role. But these factors do not fully explain difficulties with managing unpleasant feeling states, disruptive impulses, and self-defeating thoughts. The lack of consistent and sufficient nurturance early in life, and its impact on your brain development and self-regulation capabilities, must be taken into consideration.

The global obesity crisis represents, in part, a nurturance crisis of epic proportion. Many adults, including parents, teachers, and mentors, as well as the children they care for, are starving for nurturance. When our emotional needs are poorly met in childhood, we fail to learn how to connect to our inner world in a nurturing way. This disconnection can lead to a painful, desperate sense of emptiness, loneliness, and insecurity and a joyless existence that fuels emotional eating. We try to meet our needs by looking outside ourselves, erroneously believing that what we seek can be found in another person, place, or thing.

The better-than-good news is that your history is not your destiny. You can develop a relationship with food and your body that is easy, comfortable, and intuitive at any age. By making sense of your past, you can free yourself, and your loved ones, from a legacy of pain and addictive behaviors. Advances in neuroscience have given us a better understanding of how our experiences continue to change the structure and function of the brain throughout our lives. The approach I've outlined in this book works because it addresses the root cause of your inability to regulate your behavior: faulty neurological programming. And it offers a permanent fix: the rewiring of circuits through mindfulness and proper attunement, both external and internal.

This approach requires a shift in your thinking, a longer-term perspective, and a loving commitment to yourself. You now have access to strategies that actually sculpt your brain in positive ways so that you can guide yourself and make better food choices. It's best if you shift your focus from losing weight to gaining skills. Over time, as you apply these skills, any excess weight will come off, and you'll find, like everyone else who has lost weight with this approach, that the weight-loss part feels somewhat effortless. Rather than feeling enslaved to your favorite foods and deprived when you try to go without them, you will learn that your true source of comfort lies within.

Emotional intelligence begins with mindfulness — labeling our own feelings and then attuning ourselves to the feelings of the people around us. With the practice of mindfulness, we can calm ourselves down and understand, and bring harmony back to, the conflicting elements inside us. As we learn to access the peace, joy, and happiness that are already there, we become stronger and healthier, and a resource for others.

ACKNOWLEDGMENTS

M y deepest gratitude and heartfelt appreciation to those who helped make this book a reality:

First and foremost, my clients and every person who has attended the Twelve-Week Emotional Eating Recovery Program, my emotional-eating support groups, my workshops, and my seminars over the past twenty-seven years. You are my inspiration, and you have been my greatest teachers, helping me to clarify my thinking and refine my teaching methods. I feel blessed to have worked with each and every one of you. Thank you for placing your trust in me and allowing me to share your journeys of recovery.

Tom Silvestri, who took the time to carefully read, edit, and critique the book proposal and manuscript and offer insightful commentary and caring support. Thank you for all the helpful discussions in between sets at the gym!

Michael Gellert, for reading and editing the book proposal and manuscript. Thank you for those discussions in the wee hours of the night to get the title and subtitle just right. And thank you for your continuous and enthusiastic encouragement and support.

My wonderful and supportive publisher, New World Library: Marc Allen, for your continued support of my projects; Georgia Hughes, my editor, for your enthusiastic support of this project and your patience and incredible talent in managing the entire editorial process and shaping this book into its current form; Kristen Cashman, managing editor, for your attention to all the details and your ever kind, patient, and wonderful support; Erika Büky, copyeditor, for your keen editorial eye and skill at shaping the narratives to keep the reader's experience in focus; Vicki Kuskowski, for your talent and creativity in designing the cover; and Tona Pearce Myers, production director, for the beautiful text design.

The many talented and gifted researchers and authors, too numerous to mention, who have studied and written about overeating, weight loss, child development, trauma, neuroscience, and recovery and who have informed my life's work.

The teachers, therapists, gurus, and authors who have greatly inspired me, contributed to my evolution as a therapist, and awakened and nurtured my spirituality.

My encouraging and supportive friends and spiritual community at the Siddha Yoga Meditation Center.

My mother, for always believing in me and being my biggest supporter. Our relationship has offered me the greatest opportunity for learning about love, trauma, brain derailment, healing, compassion, and forgiveness.

My butterflies and my angels, Maurine and Joseph, who are a daily reminder that I am never alone.

My Source, who is ever present, gracing me daily with love, light, and divine guidance.

NOTES

Introduction

Page 7, *Research suggests that well into old age*: G. Flügge and E. Fuchs, "Adult Neuroplasticity: More Than Forty Years of Research," *Neural Plasticity* 2014 (2014), http://dx.doi.org/10.1155/2014/541870.

Chapter One: The Importance of Early Caregiving

Page 18, *Studies in rats have shown that those who received more licking*: C. Caldji, B. Tannenbaum, S. Sharma, D. Francis, P. M. Plotsky, and M. J. Meaney, "Maternal Care during Infancy Regulates the Development of Neural Systems Mediating the Expression of Fearfulness in the Rat," *Neurobiology* 95, no. 9 (April 1998): 5335–40.

Page 19, *Poor maternal nutrition and prenatal alcohol and drug exposure*: J. M. Soby, *Prenatal Exposure to Drugs/Alcohol: Characteristics and Educational Implications of Fetal Alcohol Syndrome and Cocaine/Polydrug Effects* (Springfield, IL: Charles C. Thomas, 2006).

Page 19, *Infants and children exposed to neglect and abuse*: G. E. Miller, E. Chen, A. K. Fok, H. Walker, A. Lim, E. F. Nicholls, S. Cole, and M. S. Kobor, "Low Early- Life Social Class Leaves a Biological Residue Manifested by Decreased Glucocorticoid and Increased Proinflammatory Signaling," *Proceedings of the National Academy of Sciences* 106 (2009): 14716–21.

Chapter Two: What's Love Got to Do with It?

Page 25, *only about one-half to two-thirds of the general population:* D. Siegel, *Brainstorm: The Power and Purpose of the Teenage Brain* (New York: Penguin, 2013), 144.

Page 26, *"toxic shame: the feeling of being flawed":* J. Bradshaw, *Homecoming: Reclaiming and Championing Your Inner Child* (New York: Bantam, 1990), 47.

Page 27, *"Cells that fire together wire together":* This phrase is generally attributed to Donald Hebb, a Canadian physician and psychologist whose book, *The Organization of Behavior: A Neuropsychological Theory* (New York: Wiley, 1949), postulates that neurons firing simultaneously once will be more likely to fire together in the future.

Page 27, *"These isolated states of being":* D. Siegel, *Mindsight: The New Science of Personal Transformation* (New York: Bantam Books, 2010), 195.

Page 29, *Research suggests that good attunement promotes:* C. Rees, "Childhood Attachment," *British Journal of General Practice* 57, no. 544 (November 1, 2007): 920–22, https://www.ncbi.nlm.nih.gov/pmc/articles/PMC2169321.

Page 29, *"Children who suffer disruptions in their attachment relationships":* G. Maté, *In the Realm of Hungry Ghosts* (Berkeley, CA: North Atlantic Books, 2008), 201.

Chapter Three: It's All in Your Head

Page 36, *optimal relationships are likely to stimulate the growth of integrative fibers:* D. Siegel, *The Developing Mind: How Relationships and the Brain Interact to Shape Who We Are* (New York: Guilford Press, 2012), 19.

Page 36, *The Triune Brain:* P. Maclean and V. Kral, *A Triune Concept of the Brain and Behaviour* (Toronto: University of Toronto Press, 1973).

Page 40, *Studies have demonstrated that 12 to 40 percent of adults in the United States:* E. P. Noble, "The DRD2 Gene in Psychiatric and Neurological Disorders and Its Phenotypes," *Pharmacogenomics* 1, no. 3 (2000): 309–33.

Page 41, *Animal studies have demonstrated that parental nurturing:* G. Maté, "Addiction: Childhood Trauma, Stress and the Biology of Addiction," *Journal of Restorative Medicine* 1, no. 1 (September 1, 2012): 56–63 (8), https://restorativemedicine.org/journal/addiction-childhood-trauma-stress-and-the-biology-of-addiction.

Page 41, *Serotonin deficiency is by far the most common cause:* J. Ross, *The Mood Cure* (New York: Penguin, 2002), 25.

Page 42, *It is critical for optimal brain function:* E. Briassouli and G. Briassoulis, "Glutamine Randomized Studies in Early Life: The Unsolved Riddle of Experimental and Clinical Studies," *Clinical and Developmental Immunology* 2012 (September 2012), http://dx.doi.org/10.1155/2012/749189.

Chapter Four: The Body Remembers

Page 52, *Infant observation studies suggest*: D. Benoit, "Infant-Parent Attachment: Definition, Types, Antecedents, Measurement and Outcome," *Paediatrics Child Health* 9, no. 8 (October 2004): 541–45, https://www.ncbi.nlm.nih.gov/pmc/articles/PMC2724160.

Page 53, *Early parental deprivation (even in mild forms) can lead to*: M. J. Essex, M. H. Klein, E. Cho, and N. H. Kalin, "Maternal Stress Beginning in Infancy May Sensitize Children to Later Stress Exposure: Effects on Cortisol and Behavior," *Biological Psychiatry* 52, no. 8 (October 2002): 776–84.

Page 55, *people can become addicted to their own stress hormones*: Hans Selye, *The Stress of Life* (New York: McGraw-Hill, 1978), 4.

Chapter Five: Yes, but I Had Great Parents

Page 66, *"nothing happening when something might profitably have happened"*: D. W. Winnicott, *Home Is Where We Start From* (New York: W. W. Norton, 1986).

Chapter Seven: Skill 1

Page 92, *Research demonstrates that the simple act of writing down*: J. W. Pennebaker, "Writing about Emotional Experiences as a Therapeutic Process," *Psychological Science* 8, no. 3 (May 1997): 162–66.

Page 99, *"High levels of arousal, freeze, and dissociation"*: L. Heller, *Healing Developmental Trauma* (Berkeley, CA: North Atlantic Books, 2012), 121.

Page 100, *"A felt sense is not a mental experience"*: E. Gendlin, *Focusing* (New York: Bantam Books, 1981).

Page 112, *the feel-good hormone oxytocin*: T. Insel and L. Young, "The Neurobiology of Attachment," *Nature Reviews: Neuroscience* 2 (2001): 129–36; S. Carter, "Neuroendocrine Perspectives on Social Attachment and Love," *Psychoneuroimmunology* 23, no. 8 (November 1998): 779–818.

Chapter Eleven: Skill 5

Page 169, *Aaron T. Beck*: A. Beck, *Cognitive Therapy and the Emotional Disorders* (New York: International Universities Press, 1976).

Page 173, *"Perfectionism is a self-destructive and addictive belief system"*: B. Brown, *The Gifts of Imperfection* (Center City, MN: Hazelden, 2010), 57.

Page 179, *"the tyranny of the shoulds"*: K. Horney, *Neurosis and Human Growth* (New York: W. W. Norton, 1950), 65–66.

Page 181, *Research suggests that women ruminate more than men*: D. Johnson and M. Whisman, "Gender Differences in Rumination: A Meta-analysis," *Personality and Individual Differences* 55, no. 4 (August 2013): 367–74, https://www.ncbi .nlm.nih.gov/pmc/articles/PMC3786159.

Page 197, *Research shows that the act of recognizing and acknowledging*: R. Kobau, M. Seligman, C. Peterson, E. Diener, M. Zack, D. Chapman, and W. Thompson, "Mental Health Promotion in Public Health: Perspectives and Strategies from Positive Psychology," *American Journal of Public Health* 101, no. 8 (August 2011): e1–e9, https://www.ncbi.nlm.nih.gov/pmc/articles/PMC3134513.

Chapter Twelve: Skill 6

Page 214, *Charles R. Snyder*: C. R. Snyder, *The Psychology of Hope* (New York: Free Press, 1994).

Chapter Fourteen: Taking It to the Street

Page 247, *Marshall Rosenberg*: M. B. Rosenberg, *Nonviolent Communication: A Language of Life* (Encinitas, CA: PuddleDancer Press, 2003).

Chapter Fifteen: Attracting Nurturing Others

Page 266, *Fritz Perls*: J. Stevens, *Gestalt Is* (Moab, UT: Real People Press, 1975), 90.

Page 267, *Rick Hanson*: R. Hanson, *Hardwiring Happiness: The New Brain Science of Contentment, Calm, and Confidence* (New York: Harmony Books, 2013).

Page 267, *Research studies demonstrate that judgment and criticism*: G. Shahar, G. C. Henrich, S. J. Blatt, R. Ryan, and T. Little, "Interpersonal Relatedness, Self-Definition, and Their Motivational Orientation during Adolescence: A Theoretical and Empirical Integration," *Developmental Psychology* 39 (2003): 470–83.

Chapter Sixteen. Nurturing Our Relationships

Page 277, *Researchers have postulated that this system*: G. Rizzolatti, L. Fogassi, and V. Gallese, "Neurophysiological Mechanisms Underlying the Understanding and Imitation of Action," *Nature Reviews Neuroscience* 2, no. 9 (2001): 661–70; V. Gallese, "Mirror Neurons, Embodied Simulation, and the Neural Basis of Social Identification," *Psychoanalytical Dialogues* 19, no. 5 (2009): 519–36.

BIBLIOGRAPHY

Alonso-Alonso, M., and A. Pascual-Leone. "The Right Brain Hypothesis for Obesity." *Journal of the American Medical Association* 297, no. 16 (April 2007): 1819–22.

Appleton, N. *Lick the Sugar Habit*. Garden City, NY: Avery, 1997.

Archer, C., C. Drury, and J. Hills. *Healing the Hidden Hurts: Transforming Attachment and Trauma Theory into Effective Practice with Families, Children and Adults*. London: Jessica Kingsley Publishers, 2015.

Arem, R. *The Thyroid Solution: A Revolutionary Mind-Body Program for Regaining Your Emotional and Physical Health*. New York: Random House, 2007.

Barnard, N. *Dr. Neal Barnard's Program for Reversing Diabetes*. New York: Rodale, 2007.

Beattie, M. *Codependent No More: How to Stop Controlling Others and Start Caring for Yourself*. Center City, MN: Hazelden, 1986.

Beck, A. *Cognitive Therapy and the Emotional Disorders*. New York: International Universities Press, 1976.

Begley, S. *Train your Mind, Change your Brain*. New York: Ballantine, 2007.

Berg, F. M. *The Health Risks of Weight Loss*. Hettinger, ND: Healthy Living Institute, 1993.

Blackburn, G. L., G. T. Wilson , B. S. Kanders, L. J. Stein, P. T. Lavin, J. Adler, and K. D. Brownell. "Weight Cycling: The Experience of Human Dieters." *American Journal of Clinical Nutrition* 49 (1989): 1105.

Blakeslee, S., and M. Blakeslee. *The Body Has a Mind of Its Own*. New York: Random House, 2007.

Bowlby, J. *A Secure Base: Parent-Child Attachment and Healthy Human Development*. London: Routledge, 1988.

Bradshaw, J. *Homecoming: Reclaiming and Championing Your Inner Child*. New York: Bantam, 1990.

Braly, J., and P. Holford. *Hidden Food Allergies: The Essential Guide to Uncovering Hidden Food Allergies and Achieving Permanent Relief*. London: Piatkus Books, 2005.

Braverman, E. *The Edge Effect*. New York: Sterling, 2005.

Braverman, E., and C. Pfeiffer. *The Healing Nutrients Within*. New Canaan, CT: Keats, 1997.

Briassouli, E., and G. Briassoulis. "Glutamine Randomized Studies in Early Life: The Unsolved Riddle of Experimental and Clinical Studies." *Clinical and Developmental Immunology* 2012 (September 2012), http://dx.doi.org/10.1155/2012/749189.

Brown, B. *The Gifts of Imperfection*. Center City, MN: Hazelden, 2010.

Cacioppo, J., and W. Patrick. *Loneliness: Human Nature and the Need for Social Connection*. New York: W. W. Norton, 2008.

Caldji, C., B. Tannenbaum, S. Sharma, D. Francis, P. M. Plotsky, and M. J. Meaney. "Maternal Care during Infancy Regulates the Development of Neural Systems Mediating the Expression of Fearfulness in the Rat." *Neurobiology* 95, no. 9 (April 1998): 5335–40.

Carr, L., M. Iacoboni, M. C. Dubeau, J. C. Mazziotta, and G. L. Lenzi. "Neural Mechanisms of Empathy in Humans: A Relay from Neural Systems for Imitation to Limbic Areas." *Proceedings of the National Academy of Sciences* 100, no. 9 (2004): 5497–502.

Carter, S. "Neuroendocrine Perspectives on Social Attachment and Love." *Psychoneuroimmunology* 23, no. 8 (November 1998): 779–818.

Cass, H., and P. Holford. *Natural Highs*. New York: Penguin, 2002.

Colantuoni, C., P. Rada, J. McCarthy, C. Patten, N. M. Avena, A. Chadeayne, and B. G. Hoebel. "Evidence That Intermittent, Excessive Sugar Intake Causes Endogenous Opioid Dependence." *Obesity Research* 20 (2002): 478–88.

Colantuoni, C., J. Schwenker, J. McCarthy, P. Rada, B. Ladenheim, J. L. Cadet, G. J. Schwartz, T. H. Moran, and B. G. Hoebel. "Excessive Sugar Intake Alters Binding to Dopamine and Mu-opioid Receptors in the Brain." *NeuroReport* 12 (2001): 3549–52.

Cousens, G. *Depression-Free for Life*. New York: HarperCollins, 2001.

Cozolino, L. *The Healthy Aging Brain*. New York: W. W. Norton, 2007.

———. *The Neuroscience of Human Relationships*. New York: W. W. Norton, 2014.

Craig, G. *EFT for Weight Loss*. Fulton, CA: Energy Psychology Press, 2010.

Doidge, N. *The Brain That Changes Itself*. New York: Penguin, 2007.

Drenowski, A., D. D. Krahn, M. A. Demitrack, K. Nairn, and B. A. Gosnell, "Nalox-one, an Opiate Blocker, Reduces the Consumption of Sweet High-Fat Foods in Obese and Lean Female Binge Eaters." *American Journal of Clinical Nutrition* 61 (1995): 1206–12.

Duncan, K. "The Effects of High and Low Energy Density Diets on Satiety, Energy Intake, and Eating Time of Obese and Nonobese Subjects." *American Journal of Clinical Nutrition* 37 (1983): 763.

Dupont, R. *The Selfish Brain: Learning from Addiction.* Center City, MN: Hazelden, 2000.

Ellis, A. *A New Guide to Rational Living.* North Hollywood, CA: Wilshire Books, 1975.

Ellis, A., and M. Powers. *The Secret of Overcoming Verbal Abuse.* North Hollywood, CA: Wilshire Books, 2000.

Essex, M. J., M. H. Klein, E. Cho, and N. H. Kalin. "Maternal Stress Beginning in Infancy May Sensitize Children to Later Stress Exposure: Effects on Cortisol and Behavior." *Biological Psychiatry* 52, no. 8 (October 2002): 776–84.

Fosha, D., and D. Siegel. *The Healing Power of Emotion.* New York: W. W. Norton, 2009.

Fuhrman, Joel. *Eat to Live.* Boston: Little, Brown, 2003.

Fung, J. *The Obesity Code.* Vancouver, BC: Greystone Books, 2016.

Gaesser, G. A. *Big Fat Lies: The Truth about Your Weight and Your Health.* New York: Ballantine, 1998.

Gendlin, E. *Focusing.* New York: Bantam, 1981.

———. *Focusing-Oriented Psychotherapy: A Manual of the Experiential Method.* New York: Guilford, 1996.

Germer, C. *The Mindful Path to Self-Compassion: Freeing yourself from Destructive Thoughts and Emotions.* New York: Guilford, 2009.

Gilbert, D. *Stumbling on Happiness.* New York: Random House, 2006.

Goleman, D. *Emotional Intelligence.* New York: Bantam, 1994.

Hanson, R. *Hardwiring Happiness: The New Brain Science of Contentment, Calm, and Confidence.* New York: Harmony, 2013.

Heller, L. *Healing Developmental Trauma.* Berkeley, CA: North Atlantic Books, 2012.

Herman, J. *Trauma and Recovery.* New York: Basic Books, 1992.

Horney, K. *Neurosis and Human Growth.* New York: W. W. Norton, 1950.

Horwath, N. C., E. Saltzman, and S. B. Roberts. "Dietary Fiber and Weight Regulation." *Nutrition Reviews* 59 (2001): 129–39.

Iacoboni, M. *Mirroring People.* New York: Picador, 2008.

Insel, T., and L. Young. "The Neurobiology of Attachment." *Nature Reviews: Neuroscience* 2 (2001): 129–36.

Johnson, P. M., and P. J. Kenny. "Dopamine D2 Receptors in Addiction-Like Reward Dysfunction and Compulsive Eating in Obese Rats." *Nature Neuroscience* 13 (2010): 645–41.

Kabat-Zinn, J. *Mindfulness for Beginners*. Boulder, CO: Sounds True, 2012.

Kessler, D. A. *The End of Overeating*. New York: Rodale, 2009.

Kress, Diane. *The Metabolism Miracle*. Philadelphia: Da Capo Press, 2009.

Langer, E. *Counterclockwise: Mindful Healing and the Power of Possibility*. New York: Ballantine, 2009.

Levine, P. *In an Unspoken Voice: How the Body Releases Trauma and Restores Goodness*. Berkeley, CA: North Atlantic Books, 2010.

———. *Waking the Tiger: Healing Trauma*. Berkeley, CA: North Atlantic Books, 1997.

Lieberman, H. "The Effects of Dietary Neurotransmitter Precursors on Human Behavior." *American Journal of Clinical Nutrition* 42 (1985): 366.

Lisle, D. J., and A. Goldhamer. *The Pleasure Trap*. Summertown, TN: Healthy Living Publications, 2003.

Lissau, I., and T. Sorensen. "Parental Neglect during Childhood and Increased Obesity in Young Adulthood." *Lancet* 343 (1994): 324–27.

Maclean, P., and V. Kral, *A Triune Concept of the Brain and Behaviour*. Toronto: University of Toronto Press, 1973.

Mann T., A. J. Tomiyama, E. Westling, A. M. Lew, B. Samuels, and J. Chatman. "Medicare's Search for Effective Obesity Treatments: Diets Are Not the Answer." *American Psychology* 62 (2007): 220–33.

Maté, G. *Scattered: How Attention Deficit Disorder Originates and What You Can Do about It*. New York: Penguin, 1999.

———. *In the Realm of Hungry Ghosts*. Berkeley, CA: North Atlantic Books, 2008.

———. *When the Body Says No: Exploring the Stress-Disease Connection*. Hoboken, NJ: Wiley, 2011.

Mellin, L. *The Solution: 6 Winning Ways to Permanent Weight Loss*. New York: HarperCollins, 1997.

Miller, G. E., E. Chen, A. K. Fok, H. Walker, A. Lim, E. F. Nicholls, S. Cole, and M. S. Kobor. "Low Early-Life Social Class Leaves a Biological Residue Manifested by Decreased Glucocorticoid and Increased Proinflammatory Signaling." *Proceedings of the National Academy of Sciences* 106 (2009): 14716–21.

Miller, W. C. "How Effective Are Traditional Dietary and Exercise Interventions for Weight Loss?" *Medicine and Science in Sports Exercise* 31 (1999): 1129–34.

Montgomery, A. *Neurobiology Essentials for Clinicians: What Every Therapist Needs to Know*. New York: W. W. Norton, 2013.

Moore, R. Y. "Circadian Rhythms: Basic Neurobiology and Clinical Applications." *Annual Review of Medicine* 48 (1997): 253–66.

Nader, M. A., D. Morgan, H. D. Gage, S. H. Nader. T. L. Calhoun, N. Buchheimer, R. Ehrenkaufer, and R. H. Mac. "PET Imaging of Dopamine D2 Receptors during Chronic Cocaine Self-Administration in Monkeys." *Nature Neuroscience* 8 (August 2006): 1050–56.

Neff, K. *Self-Compassion: The Proven Power of Being Kind to Yourself*. New York: HarperCollins, 2011.

Neufeld, G., and G. Maté. *Hold On to Your Kids: Why Parents Need to Matter More Than Peers*. New York: Ballantine, 2006.

Noble, E. P. "The DRD2 Gene in Psychiatric and Neurological Disorders and Its Phenotypes." *Pharmacogenomics* 1, no. 3 (2000): 309–33.

Ogden, P. *Trauma and the Body: A Sensorimotor Approach to Psychotherapy*. New York: W. W. Norton, 2006.

———. *Sensorimotor Psychotherapy: Interventions for Trauma and Attachment*. New York: W. W. Norton, 2015.

Panksepp, J. "Social Support and Pain: How Does the Brain Feel the Ache of a Broken Heart?" *Journal of Cancer Pain and Symptom Palliation* 1, no. 1 (2005): 29–65.

Peck, M. Scott. *The Road Less Traveled*. New York: Simon and Schuster, 1978.

Philpott, W., and D. Kalita. *Brain Allergies: The Psychonutrient Connection*. New Canaan, CT: Keats, 1987.

Randolph, T., and R. Moss. *An Alternative Approach to Allergies*. New York: Bantam, 1980.

Rapp, D. *Is This Your Child? Discovering and Treating Unrecognized Allergies in Children and Adults*. New York: William Morrow, 1992.

Rivera, R., and F. Deutsch. *Your Hidden Food Allergies Are Making You Fat*. Rocklin, CA: Prima, 1998.

Rosenberg, M. B. *Nonviolent Communication: A Language of Life*. Encinitas, CA: PuddleDancer Press, 2003.

Ross, J. *The Diet Cure*. New York: Penguin, 1999.

———. *The Mood Cure*. New York: Penguin, 2002.

Sakyong, M. *Turning the Mind into an Ally*. New York: Riverhead Books, 2003.

Schore, A. *Affect Dysregulation and Disorders of the Self*. New York: W. W. Norton, 2003.

———. *Affect Regulation and the Repair of the Self*. New York: W. W. Norton, 2003.

———. *Affect Regulation and the Origin of the Self: The Neurobiology of Emotional Development*. New York: Routledge, 2016.

Seligman, M. *Authentic Happiness*. New York: Free Press, 2002.

Selye, H. *The Stress of Life*. New York: McGraw-Hill, 1978.

Shames, R., and K. Shames. *Feeling Fat, Fuzzy, or Frazzled? A Three-Step Program to Restore Thyroid, Adrenal, and Reproductive Balance*. London: Penguin, 2005.

Shapiro, S., L. E. Carlson, J. A. Astin, and B. Freedman. "Mechanisms of Mindfulness." *Journal of Clinical Psychology* 62, no. 3 (2006): 373–86.

Shell, E. R. *The Hungry Gene*. New York: Atlantic Monthly Press, 2002.

Siegel, D. *Mindsight: The New Science of Personal Transformation*. New York: Bantam, 2010.

———. *The Developing Mind: How Relationships and the Brain Interact to Shape Who We Are*. New York: Guilford, 2012.

———. *Brainstorm: The Power and Purpose of the Teenage Brain*. New York: Penguin, 2013.

Siegel, D., and T. Bryson. *The Whole-Brain Child: 12 Revolutionary Strategies to Nurture Your Child's Developing Mind*. New York: Bantam, 2011.

———. *No-Drama Discipline: The Whole-Brain Way to Calm the Chaos and Nurture Your Child's Developing Mind*. New York: Bantam, 2014.

Simon, Julie M. *The Emotional Eater's Repair Manual: A Practical Mind-Body-Spirit Guide for Putting an End to Overeating and Dieting*. Novato, CA: New World Library, 2012.

Slagle, P. *The Way Up from Down*. New York: St. Martin's, 1994.

Snyder, C. R. *The Psychology of Hope*. New York: Free Press, 1994.

Soby, J. M. *Prenatal Exposure to Drugs/Alcohol: Characteristics and Educational Implications of Fetal Alcohol Syndrome and Cocaine/Polydrug Effects*. Springfield, IL: Charles C. Thomas, 2006.

Stevens, J. *Gestalt Is*. Moab, UT: Real People Press, 1975.

Tronick, E. *The Neurobehavioral and Social-Emotional Development of Infants and Children*. New York: W. W. Norton, 2007.

van der Kolk, B. *The Body Keeps the Score: Brain, Mind, and Body in the Healing of Trauma*. New York: Penguin, 2014.

Wang, G. J. "The Role of Dopamine in Motivation for Food in Humans: Implications for Obesity." *Expert Opinion on Therapeutic Targets* 9, no. 5 (October 2002): 601–9.

Williamson, D. F., T. J. Thompson, R. F. Anda, W. H. Dietz, and V. Felitti. "Body Weight and Obesity in Adults and Self-Reported Abuse in Childhood." *International Journal of Obesity* 26 (2002): 1075–82.

Wilson, James L. *Adrenal Fatigue: The 21st-Century Stress Syndrome*. Petaluma, CA: Smart Publications, 2001.

Winnicott, D. W. *Home Is Where We Start From*. New York: W. W. Norton, 1986.

Wurtman, J. J., R. J. Wurtman, J. H. Growdon, P. Henry, A. Lipscomb, and S. H. Zeisel. "Carbohydrate Craving in Obese People: Suppression by Treatments Affecting Serotoninergic Transmission." *International Journal of Eating Disorders* 1, no. 1 (1981): 2–15.

INDEX

ABOUT THE AUTHOR

J ulie M. Simon, MA, MBA, LMFT, is a psychotherapist and life coach and the bestselling author of *The Emotional Eater's Repair Manual: A Practical Mind-Body-Spirit Guide for Putting an End to Overeating and Dieting*. For more than twenty-seven years, Julie has been helping overeaters and imbalanced eaters to heal their relationships with themselves, their bodies, and food, and to stop dieting, lose excess weight, and keep it off. A lifelong fitness enthusiast, she is also a certified personal trainer with over twenty-five years of experience designing personalized exercise and nutrition programs.

A two-time summa cum laude graduate of UCLA, Julie is also the founder and director of the Twelve-Week Emotional Eating Recovery Program, an alternative to dieting that addresses the true causes of overeating and weight gain: emotional and spiritual hunger and body imbalance. The program grew out of her professional experience with and personal journey through childhood trauma, weight challenges, and body, brain, and spiritual imbalances. She is also the creator of the Women Who Use Food for Emotional Comfort support groups.

For over two decades, Julie has presented seminars and workshops on overcoming overeating and on associated mental health topics to both lay and professional audiences. Julie has appeared on numerous TV and radio shows and at live events, encouraging people to pay attention to their phenomenal mind, body, and spirit signals and teaching them to nurture themselves mindfully and stop turning to food for comfort.

For many years Julie served in different capacities on the board of the Los Angeles Chapter of the California Association of Marriage and Family Therapists. She lives and practices in Los Angeles.

For more information and inspiration,
visit Julie's website at www.overeatingrecovery.com.